Creating Effective Undergraduate Research Programs in Science

Creating Effective Undergraduate Research Programs in Science

THE TRANSFORMATION FROM STUDENT TO SCIENTIST

Edited by Roman Taraban and Richard L. Blanton

Teachers College, Columbia University
New York and London

Published by Teachers College Press, 1234 Amsterdam Avenue, New York, NY 10027

Library of Congress Cataloging-in-Publication Data

Creating effective undergraduate research programs in science : the transformation
from student to scientist / edited by Roman Taraban and Richard L. Blanton.
    p.   cm.
  Includes bibliographical references and index.
  ISBN 978-0-8077-4877-0 (pbk : alk. paper)
  1. Research. 2. Science—study and teaching (Higher) I. Taraban, Roman (Roman
Myron), 1952– II. Blanton, Richard L. (Richard Lawrence)

  Q180.A1C74 2008
  507.1'l—dc22

2007047082

ISBN 978-0-8077-4877-0 (paper)

Printed on acid-free paper
Manufactured in the United States of America

15 14 13 12 11 10 09 08   8 7 6 5 4 3 2 1

Contents

PART III
The Experience of Science

PART IV
Women in Science

PART V
Looking Back and Looking Forward

Preface

RESEARCH EXPERIENCES for students entail building domain knowledge and skills and actively participating in authentic research. This book is the first thorough and unified treatment of research experiences for undergraduates. It provides detailed qualitative and quantitative descriptions of the nature and benefits to college students of participating in research, and describes the postbaccalaureate outcomes of research participation. It also discusses faculty and mentors' perspectives on students' gains, gender differences, and drawing students into science. This is a much-needed volume in the current climate of extensive government and foundation funding of research experiences for students at all grade levels, the proliferation of summer research minicourses for rising high school seniors at colleges and universities around the country, and the growing commitment by faculty and school administrators at all levels of instruction to the experiences and benefits that come when students actively participate in authentic research.

The primary audience for this book is college faculty who currently support students, or who have supported students, through direct mentoring relationships in research experiences, including the support of college and high school students in summer programs and college students in academic-year programs. Related to this faculty cohort are faculty, administrators, and program staff who are currently managing undergraduate research experience programs or who are developing such programs for future implementation.

Undergraduate research is undergoing a transition from a cottage industry to a significant movement. There are increasing numbers of formal undergraduate research programs and a perception that they are important for student recruitment. There is interest in how to design programs. This book serves as a how-to guide not only for creating programs, but also for determining their effectiveness.

This book was supported in part by a Howard Hughes Medical Institute grant through the Undergraduate Science Education Program to Texas Tech University and by the Center for the Integration of Science Education and Research at Texas Tech University.

We dedicate this book with deep appreciation to Dr. John M. Burns, who initiated and facilitated programmatic implementation of research opportunities for undergraduates in the life sciences at Texas Tech University, to Julie Isom, Associate Director of the Howard Hughes Medical Institute grant program at Texas Tech, to the dedicated faculty mentors and staff who have sustained this program over the years, and to faculty and administrators who are envisioning new research opportunities for students at Texas Tech and elsewhere.

A Context for Curriculum Change

CHAPTER 1

What Is Undergraduate Research, and Why Should We Support It?

Roman Taraban

SEVERAL ELEMENTS in the recent history of American education have worked together to provide students with a more active role in learning about science and participating in research. Over the past several decades, educators at all academic levels have dedicated themselves to developing inquiry skills and knowledge of the scientific method in students. Inquiry-oriented curricula at the elementary and secondary levels have evolved from the "alphabet" curricula of the 1960s and 1970s (CBA, ESS, PSSC, SAPA) to curricula designed with teacher input, active student participation, and expert/faculty mentorship. In the 1960s and 1970s the National Science Foundation (NSF) through the Undergraduate Research Program provided funding to institutions—typically research universities—that allowed undergraduates to spend a summer in an active research lab. Then in 1987 the National Science Foundation funded the first site in the Research Experiences for Undergraduates (REU) program, a program that was important because it recognized the importance of undergraduate research experiences and made a commitment to supporting those experiences. Beginning in the 1980s, various reports and national forums raised serious concerns about undergraduate education in the United States, among them the influential Boyer Commission Report. These reports and discussions, along with the work of national organizations, such as the Council on Undergraduate Research (http://cur.org), the National Council on Undergraduate Research (www.ncur.org), Project Kaleidoscope (www.pkal.org), the National Science Foundation, the Howard Hughes Medical Institute, the Reinvention Center (founded to support the aims of the Boyer Commission), have produced significant reform in colleges and universities directed toward developing in students an understanding and appreciation of scientific methodology, the creation of new knowledge, and the role of science in society.

A significant facet of this decades-long effort to reform education has been to get students directly involved in research labs. Providing research experiences for students has become a widely recognized and accepted goal of science education. The National Science Foundation has invested millions of dollars in support of undergraduate research through Research Experiences for Undergraduates (REU) programs. The Howard Hughes Medical Institute (HHMI) began supporting science education in 1988 and since then has invested heavily to support students in research labs. Increasing numbers of institutions are establishing internally funded undergraduate research programs. Supporting student research is a significant activity of many honors programs and colleges. There are currently hundreds of summer research-oriented programs for precollege students, and the numbers are growing: These include summer internships that provide financial support through stipends, summer courses and programs for which students pay tuition and fees, and school-to-work programs.

Through what is termed here as the *undergraduate research experience*, significant numbers of undergraduate students participate in a range of activities that draw them into the contemporary culture of science and integrate them more fully into the practice of inquiry and research. "The undergraduate research experience [is] a concept that integrates the authenticity of research with the education of novice scientists" (Lopatto, Chapter 6, p. 112). The National Research Council, the National Science Foundation, the American Association for the Advancement of Science, and other organizations recommend that all undergraduate students be encouraged to pursue research projects, and that they get involved in research as early as is practical in their school programs. This has been achieved, in part, by getting students to work on research projects in lab and field settings under the guidance of faculty mentors beginning as early as their freshman and sophomore years. When one examines science reform initiatives at the middle and high school levels one sees efforts comparable to those at the college level, that is, efforts to provide students with "driving questions," rich data sets, sophisticated measuring instruments, and an emphasis on the scientific method and authentic research.

In spite of the widespread success in implementing science education reform through federal and institutional initiatives, there is at present no unified presentation of the organization, nature, benefits, and challenges associated with student research experiences that is based on evidence. Faculty members, graduate students, and postdocs who mentor students, administrators who initiate and manage student research programs, and foundations that financially support student research are currently without essential information about the organization and administration of research opportunities, the benefits that students gain from par-

ticipation in research, and the challenges to creating and sustaining viable research opportunities for students. Further, although there is growing support for student research experiences, providing these experiences is not without problems, including a constant pull on the part of faculty to demonstrate student achievement through test results that typically focus on content knowledge (e.g., concepts and facts) and not the design, procedural, and analytic skills of the lab. There are material and facility costs associated with providing research experiences. And, finally, there are substantial costs of faculty time and effort that are often perceived as detracting from effort that should be devoted to traditional teaching, research, and service. Therefore, as a teacher or administrator, one can legitimately ask about the costs and benefits of providing student research experiences.

Many practical questions await answers. In what ways do research experiences affect student achievement? What institutional supports are necessary to provide research experiences, and how does one go about establishing a program with wide student impact? Are there racial and gender differences in the success of research programs, and what do we still need to learn about the pedagogy of research experiences? These are practical questions that need to be addressed in curriculum policy and implementation, and they are the kinds of questions that motivated the present collection of papers by well-known researchers and practitioners.

A major goal in compiling this volume was to gather together the best empirical evidence currently available about the effects of research experiences on college students. This evidence includes data about student change and development during the college years, as well as the impact of research experiences on the academic and research paths that students follow after graduation. A second goal was to clearly describe research opportunity programs that have worked, as well as to inspire faculty with new ideas for research and course reorganizations and new methods of assessing student learning in research contexts. A third goal was to use this work to set a firm foundation for an animated and productive discussion of the topics of this book and to spur a wide and rich range of subsequent research on student research experiences.

SOME SIGNIFICANT FINDINGS

In the remainder of this chapter, I will provide pointers to some of the significant findings reported in this book. In some cases, the data relate primarily to STEM (science, technology, engineering, math) disciplines (Bauer & Bennett, Chapter 5; Campbell & Skoog, Chapter 10; Henne et al., Chapter 11; Kardash et al., Chapter 9; Lopatto, Chapter 6; Trosset et al., Chapter 3). In other cases the data address the impact of undergraduate research across a broad range of disciplines (Locks & Gregerman, Chapter 2; Russell, Chapter 4; Taraban et al., Chapter 8).

The Basis of a Successful Research Experience

Consistent with expectations, the length of students' research experiences and the number of activities they engage in are some of the strongest predictors of positive outcomes of a research experience (Bauer & Bennett, Chapter 5; Russell, Chapter 4; Taraban et al., Chapter 8). "Involvement with the process and culture of research" and "the development of interest and curiosity followed by an acculturation process" are the most prominent outcomes of successful participation in research (Russell, Chapter 4; also Hunter et al., Chapter 7, p. 75). Students are motivated to do research when it is voluntary and they engage in the process out of genuine interest; requiring students to do research does not appear beneficial (Russell, Chapter 4). However, it is possible to maintain a sense of voluntary participation while offering students authentic research activities in the context of organized courses (Trosset et al., Chapter 3).

The Roles of Mentors and Peers

Talented mentors create successful student research experiences (Campbell & Skoog, Chapter 10; Henne et al., Chapter 11; Hunter et al., Chapter 7; Kardash et al., Chapter 9; Russell, Chapter 4). Students develop supportive peer relations as part of their research experiences (Henne et al., Chapter 11; Kardash et al., Chapter 9; Locks & Gregerman, Chapter 2). Engaging in undergraduate research promotes proactive behaviors, promotes interactions, and strengthens relations with faculty and peers (Locks & Gregerman, Chapter 2).

On the other hand, poor mentoring was voiced by some students (Kardash et al., Chapter 9), and by far the most frequent suggestion in students' postexperience surveys was to better prepare mentors to guide students. Students want mentors with good interpersonal skills who provide effective guidance (Russell, Chapter 4).

Student Satisfaction with Research Experiences

Perhaps the most common assessment question asked of students involved in research is whether they found the experience worthwhile. Students' response has been a definite yes (Campbell & Skoog, Chapter 10; Henne et al., Chapter 11; Hunter et al., Chapter 7; Kardash et al., Chapter 9; Locks & Gregerman, Chapter 2; Lopatto, Chapter 6; Russell, Chapter 4). As one might expect, disappointments do arise from experiments that fail, broken equipment, and other sources of frustration (Kardash et al., Chapter 9; Trosset et al., Chapter 3).

Student Achievements

Regardless of academic major or gender, students who have had research experiences are more academically motivated and achieve higher levels of technical skills

and scientific understanding (Bauer & Bennett, Chapter 5; Russell, Chapter 4). Undergraduate research participation increases students' awareness of and commitment to research and science, and increases their confidence in carrying out research (Campbell & Skoog, Chapter 10; Henne et al., Chapter 11; Hunter et al., Chapter 7; Russell, Chapter 4; Taraban et al., Chapter 8). Students report high levels of achievement in analytic and procedural skills necessary for success in science, including "understanding the research process," "readiness for more demanding research," "understanding how scientists work on real problems," and "learning laboratory techniques" (Lopatto, Chapter 6, p. 117; see also Trosset et al., Chapter 3). Through research experiences, students recognize and learn to overcome obstacles in the lab (Campbell & Skoog, Chapter 10; Hunter et al., Chapter 7). There is only suggestive evidence that students who engage in intense research experiences show significant gains in critical thinking, logical reasoning, and reflective judgment from freshman to senior years (Bauer & Bennett, Chapter 5). Research experiences increase retention rates, particularly for minorities (Locks & Gregerman, Chapter 2). Undergraduate research experiences are important to students in making career decisions (Russell, Chapter 4).

Building Successful Programs

Through deliberate planning and actions, it is possible to establish highly successful undergraduate research programs at universities and smaller colleges (Blanton, Chapter 12; Locks & Gregerman, Chapter 2; Lopatto, Chapter 6), but this depends critically on providing students with extensive supports for entering into and succeeding in a research lab setting (Locks & Gregerman, Chapter 2; Henne et al., Chapter 11).

The University of Michigan (UM) program (Locks & Gregerman, Chapter 2) stands as an exemplary model for recruiting students of all abilities into research and providing them with an effective research experience. In order to maximize the benefits of a research experience, students are invited to get involved in research in their freshman and sophomore years. In contrast, data from broad-based national surveys (Russell, Chapter 4) indicate that students typically get involved in their junior and senior years. Through peer mentoring, UM students identify research projects, develop a résumé, and practice interviewing, in order to gain a lab position. Peer mentors conduct monthly meetings with individual students to work on time management and to address any concerns that faculty sponsors may have with students. Students participate in biweekly research seminars led by peer mentors in order to learn about research responsibilities, faculty expectations, and research ethics, and they also discuss research methods and talk to one another about their projects. During alternate weeks, students attend skill-building workshops around campus to learn about library use, Web resources, software programs, and poster presentations. Each year, the majority of these students present posters and oral papers in a research symposium.

Drawing Students Into the Culture and Practice of Science

Data in Russell (Chapter 4) suggest that the majority of students who get involved in STEM (science, technology, engineering, and math) research in college, became interested in research when they were kids; only 8% to 10% first became interested in college. About 25% of students in SBES (social, behavioral, and economic sciences) reported becoming interested in research during childhood. In both cases, the data indicate the importance of reaching students in their elementary school years in order to attract them to research careers. Research experiences lead a small percentage of students to consider a science career for the first time, and an equally small percentage to decide against a science career (Hunter et al., Chapter 7; Lopatto, Chapter 6). Lopatto (Chapter 6) indicates that students who decided against a research career after a research experience could not be characterized by ethnicity or gender; however, Kardash and colleagues (Chapter 9) report that a higher percentage of women than men expressed a decreased interest in pursuing a career in research science after a research experience. Research experiences typically confirm students' existing interests in science careers, rather than sparking a new interest (Lopatto, Chapter 6; Russell, Chapter 4; Trosset et al., Chapter 3). Nevertheless, long-term, multifaceted experiences, draw students more deeply into the culture and practice of science (Bauer & Bennett, Chapter 5; Russell, Chapter 4). This may be the single most important benefit of these experiences.

Racial and Gender Effects

In broad-based national surveys, Hispanic/Latino and Black participation in research was as high as or higher than that of non-Hispanic Whites, and participation rates for men and women were nearly identical (Russell, Chapter 4). Males of color and Hispanics achieved the greatest academic and career gains from research experiences (Locks & Gregerman, Chapter 2). In general, career plans did not differ greatly because of gender or ethnicity (Lopatto, Chapter 6). Among students retained through graduation, underrepresented students of color were as likely to pursue graduate education as White and Asian American students (Locks & Gregerman, Chapter 2).

Minorities do not benefit more from same race/ethnicity compared to mentors of a different race/ethnicity. Women do not benefit more from female mentors than from male mentors (Russell, Chapter 4). When there are differences, the greatest gains were associated with Hispanics and Latinos (Russell, Chapter 4). On most measures, women did not differ from men (Kardash et al., Chapter 9; Russell, Chapter 4). One difference may be that research experiences increase self-efficacy for women more than for men (Kardash et al., Chapter 9). When underrepresented students participate in research, faculty mentors gain a deeper appreciation of diversity and the challenges faced by underrepresented students (Locks & Gregerman, Chapter 2).

Postbaccalaureate Gains

Most students who engaged in research reported having a plan for postgraduate education in science (Russell, Chapter 4). Students credit research experience for making them aware of new career opportunities (Kardash et al., Chapter 9). Students with undergraduate research experiences are more likely to pursue postgraduate education, including PhD programs, law, and medicine (Campbell & Skoog, Chapter 10; Henne et al., Chapter 11; Locks & Gregerman, Chapter 2; Russell, Chapter 4). Career plans, learning gains, and overall satisfaction with the research experience did not differ among research universities and colleges (Lopatto, Chapter 6).

Faculty Costs and Benefits

Bauer and Bennett (Chapter 5) found that faculty are sensitive to the costs, in terms of time required, associated with mentoring students in the lab. They regard the financial costs as being high (Bauer & Bennett, Chapter 5; Russell, Chapter 4. More students could be accommodated with additional financial support. Blanton (Chapter 12) and Hunter and colleagues (Chapter 7) echo similar concerns and recommendations.

AN INVITATION TO READ ON

Research experiences help students understand the methods of science, develop skills in conducting research, and work collaboratively with peers and mentors. Providing research experiences contributes to an institution's goals of educating students who are scientifically literate and capable of pursuing advanced degrees, and preparing them to assume leadership positions in research, teaching, and health professions. Barriers remain to the widespread availability of student research opportunities, including lack of departmental and institutional resources and compensation to faculty for mentoring students (Blanton, Chapter 12). This book presents compelling evidence favoring research experiences and ideas for sustainable research opportunities that can help to improve departmental and disciplinary culture to make it more supportive of student research opportunities. The greatest shortcoming associated with undergraduate research may be getting information out to students about available opportunities (Russell, Chapter 4). Making students aware of research opportunities on their campus and making those opportunities accessible to all students may be the most important curricular change we can make in our schools. Students are asking for more mentors who are socially adept and can provide effective guidance. To develop more mentors like this will require a variety of supports from college and university administrators.

This book will surely fall into the hands of those who have been leaders and significant contributors to science curriculum reform, as well as into the hands of those who believe in this movement and want to promote it. Apart from pedantic pedagogical concerns with restructuring schools, many of us are driven by a sincere concern with student outcomes—with promoting the professional success, the personal joy and satisfaction, and in some cases the upward social mobility that come to students from motivating and inspiring school experiences.

Until recently, research opportunities on my campus were communicated to students by faculty members and in select venues, such as the Honor's College. A new initiative is afoot to make research opportunities more visible and accessible to all students, through a university Web site and departmental ones. These changes, while small, are a start in the right direction, and could have a significant impact over time. Modest initiatives like this one, multiplied over and across campuses, could add up to significant curricular change.

It is my sincere hope that in reading this book, from cover to cover or selectively, you will become more fully committed to moving education in new directions. The programs described in this volume, the supporting data, and the words of the students themselves indicate several related benefits of research involvement. Students become fully integrated into the goals of the academy, they passionately pursue knowledge through research and scholarship, and they amplify their prospects of contributing substantively to discoveries in their disciplines and for the benefit of society in general.

Can administrators ignore the significant findings calling for a transformation of the academy from an institution of observation to a body of participation? Can teachers continue to try to educate by the passive transmission of knowledge? Probably—but it will be to the detriment of all involved.

CHAPTER 2

Undergraduate Research as an Institutional Retention Strategy: The University of Michigan Model

Angela M. Locks and Sandra R. Gregerman

IN THE PAST 15 years, the popularity of undergraduate research programs has grown tremendously, particularly at large research universities. The Undergraduate Research Opportunity Program (UROP) was one of the earlier such initiatives, begun in 1989 with 14 research partnerships between first- and second-year students and social science faculty in the College of Literature, Science, and the Arts (LSA) at the University of Michigan. In 2006 the program served over 1,000 undergraduates and 600 faculty members from all University of Michigan (UM) schools and colleges and all academic disciplines. Initially the program served students of color exclusively. In 1992 the program expanded research opportunities to all students with any first- or second-year student being eligible for participation. Since its inception, the program has added a comprehensive peer advising program, research and learning skills workshops, curricula, and a formal research seminar. Additionally, the permanent staff size has increased from one to five. Tangential programs include a number of summer research fellowship programs; two smaller academic-year programs, one for sophomores participating in UROP for a second academic year, and one for junior and senior students participating in a formal research experience for the first time; and a residential learning community called the Michigan Research Community. Summer research programs include those focused on the biomedical and health sciences, physical sciences, engineering, social sciences, and community-based research. The aforementioned program features make UROP distinct.

Early on, UROP received significant grants from the Howard Hughes Medical Institute and the Michigan Department of Equity. The program also received two successive grants from the Fund for the Improvement of Postsecondary Education to study itself and a grant from the National Science Foundation. Evidence from research and evaluative efforts show that UROP has several positive outcomes for students and there is evidence that the program has an effect on faculty. These events have garnered attention and support for the undergraduate research enterprise at the University of Michigan.

UROP has been deemed a successful venture. This is mostly due to the national attention the program has received over the years, in part based on the results of a longitudinal assessment of the program's effectiveness in meeting its student retention goals. The program has also been highlighted in several campus reports seeking to improve undergraduate education including the President's Undergraduate Commission Report. Moreover, the last two provosts and the current Dean of LSA have publicly expressed interest in making research opportunities more readily available. Conversations have occurred between UROP staff, LSA, and central administration about how to best achieve this goal. In support of the call for more undergraduate research opportunities, at the start of the 2007–08 academic year over 500 students were on the UROP wait-list.

INSTITUTIONAL CONTEXT

Under the leadership of former University of Michigan President James Duderstadt in the late 1980s and early 1990s, the University of Michigan instituted a comprehensive action plan called the Michigan Mandate to increase campus racial and ethnic diversity at all levels—faculty, students, and staff. The Michigan Mandate was successful in several ways, as it engaged all schools and colleges in a comprehensive plan to develop effective recruitment programs to attract diverse undergraduate and graduate students. As a result, the number of historically underrepresented students on campus increased at all academic levels, and collaborative plans were implemented to recruit and create new faculty positions that increased diversity. At the same time that the campus was enrolling a more ethnically diverse undergraduate student population, the university was not as successful in the retention of these ethnically diverse students when compared to White students on the campus.

In the late 1980s the campus experienced differential retention rates of approximately 25 points, with White student retention hovering around 90%, while the retention of historically underrepresented students of color reflected a significant disparity at 65%. This occurred despite numerous programs that were implemented to address student needs. Developmental retention programs addressed academic preparation, lack of access to advanced placement courses, and the overall effects of attending underresourced school systems. During this period, these initiatives incorporated supplemental sections of specific subjects, high school review courses, and intensive tutoring programs. Other approaches included programs that addressed a poor climate as well as those designed to provide students social support and cultural affirmation. For example, mentorship programs, living-learning programs, and support groups focused on race and ethnicity fell under the umbrella of retention efforts. Other programs provided support services to improve the transition from high school to college; hence, support services like mentoring from faculty and peers and academic enrichment activities mediated the potentially poor adjustment to the university environment (see Figure 2.1).

PROGRAM RATIONALE

Most campuses across the country are grappling with the issue of student retention and, in particular, the differential retention rates of students from different racial and socioeconomic backgrounds. To this end, they have employed and instituted a variety of programs and initiatives to address differential retention rates between White students and historically underrepresented students. At the University of Michigan, a large public research university enrolling 25,000 undergraduate students, the Undergraduate Research Opportunity Program was developed as a different approach to student retention. The use of undergraduate research to improve student retention was based on lessons learned from higher education scholars who focus on the retention of ethnically diverse students on predominantly White campuses. The program was not initially developed to address the retention of students in STEM (science, technology, engineering, math) fields; however, a significant percentage of historically underrepresented students enter the University of Michigan interested in science and engineering.

Astin (1993), Kuh, Kinzie, Schuh, and Whitt (2005), and Pascarella and Terenzini (1991, 2005), among other scholars, have completed longitudinal studies and literature reviews pertaining to the impact of college on students. Collectively, their work looked specifically at social and academic influences and found several factors that affect student retention. These include (1) the nature of a student's peer group; (2) the quality and quantity of student interactions with faculty outside the classroom setting; (3) the balancing of students' academic and social lives; (4) experiences that make coursework more relevant, especially coursework in the gateway courses to STEM fields; and (5) the invitation from faculty to participate in research, one of the core academic missions of the campus.

BENEFITS OF UNDERGRADUATE RESEARCH

As Lopatto (Chapter 6) and Hunter et al. (Chapter 7) discuss in their chapters, and based on the experience at the University of Michigan engaging first- and second-year students in research, undergraduate research addresses many of the key

Figure 2.1. Predominant explanations of college dropout rates among minority students in the late 1980s and early 1990s.

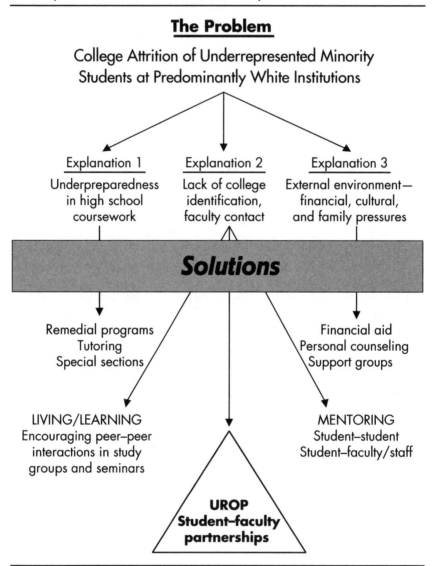

factors that impact student retention. It provides opportunities for students to interact with faculty outside the classroom and around a common intellectual activity; it increases students' engagement and involvement in their own learning; it has the potential to change the students' peer group depending upon how the program is structured to create a community of young researchers; and it makes coursework more relevant. Additionally, it provides opportunities for students to see the entire academic pipeline, especially students who may not be familiar with the process of pursuing a PhD. The types of college student outcomes identified by Astin (1993), Kuh and colleagues (2005), Pascarella and Terenzini (1991, 2005), and others, clearly support the relevance of undergraduate research programs. Such programs are intentionally structured to provide meaningful opportunities that foster the college student outcomes mentioned above.

The Undergraduate Research Opportunity Program creates research partnerships between first- and second-year students and faculty researchers campuswide. The program runs during the academic year and in the case of first-year students engages these students in research when they initially arrive on campus. In addition to all the benefits of undergraduate research, in the context of what is generally understood about student success, this early engagement in research also engages a nonremedial approach to retention. A faculty invitation to participate in research projects includes students in one of the core missions of a large research university. This nonremedial approach is critically important in light of the fact that campuses such as the University of Michigan lose historically underrepresented students who enter with excellent academic preparation and demonstrate high levels of achievement.

In the early years, the program was only open to historically underrepresented students. In addition to an interest in the positive benefits for student retention, there was also great interest in looking at the faculty's role in student retention and the impact of programs such as UROP on faculty perceptions and beliefs about diversity. During this period, faculty participants in the program were included in assessment and evaluation efforts. The study was particularly interested in looking at how faculty attitudes about diversity might change after working closely with diverse students. Would faculty gain a better understanding of the obstacles and barriers facing diverse students? Would faculty value the contributions diverse students bring to the research enterprise? Would they view these students and their academic strengths differently in their classes? Would participation in UROP encourage faculty to invite a more diverse cadre of students into their laboratories in the future? The study did not answer all of these questions, but the study revealed that faculty gained a greater appreciation of both diversity and the special challenges faced by underrepresented students on the University of Michigan campus. The program now has over 600 faculty participants annually engaged in what has become a major campus retention program.

UROP PROGRAM COMPONENTS

UROP focuses on first- and second-year students, involving them in ongoing faculty research programs during the academic year. Unlike many NSF, REU, NIH, and other summer research programs, the intent of the UROP program is to engage students in research while they are concurrently enrolled in traditional academic courses. Students identify research projects in September, typically begin their projects by October, and work on a specific project with their faculty member and research teams for the entire academic year.

Faculty Sponsors and Research Projects

UROP students spend anywhere from 6–12 hours per week engaged in ongoing or developing faculty research projects. Projects are solicited from the faculty through a variety of methods including presentations at faculty meetings, targeted mailings, colleague referrals, and other recruitment methods. The descriptions of faculty research are then compiled and published in a project book available for admitted UROP students in early September. The students then contact the research sponsors, who can be tenure-track faculty, research scientists, or post-doctoral fellows, and set up interviews. Finally, the research sponsors decide which students will work with them. Because the majority of UROP students are first- and second-year students, they are not expected to conduct independent research. However, some students remain involved in the same project for more than one year, at which point they often pursue an independent project and possibly coauthor a paper, depending upon the field.

Peer Advisors

An important component of the UROP program is the peer advising program. All UROP students are assigned to a peer advisor, who is a junior or senior and an alumnus of UROP. As the program grew beyond the original 15 students and their faculty partners, the peer advising component was developed to provide the student with guidance in the research culture, monitor the research partnerships, develop student leaders, and work with students on typical transition issues faced by first- and second-year students that could impact the research partnerships.

The amount and type of support students of color receive in college can have an effect on their desire to persist in the sciences. Specifically, Grandy (1998) found that students who had role models who were people of color who received mentorship from older students in their own ethnic group, and who had contact with staff of color were more likely to value scientific or technological contributions and want to contribute to scientific advancements. The support from other people of color is important, not because of its effect on grades (Grandy found no direct effect on grades), but because of its impact on students' positive feelings about the sciences, which may be related to students' attachment to the institution. Consequently, students and peer advisors now are matched based on common academic interests. The program hires advisors in the biomedical sciences, social sciences, humanities, natural sciences, engineering, and physical sciences. There is also an interdisciplinary group for women in the sciences. This common academic interest and focus increases peer advisors' ability to serve as research and academic guides and provides a common foundation of coursework and research interests for the peer advisors and their students.

Approximately 35 students are assigned to each peer advisor at the beginning of the academic year and peer advisors conduct an enrollment workshop to meet their students during the first week of the fall term. Immediately following the enrollment workshop, the peer advisors help their students develop a résumé, practice their interviewing skills, and provide guidance and support on how to identify research projects. All UROP students are required to meet with their peer advisors monthly to monitor the progress of these projects, discuss any time management or other related academic issues, and address any performance issues identified by a faculty research sponsor. In this way the peer advisors also serve as a resource for the faculty research sponsors when they have concerns about students. In addition to individual peer advising, advisors are also responsible for facilitating biweekly research seminars for all their students.

The peer advisors are required to attend a rigorous intensive weeklong training program in late summer. The training program includes role-playing around common student issues and intergroup relations training to prepare them to work with a diverse group of students and other staff. The staff training agenda includes program planning, syllabus development, tenets of effective peer advising, and other related topics. The UROP recruits a diverse group of peer advisors who reflect the makeup of the program. The peer advisors are highly motivated students who are proponents of the value of undergraduate research and want to give back to the program. The peer advisor position requires significant responsibility, and operating in this capacity helps prepare these upper-level students for graduate school, medical school, and other professional schools.

Research Seminars

The biweekly research seminars that the UROP peer advisors are responsible for facilitating for their students cover a range of research-related topics such as cutting edge research, research integrity and ethics, research field trips, and interactive discussions to learn about other students' research. These sessions typically involve a guest faculty lecturer or discussant. The peer research seminars serve a dual purpose; to expose students to research in their discipline and to create a community of young scholars. In some cases, a peer group serves to provide students' with an academic and social support network. Students meet ethnically and culturally similar students who are also engaged in similar academic activities on campus.

The peer advisors work with UROP staff members to design their seminars and prepare a syllabus. While the peer advisors have freedom to choose speakers and content to some extent, each peer advisor is required to cover certain topics each semester. In the fall term, the focus is on learning initial research responsibilities, faculty expectations, research integrity and ethics, cutting-edge research, research methods in the discipline, and opportunities for students to talk to each other about their respective projects. In the winter term, the seminars continue discussions on research methods, multicultural issues in research, and graduate and professional school opportunities. Additionally, a programwide career fair is held to showcase the role of research in nonacademic settings in the middle of the second semester.

Skill-Building Workshops

One of the most important and growing components of the program is a biweekly series of research-skill-building workshops created at the request of the program's faculty research partners. (These workshops alternate weeks with the reseach seminars.) Offered in collaboration with the libraries and other centers, these workshops address library use, Web research, EndNote, SPSS and STATA, GIS, MatLab, scientific writing, large-scale poster presentations, Microsoft PowerPoint, and so on. The goal is to reduce the training demands on faculty and to better facilitate student involvement with their projects. This also enables faculty to concentrate their interactions with their students on the content and research methods specific to the project.

Annual Research Symposium

The UROP year culminates with an annual research symposium. All UROP students are required to attend the symposium, where the majority of the students present research posters. Twenty to thirty students give oral presentations. The symposium provides a forum for students to share what they have learned over the course of the year and an opportunity to enhance their presentation skills.

Examples of Research Projects

Students in UROP conduct research in all fields and disciplines and with researchers in all UM schools and colleges. Student research tasks and responsibilities include development of research protocols, survey development, conducting experiments, data collection, data analysis, comprehensive literature reviews, and manuscript preparation. Although the examples given below are STEM research projects, UROP students also conduct research in the social sciences and the humanities.

- *Biomedical projects.* Students conduct hands-on laboratory work including behavioral tests, image processing, procedures such as PCR genotyping, as well as surgical and histologic studies.
- *Engineering.* Students develop computer programs and interfaces as well as working on equipment design, fabrication, and testing. They run trials and simulations, develop instrumentation, and secure related data.
- *Natural sciences.* Students engage in field and laboratory data collection and analysis, as well as sequencing and analysis of plant and animal DNA and other laboratory procedures. They observe insect and animal behavior; record and analyze observations; and input, analyze and display information, using GIS and remote sensing tools.

Lessons Learned

There are several key lessons that have informed the program's development and expansion over the years. First, early identification of students is critical in maintaining a diverse group of students in the academic and STEM pipeline. Typically, campuses wait until students reach their junior or senior year before inviting students into the research process. Therefore, an opportunity is lost to invite diverse students into the research process during the first and second years of college, one of the most critical junctures of their undergraduate careers. Furthermore, departments miss chances to enlist such students as concentrators and potential contributors to their field. It is critical that staff and faculty identify and engage students who indicate interest in certain fields in the early stages of their undergraduate careers.

Second, program staff members, who are dedicated and capable of providing personalized academic advising to support students' academic success, are key contributors. Not all first- and second-year students are familiar with the necessary skills to navigate the process of interacting with faculty as part of the interview and research processes comfortably and successfully. Therefore, the program staff, including peer advisors, plays a key role in making UROP accessible regardless of a students' familiarity with university norms.

Third, providing pathways into research labs and teams is extremely valuable to students as they leverage their UROP experience into professional and academic development and continue their undergraduate research careers. For example, the program is structured so that many UROP students have ample interactions in their seminars with their peers who are also engaged in research. In this context, students are also exposed to graduate students in research placements and through their appearances as guest speakers in the biweekly research seminars. The program also provides monetary support for UROP students to attend professional meetings.

ASSESSMENT AND EVALUATION

Undergraduate research programs have gained increasing amounts of attention for their contribution to undergraduate education (Pascarella & Terenzini, 2005). Braxton, Hirschy, and McClendon (2004), in their monograph on college student departure, cite the Undergraduate Research Opportunity Program at the University of Michigan as an exemplary retention program. Nagda, Gregerman, Jonides, von Hippel, and Lerner (1998) found that participating in such a program has a positive effect on retention, especially for African American sophomores who had not excelled academically in their first year in college. Involvement with undergraduate research is also positively correlated with the pursuit of postgraduate education (Hathaway, Nagda, & Gregerman, 2002).

Evaluation of minority-centered retention programs present a host of challenges. Most of the claims of program effects are anecdotal and present methodological challenges, including defining program goals and effectiveness, assumptions of inferential statistics, and lack of data (Levin & Levin, 1991, 1993). To address these and other challenges, Levin and Levin recommend using quasi-experimental designs (i.e., wait-list program controls) and time-series designs. In fact, a major strength of the studies by Nagda and colleagues (1998) and Hathaway and colleagues (2002) mentioned above is their quasi-experimental design. The challenge of assessing the impact of minority-centered programs is gaining increasing attention as various entities begin to challenge colleges and universities on their use of minority-centered services in retaining underrepresented racial and ethnic groups and women, particularly in the sciences.

Program assessment and evaluation has been an integral part of the University of Michigan's Undergraduate Research Opportunity Program. Assessment and evaluation activities, summarized in the next section, are distinct from other studies included in this volume because this work focuses on one program within a single institution's context. The following questions guide the assessment and evaluation of UROP:

- To what degree does UROP enhance the retention of underrepresented students' year-to-year retention and graduation rates?
- To what extent does undergraduate research facilitate student adjustment to college and socialization into academic life, campus life, and fields of study?

- What role does undergraduate research play in students' decisions to pursue graduate education?
- Do any of the aforementioned outcomes differ by race, ethnicity, or gender?

Mixed Methods Approach to Assessment and Evaluation

Collectively, the entire UROP assessment and evaluation program represents a mixed methods approach. Initially, quantitative research methods were used, collecting and analyzing survey and institutional data. These initial studies demonstrated that UROP had a positive effect on retention (Nagda et al., 1998). However, an important question remained: Which aspects of the program and student behaviors were associated with these positive outcomes? It was determined that this process-oriented question would best be answered through qualitative approaches; thus individual and small-group semistructured interviews were conducted. Experiential sampling and institutional academic data were used to explore certain questions: Are students still enrolled at UM? In what disciplines and fields are UROP students concentrating? What is the nature of UROP students' academic records (i.e., grades, course-taking patterns, and so on)? Finally, a survey of alumni was used to find out if UROP students pursued postgraduate degrees. These three key areas of UROP's assessment and evaluation are discussed in more detail below.

Retention studies. UROP was created to address differential retention rates of historically underrepresented students of color and their White counterparts. Initial research activities were designed to evaluate the program's effectiveness as a retention intervention. Evaluation team members understood it was critical, to the best of their ability, to discern whether UROP was having an impact on its participants. Because there were more applicants than available spaces in the program, the team took advantage of the natural experiment presented to them. The original retention study had experimental and control groups created from the entire pool of UROP applicants. Out of 2,873 applications, 1,280 were selected for inclusion in the study; 613 were UROP participants and 667 were non-UROP students (Nagda et al., 1998).

UROP applicants were matched by standardized test scores, grade point average, race, gender, and type of high school attended, and then randomly assigned to the experimental (admitted to UROP) or the control group (not admitted to UROP) (see Table 2.1). Both the control and experimental groups were administered a pre- and postsurvey, using a set of items comprised of psychological scales and measures designed to measure the psychosocial adjustment to college. Surveys were administered prior to students beginning their UROP experience at the start of the academic year and near the end of that academic year. The dean's office in the College of Literature, Science, and the Arts sent

Table 2.1. Sample profile on randomized selection criteria.

	African American Students			Hispanic Students			White Students		
	Participant	Control	t-stat	Participant	Control	t-stat	Participant	Control	t-stat
Sample size (n)	237	153		95	71		281	443	
High school GPA	1.871	2.040	−1.043	1.946	2.209	−1.046	3.669	3.682	−.481
SAT composite	972.03	948.32	1.178	1045.9	1076.7	−1.132	1205.4	1205.4	−.036
ACT composite	22.39	22.47	−.209	25.00	25.33	−.472	28.41	28.12	1.071

Note: From "Undergraduate Student–Faculty Research Partnerships Affect Student Retention," by B. A. Nagda, S. Gregerman, J. Jonides, W. von Hippel, and J. S. Lerner, 1998, *Review of Higher Education, 22*(1), pp. 55–72. Copyright 1998 by Johns Hopkins University Press. Reprinted with permission.

letters requesting students' participation in the study to assess their transition to the University of Michigan.

Findings from this initial study indicated that UROP students had higher retention rates compared to their matched non-UROP counterparts. These retention rate effects were strongest for African American students, and even more so for students who participated in UROP their sophomore year (Nagda et al., 1998). (See Tables 2.2–2.4.)

In 2003 a follow-up study was conducted using the same measures but with an outcome for 6-year graduation rates. This second study revealed that African American men had the highest graduation rates: 75.3% for those who participated in UROP, versus 56.2% for those in the control group (Hathaway, Nagda, & Gregerman, 2007). It is clear from these retention studies that UROP has a progressive effect on students; of note are the differential and positive effects for African American students and African American male students in particular.

Qualitative study. While the first retention study made known that UROP students had higher retention rates, the reasons for these effects were not clear, so a qualitative study was launched in 1996. As with the original retention study, experimental and control groups were established. Students were invited to

Table 2.2. Attrition rates of UROP participant and control groups.

	African American Students		Hispanic Students		White Students	
	Participant	Control	Participant	Control	Participant	Control
Sample size (n)	237	153	95	71	281	443
Nonpersisters (n)[a]	24	28	11	8	9	27
Percentage attrition	10.1	18.3	11.6	11.3	3.2	6.1
x^2-statistic ($df = 1$)	4.809		0.034		2.611	
p-value	.03		.85		.11	

Note: From "Undergraduate Student–Faculty Research Partnerships Affect Student Retention," by B. A. Nagda, S. Gregerman, J. Jonides, W. von Hippel, and J. S. Lerner, 1998, *Review of Higher Education, 22*(1), pp. 55–72. Copyright 1998 by Johns Hopkins University Press. Reprinted with permission.

[a] Defined as students who did not return the following semester.

Table 2.3. Attrition rates by academic performance of UROP participant and control groups.

	African American Students		Hispanic Students		White Students	
	Participant	Control	Participant	Control	Participant	Control
Low-GPA students (n)	111	85	40	33	112	220
Nonpersisters (n)	17	23	8	5	4	19
Percentage attrition	15.3	27.1	20.0	15.2	3.6	8.6
x^2-statistic ($df = 1$)	3.396		0.054		2.220	
p-value	.07		.82		.14	
High-GPA students (n)	115	61	49	32	146	183
Nonpersisters (n)	6	4	3	2	5	5
Percentage attrition	5.2	6.6	6.1	6.3	3.4	2.7
x^2-statistic ($df = 1$)	0.001		0.172		0.002	
p-value	.98		.68		.97	

Note: From "Undergraduate Student–Faculty Research Partnerships Affect Student Retention," by B. A. Nagda, S. Gregerman, J. Jonides, W. von Hippel, and J. S. Lerner, 1998, *Review of Higher Education, 22*(1), pp. 55–72. Copyright 1998 by Johns Hopkins University Press. Reprinted with permission.

participate in conversations about their first year at Michigan. In a letter sent from the dean's office, students were invited to participate in a series of semistructured group interviews; letters were sent to UROP students, students in other learning communities, and students not participating in any formal learning community. The primary interest was finding out if there were certain behaviors that UROP participants demonstrated that could help explain their higher retention rates. More specifically, the program staff and research team sought to better understand the nature of student-faculty interactions and the process by which students make their transition to college and become part of the academic and social realms of campus.

Table 2.4. Attrition rates by first-year/sophomore status.

	African American Students		Hispanic Students		White Students	
	Participant	Control	Participant	Control	Participant	Control
First-year students (n)	149	88	58	42	141	242
Nonpersisters (n)	14	15	11	4	7	16
Percentage attrition	9.4	17.0	19.0	9.5	4.9	6.6
x^2-statistic ($df = 1$)		2.344		1.043		0.186
p-value		.13		.31		.66
Second-year students (n)	81	65	36	29	141	201
Nonpersisters (n)	9	13	0	4	2	11
Percentage attrition	11.1	20.0	0.0	13.8	1.4	5.5
x^2-statistic ($df = 1$)		1.586		3.172		2.699
p-value		.21		.07		.10

Note: From "Undergraduate Student–Faculty Research Partnerships Affect Student Retention," by B. A. Nagda, S. Gregerman, J. Jonides, W. von Hippel, and J. S. Lerner, 1998, *Review of Higher Education, 22*(1), pp. 55–72. Copyright 1998 by Johns Hopkins University Press. Reprinted with permission.

In the qualitative study, the inquiry focused on issues relevant to students' interactions with their peers, faculty, and graduate students; students' academic experiences; and students' interaction with staff and use of program offices and units. Through a qualitative, inductive approach, these processes were explored. Using a grounded theory approach (Glaser & Strauss, 1967; Strauss & Corbin, 1990), this inquiry began with a broad interest in the transition to college. Through the analyses of data, student behavior was categorized in three distinct ways: (1) proactive, (2) reactive, and (3) inactive (Locks, Moldenhauer-Salazar, Hathaway, Gregerman, & Jonides, 2005). Proactive students were engaged in problem solving and often anticipated problems, while reactive students responded to events and situations without anticipating challenges. Inactive students did not respond to challenges they faced, often reporting that there was little they could to do to change their circumstances (Locks et al., 2005).

UROP students were disproportionately more likely to talk about their first year in proactive terms. In addition, UROP students were more likely to use proactive comments, talk to and meet with people, and anticipate future events such as exams and applying to graduate school. Moreover, proactive students regarded the faculty and graduate students as helpful, positive influences. In addition, these students were much more likely to create and sustain a network of people compared to non-UROP students. Students not in UROP were more likely to make reactive or inactive comments and were much more likely to visit campus offices or units but less likely to seek out specific individuals. Reactive and inactive students did not see faculty or staff as instrumental to their navigation of the campus nor as a potential source for assistance. In contrast to reactive and inactive students, proactive students, who were mostly UROP students, perceived their faculty as caring and interested in their success. Consequently, proactive students were more likely to access faculty in office hours. UROP students viewed university personnel as resources to help them navigate the college environment. These findings may be explained by students' working relationships with faculty as members on research teams (see Kuh & Hu, 2001) or because of their affiliation with a UROP peer advisor.

Alumni survey. Hathaway and colleagues (2002) conducted an alumni survey of UROP participants in order to ascertain if those students retained through graduation were more likely to pursue postgraduate degrees. Again, an experimental control design was used, with a smaller sample size of 288, with a significant return rate of 58.55% of the surveys (see Table 2.5). The survey questioned alumni about their undergraduate experiences and activities, not unlike Russell (Chapter 4). Students in the sample who participated in undergraduate research are similar to those discussed in Bauer and Bennett (Chapter 5). Undergraduate research experiences influenced students' likelihood to pursue a postgraduate education, regardless of their UROP status (see Tables 2.6 and 2.7). However, UROP students were more likely to pursue medical, law, or PhD programs than students in the control group, and no differences across race and gender were detected (see Table 2.8). As previous research has shown (Ethington & Smart, 1986; Hearn, 1987), undergraduate research experiences seem to equalize the path to graduate and professional schools.

NEW RESEARCH DIRECTIONS

Under the direction of Deborah Faye Carter, associate professor and director of the Center for the Study of Higher and Postsecondary Education, University of

Table 2.5. Research participation by key outcome variables (*N* = 288).

	Group (%)			
Variable	UROP (*n* = 81)	Other Research (*n* = 100)	No Research (*n* = 107)	Chi-Square
Graduate education	81.5	82.0	65.4	9.77**
Professional education	71.2	58.5	41.4	12.43**
Research activity	51.9	56.6	30.1	16.04***
Faculty recommendation	43.9	48.2	22.1	14.70***
Faculty contact	18.5	36.7	19.2	10.83**

Note: From "The Relationship of Undergraduate Research Participation to Graduate and Professional Education Pursuit: An Empirical Study," by R. S. Hathaway, B. R. A. Nagda, and S. R. Gregerman, 2002, *Journal of College Student Development, 43*(5), pp. 614–631. Copyright 2002 by American College Personnel Association. Reprinted with permission.

** $p < .01$.   *** $p < .001$.

Michigan, two new assessment and evaluation projects concerning UROP are underway. First, the role that participation in undergraduate research has on students' educational goals is under investigation. Specifically, the relationship between what students learn in classroom environments and what they learn through undergraduate research projects is of interest. The students in this study are involved in a summer research program, most of whom have previously engaged in undergraduate research, but not necessarily through UROP. The second related study involves students' first-year college experiences and how participation in undergraduate research affects their transition to college. The students in this latter study are academic-year UROP participants. As this second study is a mixed methods study, students will be asked to complete online surveys and participate in one-on-one interviews and focus groups. The program staff is particularly interested in learning what expectations students have when they arrive on campus and how those expectations evolve during their first year of college.

EXPANDING UNDERGRADUATE RESEARCH AS A PIPELINE AND RETENTION EFFORT

The mission of the University of Michigan's UROP is to become one of the leading undergraduate research programs, engaging and serving a diverse student population. Below, we outline strategic imperatives that will allow for the expansion of undergraduate research opportunities at the University of Michigan.

Table 2.6. Research participation by key outcome variables among underrepresented students of color (N = 136).

| | Group (%) | | | |
| | --- | --- | --- | |
Variable	UROP (n = 42)	Other Research (n = 41)	No Research (n = 53)	Chi-Square
Graduate education	78.6	82.9	56.6	9.39**
Professional education	66.7	38.2	36.7	7.44*
Research activity	50.0	50.0	25.5	7.83*
Faculty recommendation	41.4	55.3	16.0	15.30***
Faculty contact	19.0	45.0	20.0	9.10**

Note: From "The Relationship of Undergraduate Research Participation to Graduate and Professional Education Pursuit: An Empirical Study," by R. S. Hathaway, B. R. A. Nagda, and S. R. Gregerman, 2002, *Journal of College Student Development, 43*(5), pp. 614–631. Copyright 2002 by American College Personnel Association. Reprinted with permission.

$*p < .05.$ $**p < .01.$ $***p < .001.$

Table 2.7. Research participation by key outcome variables among White and Asian American students (N = 152).

| | Group (%) | | | |
| | --- | --- | --- | |
Variable	UROP (n = 39)	Other Research (n = 59)	No Research (n = 54)	Chi-Square
Graduate education	84.6	81.4	74.1	1.73
Professional education	75.8	72.9	45.0	9.95**
Research activity	54.1	61.0	34.6	8.03*
Faculty recommendation	46.4	42.2	28.9	2.77
Faculty contact	17.9	31.0	18.5	3.27

Note: From "The Relationship of Undergraduate Research Participation to Graduate and Professional Education Pursuit: An Empirical Study," by R. S. Hathaway, B. R. A. Nagda, and S. R. Gregerman, 2002, *Journal of College Student Development, 43*(5), pp. 614–631. Copyright 2002 by American College Personnel Association. Reprinted with permission.

$*p < .05.$ $**p < .01.$

Table 2.8. Pursuit of graduate education by race/ethnicity.

| | Group (%) | | |
Variable	White and Asian American Students	Underrepresented Students of Color	Chi-Square
No research			
Graduate education	74.1	56.6	3.61
Professional education	45.0	36.7	0.49
UROP			
Graduate education	84.6	78.6	0.49
Professional education	75.8	66.7	0.67
Other research			
Graduate education	81.4	82.9	0.04
Professional education	72.9	38.2	9.86**

Note: From "The Relationship of Undergraduate Research Participation to Graduate and Professional Education Pursuit: An Empirical Study," by R. S. Hathaway, B. R. A. Nagda, and S. R. Gregerman, 2002, *Journal of College Student Development, 43*(5), pp. 614–631. Copyright 2002 by American College Personnel Association. Reprinted with permission.

** $p < .01$.

Create a Center for Undergraduate Research

This center will serve as a clearinghouse for on- and off-campus research opportunities that includes UROP, international research, small research grants programs, and other best practices from around the country.

1. Support summer research fellowships and a small grants program for students interested in conducting independent research projects.
2. Provide support and advising services to UROP alumni starting with a pilot program during the 2008–09 academic year.
3. Develop a series of Introduction to Research Methods courses beginning with physics and astronomy in fall 2007; add a new disciplinary area each year over the next 5 years. These courses will be designed to prepare students for research projects in disciplines with limited undergraduate research opportunities.
4. Expand skill-building workshop offerings based on faculty input from the 8 workshops currently offered to provide 10–12 per year. Examples include scientific/technical writing, how to evaluate journal articles, grant

writing, honors theses, and applying for prestigious fellowships such as Rhodes, Marshall, Mitchell, and Watson.

Increase Off-Site Research Placements

1. Identify corporations, nonprofit organizations, and government agencies interested in establishing an ongoing relationship with UROP and in recruiting UROP alumni for summer placements.
2. Develop external research internships for students with financial need through alumni contacts of the College of Literature, Science, and the Arts and the University of Michigan.
3. Support 50 summer fellowships annually.

Increase Student/Faculty Research Partnerships

The number of faculty projects must increase by 25–40 projects annually in order to meet the growing demand for UROP participation.

1. Give UROP presentations annually in departments in which additional research placements are needed and identify current UROP faculty members in these departments who can assist with these presentations.
2. Develop an active faculty advisory group with representatives from every UM school and college who can assist with faculty recruitment through presentations at faculty meetings, e-mail recruitment, and so on.

Develop a Summer Research Program for Diverse High School Students

1. Identify faculty members willing to provide research opportunities for this cohort during the summers.
2. Seek corporate/foundation support for this initiative to be used to develop a pilot program, including funds for research scholarships.
3. Start with a small pilot program of 5–10 students during summer 2008 and expand incrementally over the next 5 years as external support allows.

The above plans will allow UROP to realize a number of goals, including developing and nurturing corporate relationships for internship programs. Additionally, the number and quality of student research partnerships would increase and would result in new research courses. Finally, such structures would allow for the development of high school recruiting expertise for a more diverse student population at the University of Michigan.

ACKNOWLEDGMENTS

UROP's program assessment and evaluations were funded by the following University of Michigan Units: Office of the Vice President for Research, Office of Minority Affairs, Office of the Vice President for Student Services, Center for the Study of Higher and Postsecondary Education, and National Center for Institutional Diversity. Funding sources external to the University of Michigan have included the State of Michigan's Equity Office, the U.S. Department of Education's Fund for the Improvement of Postsecondary education, the Howard Hughes Medical Institute, General Electric Foundation, Baldwin Foundation, Coca Cola Foundation, Daimler Chrysler Foundation, Dupont Foundation, General Electric Foundation, Microsoft Corporation, Motorola Foundation, Picower Foundation, Towsley Foundation, W. K. Kellogg Foundation, Intel Foundation, and other private and individual sponsors. In addition, the National Science Foundation recognized UROP with a Recognition Award for the Integration of Research and Education.

Alba Rueda-Riedle and Dr. Melba Joyce Boyd provided invaluable feedback on earlier versions of this work.

REFERENCES

Astin, A. (1993). *What matters in college? Four critical years revisited* (2nd ed.). San Francisco: Jossey-Bass.

Braxton, J. M., Hirschy, A. S., & McClendon, S. A. (2004). Understanding and reducing college student departure. *ASHE-ERIC Higher Education Report, 30*(3).

Ethington, C. A., & Smart, J. C. (1986). Persistence to graduate education. *Research in Higher Education, 24*(3), 287–303.

Glaser, B. G., & Strauss, A. L. (1967). *The discovery of grounded theory: Strategies for qualitative research.* Chicago: Aldine.

Grandy, J. (1998). Persistence in science of high-ability minority students: Results of a longitudinal study. *Journal of Higher Education, 69*(6), 589–620.

Hathaway, R. S., Nagda, B. R. A., & Gregerman, S. R. (2002). The relationship of undergraduate research participation to graduate and professional education pursuit: An empirical study. *Journal of College Student Development, 43*(5), 614–631.

Hathaway, R. S., Nagda, B. R. A., & Gregerman, S. R. (2007). *Student-faculty research partnerships and undergraduate degree completion.* Manuscript in preparation

Hearn, J. C. (1987). Impacts of undergraduate experiences on aspirations and plans for graduate and professional education. *Research in Higher Education, 27*(2), 119–141.

Kuh, G. D., & Hu, S. (2001). The effects of student-faculty interaction in the 1990s. *The Review of Higher Education, 24*(3), 309–332.

Kuh, G. D., Kinzie, J., Schuh, J. H., & Whitt, E. J. (2005). *Student success in college: Creating conditions that matter.* San Francisco: Jossey-Bass.

Levin, M. E., & Levin, J. R. (1991). A critical examination of academic retention programs for at-risk minority college students. *Journal of College Student Development, 32*, 323–334.

Levin, J. R., & Levin, M. E. (1993). Methodological problems in research on academic retention programs for at-risk minority college students. *Journal of College Student Development, 34*, 118–124.

Locks, A. M., Moldenhauer-Salazar, J., Hathaway, R., Gregerman, S. R., & Jonides, J. (2005). *Proactive attitudes amongst first year college students: Exploring potential effects of participation in an undergraduate research program.* Manuscript in preparation.

Nagda, B. A., Gregerman, S., Jonides, J., von Hippel, W., & Lerner, J. S. (1998). Undergraduate student-faculty research partnerships affect student retention. *Review of Higher Education, 22*(1), 55–72.

Pascarella, E. T., & Terenzini, P. T. (1991). *How college affects students.* San Francisco: Jossey-Bass.

Pascarella, E. T., & Terenzini, P. T. (2005). *How college affects students: A third decade of research* (Vol. 2). San Francisco: Jossey-Bass.

Strauss, A. L., & Corbin, J. M. (1990). *Basics of qualitative research: Grounded theory procedures and techniques.* Newbury Park, CA: Sage.

Implementation and Assessment of Course-Embedded Undergraduate Research Experiences: Some Explorations

Carol Trosset, David Lopatto, and Sarah Elgin

CHANGES IN science education often follow an evolutionary pattern. Undergraduate research experiences, in which a student assumes the role of apprentice in an ongoing research program, have existed for many years but now have expanded into new niches (Fortenberry, 1998). Formerly content with anecdotal or biographical accounts of the significance of the undergraduate research experience in the recruitment and training of scientists, educators and administrators reacted to the growing popularity of undergraduate research experiences with demands for credible assessment of the benefits. Authoritative accounts of the benefits of undergraduate research experiences are relatively recent (see Lopatto, Chapter 6; Russell, Chapter 4). Even as these benefits are assimilated into our general knowledge about science education, a more recent evolution has occurred. Convinced of the benefits of providing students with research experiences, science educators are bringing such research experiences into the organized course curriculum of the university or college. As this continuing evolution occurs, the need for assessment of the benefits of course-embedded research experiences grows.

Lopatto (2006) has summarized the current state of assessments of undergraduate research experiences. Long considered a compelling stimulus for choosing a career in science (Roe, 1952), undergraduate research experiences yield benefits beyond career clarification. Data derived from both qualitative and quantitative methodology converge on the finding that undergraduate research experiences set the occasion for personal as well as professional development (Lopatto, 2004; Seymour, Hunter, Laursen, & DeAntoni, 2004). Benefits include the growth of self-confidence, ability to work independently, and tolerance for obstacles that occur in research, coupled with an increased understanding of the research process, of how scientists work on problems, and of the need to support conclusions with evidence. As research experiences become embedded in courses in the science curriculum, we need to ask if the benefits of such experiences are similar to the benefits of full-time summer research experiences, and if so, to what degree.

THE ESSENTIAL FEATURES OF UNDERGRADUATE RESEARCH

When asked "What are the essential features of undergraduate research projects?" science faculty from three undergraduate institutions responded:

> Students should read scientific literature.
> Students should design some aspect of the project.
> Students should work independently.
> Students should feel ownership of the project.
> Students should use careful and reproducible lab techniques.
> Students should have a meaningful research question.
> Students should strive to produce a significant finding.
> Students should have an opportunity for oral communication.
> Students should have an opportunity for written communication.
> Students should work in a good (state of the art) environment. (Lopatto, 2003).

Key features include generating findings that were previously unknown, student input, independence, engagement, and communication. It is also perceived as messy, work intensive, and defiant of deadlines and schedules.

Because of the associated unpredictability, the essential features of research and the undergraduate research experience are difficult to configure into a regular science curriculum. A regular science curriculum consists of courses that designate set contact time for lecture, discussion, recitation, or laboratory work. The course has an inviolate set of deadlines determined by the institution's schedule. The course may be populated by a large number of students, precluding the sort of personal mentoring that undergraduate researchers might expect. These students are expected to learn a common framework of content and methods and to proceed more or less at the same pace. Their learning usually must be assessed and assigned a letter grade at the end of the course.

To the extent that the features of research experiences are successfully assimilated into a course, the benefits of undergraduate research experiences should occur. One purpose of the research reported here is to compare the benefits of course-embedded research experiences to those reported for summer undergraduate research experiences in which students spend 6 to 10 weeks working exclusively on research (Lopatto, 2004). This constellation of benefits has been enlarged in this study to incorporate other educational benefits normally associated with science courses. In addition, previous investigations (e.g., Lopatto & Trosset, 2001) have indicated that the student's preferred learning style is related to the benefits they may gain in a course. For that reason, we explored student learning style using a brief learning style survey (Romero, Tepper, & Tetrault, 1992). We examined the reliability and validity of student reports by employing pretest-posttest measures, obtaining corroborating data from faculty, and triangulating quantitative data with interviews. We begin by clarifying the nature of course-embedded research experiences with a description of three courses at our research site, Washington University in St. Louis, Missouri.

WASHINGTON UNIVERSITY ADVANCED LAB CLASSES

While the summer undergraduate research experience remains an important part of a science major at Washington University, the faculty recognizes that not all students will avail themselves of this opportunity, for a variety of reasons. Nonetheless, it is important that all majors develop an understanding of how new knowledge is generated in their field, and hence other ways of providing a research experience are being explored (see Figure 3.1). A major effort at present is in

Figure 3.1. Spectrum of research-related undergraduate experiences. A one-semester upper-level laboratory course can be constructed to provide students with a collaborative research experience.

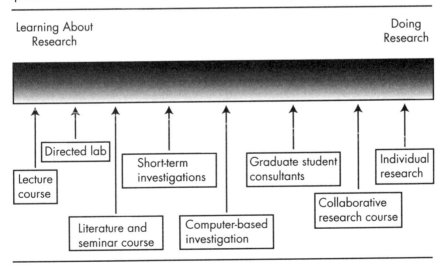

development of one-semester, upper-level laboratory courses that are built around an experimental problem or system, providing students with an opportunity to carry out research as a central part of the laboratory course (see Katkin, 2004, for examples). Typically these lab courses meet for 6 to 8 hours per week. Such laboratory courses differ conspicuously from the summer research experience in being much more structured, by necessity operating on a schedule to complete experiments within the semester. Students typically devote only a fraction (typically about a quarter) of their academic time to the effort, as opposed to having full time for research during the summer, and must earn a letter grade, a type of pressure absent during the summer. In what way do the gains made by these students mimic, and in what way do they differ from, the learning gains reported for the summer experience?

Biology 4342: Research Explorations in Genomics

The life sciences are undergoing a revolution, as genome sequencing continues to become cheaper, allowing us to use genomic tools in a variety of investigations. Clearly we need to provide students with access to genomic tools, allowing them to develop their thinking to encompass this new way of approaching biological problems. For example, rather than using morphology alone, organisms are being classified and evolutionary relationships explored using their DNA. Pathogens can be rapidly identified; whole populations can be sampled. One can follow not just the changes in expression of a few genes, but changes for the genome as a whole in response to an environmental stimulus. Human genetics is now an entirely different field, as critical loci are being identified and can be routinely sampled. Because raw sequencing, now mostly an automated process, is getting cheaper, while the process of generating finished sequence and annotating the sequence data generated continues to require human input, the time is ripe for a student-scientist partnership that engages students in finishing and/or annotating genomic sequence to address a problem of interest.

Biology 4342 engages 12–14 students each semester (14 weeks) in a partnership with faculty, TAs, and staff to finish and annotate a selected portion of a eukaryotic genome. The class meets for 8 hours per week, using 2–3 hours for lecture or group instruction and devoting the rest of the time to lab work. Lab work is largely computer based, and involves very little wet bench work. During the period 2004–2006, students have been working on the smallest chromosome (the "dot chromosome") of one species of fruit flies, *Drosophila virilis*. Scientific interest in the problem comes from data indicating that while the same genes are present, the dot chromosome of *D. melanogaster* is largely packaged in a heterochromatic form, while the dot chromosome of *D. virilis* is packaged in a euchromatic form. Comparative genomic analysis may elucidate the underlying cause of this important difference in chromatin packaging. Each student takes responsibility for work on one fosmid (about 40,000 bp) of DNA from *D. virilis*. Appropriate fosmids have been identified in the faculty lab (by Dr. Sarah Elgin), and raw sequence is generated by the Washington University Genome Sequencing Center. During the first half of the semester, the student becomes the "finisher," examining the sequence data to identify areas of insufficient coverage, designing experiments to obtain the needed additional sequencing data, and checking the results to insure high-quality, finished sequence for his or her fosmid. During the second half of the semester the student becomes the "annotator," identifying genes, repeat elements, other conserved regions, and so on, within his or her fosmid. Students prepare a paper and give an oral presentation reporting their results and defending their conclusions on finishing their fosmid, in a practice analysis of genes and pseudogenes in chimpanzee, and on completing annotation of their *Drosophila* fosmid. An analysis based on the pooled data from the 2004 class (with all of these students as coauthors) has been published in the scientific literature (Slawson et al., 2006), and these data are now part of GenBank. A second publication based on the finished *D. virilis* dot chromosome is anticipated in 2008. Of the 12 students participating in 2005, 11 provided data for this study of research experiences.

Biology 3492: Laboratory Experiments with Eukaryotic Microbes

Major discoveries of fundamental biology have been made using model organisms. From a pedagogical perspective, model organisms serve well to show students how hypothesis-driven science is carried out in biological laboratories, and provide a means to engage students in original research during their undergraduate education. This course uses *Tetrahymena* and other eukaryotic microbial model organisms to explore biological questions. A major goal of the course, beyond teaching students cell and molecular techniques, is to show how to choose and employ a model organism to make novel biological discoveries. Each time the course is taught the instructor (Dr. Douglas Chalker) chooses a single aspect of biology (for example, RNA interference, nuclear localization, and so on) for the students to study. The subjects chosen are ones where the biology of *Tetrahymena* offers some particular advantage, allowing unique, but logical approaches to the work. Gene knockout technologies, molecular cloning, fluorescence microscopy, and western blot analysis have been used to give the students diverse training in current experimental approaches. The course meets twice for 3-hour lab periods and once for a 1-hour lecture per week for 14 weeks.

In spring 2005 (the class studied here), the students first searched the *Tetrahymena* genome for homologues of the nuclear import protein, importin alpha, and found that the genome encoded at least ten candidates. Each student selected one to characterize further. Students proceeded to examine expression of their candidate by rtPCR (reverse transcription Polymerase Chain Reaction) and to examine the localization of the encoded protein by creating a GFP (Green Fluorescent Protein) fusion protein. This was enabled by the use of recombination-based cloning methodologies (Gateway system by Invitrogen) that allowed efficient cloning of PCR products of genomic coding regions and creation of GFP-fusion constructs. This module served as a proof-in-principle that students in a classroom setting can perform extensive analyses of individual genes. The students all performed significant original research that should earn them authorship of a planned scientific publication. Six students out of ten enrolled in this course contributed data to this study of research experiences.

Chemistry 445: Instrumental Methods in Physical Chemistry Laboratory

This is a structured laboratory course that aims to develop the research skills of students, with the following goals: (1) increased understanding of concepts in physical chemistry via hands-on experience; (2) gaining an appreciation of the applications of physical chemistry concepts in other areas of chemistry, in other disciplines such as biology, medicine, and materials science, and in everyday life; (3) gaining a firsthand understanding of the instrumentation, techniques, and methods utilized by researchers in physical chemistry and at its interfaces with other disciplines (including the use of a wide variety of research-grade instruments); (4) developing better understanding of the scientific method; (5) developing skills in problem solving via enquiry-based exercises built upon the structured components of certain experiments; (6) developing and honing skills in scientific writing through reports submitted in publication format (abstract, introduction, methods, results, conclusions); and (7) complementing and enhancing the breadth and depth of skills obtained in more unstructured, independent research experiences.

The class typically enrolls 15–20 students. It meets each week for a 1-hour lecture, and for a 5-hour laboratory period. The students work in pairs, but analyze their data and submit reports independently. They submit seven reports during the semester, and considerable emphasis is placed on good scientific writing. The students are first introduced to a group of measurement techniques and analytical tools, and then carry out a series of investigations. Section 1, Electronics and Measurement Methods, covers resistor networks, semiconductor devices and the operational amplifier, digital electronics, computer hardware concepts, and time- and frequency-domain electronics. Section 2, Physical Chemistry Concepts and Measurements, covers listening for gas non-ideality, investigating the speed of sound, investigating the thermochemistry of the tricarboxylic acid cycle using bomb calorimetry, electron spin resonance spectroscopy, using nuclear magnetic resonance spectroscopy to analyze enzyme kinetics, using electronic absorption and emission spectroscopy to analyze chlorophyll, rotation-vibration (infrared) spectroscopy, thermodynamics of anthracycline/DNA interactions, time-resolved optical spectroscopy, and electrochemistry-cyclic voltammetry. Thirteen students out of twenty enrolled in this course contributed data for this study of research experiences.

ASSESSMENT METHODOLOGY

One of our objectives was to compare the learning gains students experience during research-focused coursework with that in mentored summer projects. Therefore our methodology included a postcourse survey in which students were asked to reflect on their own learning gains with items that paralleled the SURE survey (Summer Undergraduate Research Experiences survey; Lopatto, 2004) used to evaluate summer research experiences. The approach followed Alexander Astin's (1993) model of the educational process, abbreviated as I-E-O, standing for Inputs (students with preexisting abilities and prior experiences) that experience an Environment (the courses described above) resulting in Outcomes (learning gains). In this study we had four input measures: self-reported entry level skills, prior experiences in research, learning styles, and career plans. We had three outcome measures: self-reported learning gains on a survey, student statements about their gains and experiences during interviews, and faculty evaluations of each student's abilities.

Twenty-eight students completed the precourse survey, and twenty-five completed the postcourse survey. Twenty-one students were interviewed by Trosset during the last week of classes. Each student was identified by a confidential number, so that data from the precourse and postcourse student surveys, postcourse student interviews, and the postcourse faculty evaluations of students could be linked for analysis.

Our interest in evaluating multiple measures created a situation that was refractory to statistical analysis, a small sample design with too many variables to be tolerated by the number of cases. As a result, we report few statistics, relying on tabular and visual displays of results.

Student-Reported Outcomes

The evidence indicates that many positive outcomes occurred in these courses, beginning with the postcourse self-ratings of how much students felt they had gained in various possible areas of learning. Figures 3.2 and 3.3 show the overall results for the group of 25 respondents. Figure 3.2 shows the items that are common to the present study and the SURE survey. The current results are displayed as one-sample 95% confidence intervals. These intervals are displayed next to the comparable SURE survey means. The figure shows that the course

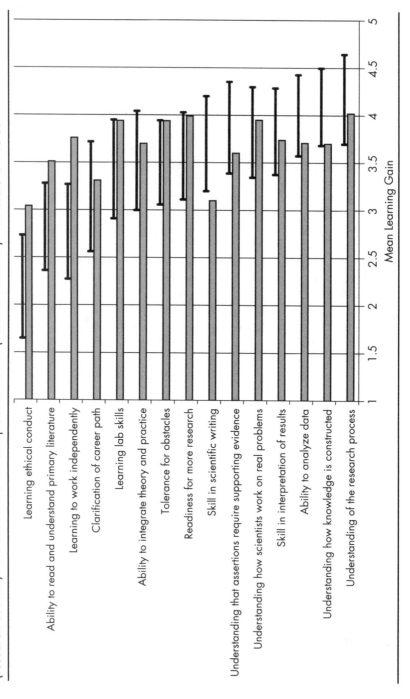

Figure 3.2. Mapping of results of student-reported learning gains in three research courses onto mean gains reported from summer research. The thin lines represent the 95% confidence interval for sample means (research courses). The bars show the comparison means (summer research). The scale is 1 to 5.

benefits and summer research benefits follow roughly the same pattern, with "understanding of the research process" the highest gain in both cases, and "learning ethical conduct" the lowest gain in both cases. The overlap of the confidence interval with the end of the bar (the SURE mean) permits judgments about statistical differences similar to that of a one-sample *t* test. Where the SURE mean lies outside the confidence interval, the mean of the current sample and the mean of the summer research comparison group are significantly different. Use the middle of the thin line as the mean for course performance and for comparison to the end of the bar.

Items on which these courses received a higher mean than summer research included understanding how knowledge is constructed, the ability to analyze data, understanding that assertions require supporting evidence, and skill in scientific writing. With respect to the last of these, it should be noted that the physical chemistry course had an especially strong focus on the writing of scientific lab reports. A number of other items received somewhat lower scores from these courses than from summer research students: readiness for more research, tolerance for obstacles, ability to integrate theory and practice, learning lab skills (note that the genomics class did not include wet-lab activities), clarification of career path, ability to read and understand primary literature, and learning ethical conduct.

Figure 3.3 displays the mean gains for the course benefits that had no comparable item on the SURE survey. The items are listed from highest to lowest gain. The highest gain, "understanding the relation of the course to other sciences," is followed by skill and self-confidence items. Among the lowest rated items are "interest in taking courses in other sciences" and "interest in taking courses in math and computer science." While understanding and self-confidence increase, students are not strongly inclined to go outside their area to other sciences.

Other types of evidence also indicated positive learning gains.

Subject matter. All the students interviewed said they had learned a great deal about the subject matter. Instructors felt that this objective had been successfully met in all three classes, and 81% of the students evaluated by faculty instructors were rated as excellent or good in their postcourse knowledge of the subject matter. Without specifically being asked, students volunteered the information that certain activities had helped—or forced—them to understand the material better. These included writing detailed formal lab reports, having to defend their work against challenges from others during oral presentations, having frequent opportunities to ask questions, and doing troubleshooting on their own projects.

Lab techniques. Wet-lab techniques, of course, were not a part of the genomics course. Students in the other two classes generally reported gains in lab techniques. Those with prior experience in lab jobs indicated that the classroom experience gave them broader exposure to more different techniques, while a job gave them

Figure 3.3. Mean gains on additional learning items reported by students in three research courses. The scale is 1 to 5.

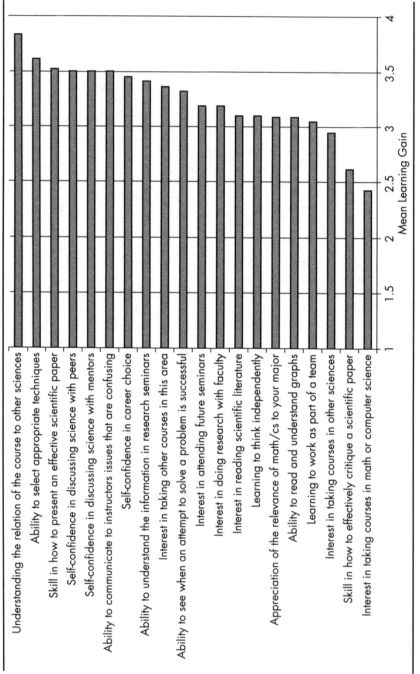

the opportunity to develop higher levels of expertise in a smaller number of techniques (sometimes only one). Of the students evaluated, 92% were rated as excellent or good in their postcourse lab techniques.

Understanding scientific research. In the postcourse student survey, "understanding the research process" received the highest average score. In fact, 77% of the students evaluated by their instructors were rated as excellent or good in their understanding of the research process. In postcourse interviews, students were asked an open-ended question about how well their course had taught them about scientific research. The most frequent responses will be described below under other learning gains, but several of the responses related to students' increased understanding of the process of doing science. Four students said they had learned that research doesn't always work, and that it goes more slowly than they had expected. Other items mentioned (by one student each) included the importance of checking everything, the fact that science is more ambiguous than it appears in lectures, that when you're doing it you can't check whether you're right, that research is collaborative, and that it leads to an increased ability to think about the big picture. (The last happened in particular because each student in the genomics course worked on a piece of the larger project; in order to talk with each other they had to fit their own pieces into the larger context.)

In order to ascertain what aspects of the research process students were aware of, the postcourse interviews also included questions about what each student liked and disliked most about doing research. Among positive comments, six students mentioned the element of discovery and learning new things. Five said they liked doing something no one had done before. Four liked working through a problem that had not been prescripted. Three said their favorite thing was when the methods worked and they got a result. Other things individuals liked were doing something useful, doing a hands-on activity, the repeated utility of the techniques, being responsible for doing things right, the importance of being organized, intellectual stimulation, and working with other people.

When asked what they disliked, six students mentioned how long it takes to do research, and an overlapping six said the repetition was tedious. Three disliked the fact that things didn't always work, and three found it frustrating that because the work had not been done before by someone else, they did not always know how to proceed. One disliked the unpredictability (not knowing what will work, what will happen, or how long it will take). Another disliked the need to work in a linear fashion; this student contrasted research to computer programming, where the programmer can skip around and work on different bits at different times. Regardless of whether students liked or disliked the different elements of research, these comments definitely indicate that many of them came to perceive research more accurately as a result of their classroom experiences.

Doing scientific research. Several elements of doing research received high scores in the postcourse self-reported learning gains, including the ability to analyze data, skill in interpretation of results, and the ability to select appropriate techniques. Faculty rated 81% of their students excellent or good in their ability to carry out research at the end of the course. In student interviews, four said they had learned a lot about why one does certain things in the course of research, and about how to choose an appropriate technique. Students were also asked to compare these courses to their other previous research experiences. Twelve of the students interviewed had had jobs in labs (most at Washington University, a few elsewhere). Nine of these described their lab jobs as teaching them less about research than their experiences in these courses. They all said some or all of the following things about their jobs: they were mostly left on their own, they were expected to learn quickly without asking questions, they had a single task which they performed repetitively, and they were not involved in the planning or design of the research. However, the other three had been involved in their research jobs in ways very similar to their involvement in the classroom projects. One was even more involved in the research on the job and preferred it to the classroom project because there was more time for deeper extended involvement.

Generally, students compared these research-based courses favorably to other science courses they had taken. They reported that other courses had prescripted labs and in those labs questions were not as welcome. Lecture courses give the same information, they reported, but you don't learn why that information is important. The research-based courses, they felt, taught them more about how things are done in science. One learning-disabled student also liked it that students could choose between various approaches in order to reach the same goals.

Writing and oral presentation skills. These were the most frequently mentioned learning gains in the interviews. Seven students said that the oral presentation skills they had learned would be useful. Most had little prior experience in this activity, and while most had not enjoyed it, they believed it was an important ability and that their skill levels had increased. Six said they had learned a lot about scientific writing. Most of these were from the physical chemistry course, which had focused heavily on the writing of research reports. Several students mentioned how different the format is for writing scientific papers from the argumentation essays they had learned to write in humanities courses. In the postcourse survey of learning gains, skill in scientific writing received one of the highest scores, and a much higher score than is generally reported by summer research students.

Interest in science and clarification of career path. Although "clarification of career path" did not receive a particularly high score on the postcourse survey of learning gains, many of the students interviewed indicated that their classroom experience had confirmed their career intentions. It is also valuable to see what types of students are attracted to a research-based science class. One junior said she would have left the sciences had she not found a research-based course that semester. Having had an excellent research experience while in high school, this student already understood what science was all about, and was very frustrated and bored during the first two years of college science courses. She acknowledged that it had helped when professors had talked about what lay ahead, but she would soon have gotten tired of waiting for it. This is not a unique motive for leaving the sciences in college, but it is not one generally mentioned in the literature. It suggests that one reason for adopting a research-based pedagogy is to avoid driving away good students who already understand and love scientific research.

INSTRUCTOR-REPORTED OUTCOMES

Twenty-six students were rated by their instructors at the end of the courses on a variety of skills. The frequencies of these ratings are summarized in Table 3.1.

The first 10 items were taken from a research assessment instrument originally developed for use at Grinnell College. The items and the behavioral anchors for the 4 levels are presented in Figure 3.4. The numbers reported in Table 3.1 represent the number of students receiving that rating from the course's instructor. Instructor ratings were reliable across items (Cronbach's alpha = .91). Interitem bivariate correlations varied from 0 to 0.7. The highest possible total evaluation score was 60. One student received a 56 (93%), ten students received between 51 and 55 (85–92%), eight received between 45 and 49 (75–82%), four received 40–44 (67–73%), and three scored below 40 (less than 67%). Instructors reported greatest satisfaction in the abilities of the students at the end of the courses to judge information, provide argumentation, and display appropriate use of evidence.

IMPLICATIONS FOR LEARNING OUTCOMES ASSESSMENT

Students from three advanced science courses reported a variety of learning gains. The pattern of gains, where comparison was possible, resembled those reported by students engaging in summer undergraduate research experiences. Course instructors reported gains for students as well, although differences in the form of the evaluation precluded a correlation between the two reports. Cognitive interviews allowed for elaboration on survey results. The nature of the gains seems consistent with the placement of research-oriented courses near research experiences in the spectrum of experiences (see Figure 3.1).

The fact that most of the students in this study already had research experience made it difficult to ascertain the origins of learning gains. Learning may depend on experience, be independent of it, or combine with experience to produce a joint effect.

Table 3.1. Frequency of research-skills ratings by instructors.

	Excellent	Good	Fair	Poor	
Independence	4	8	11	3	
Research design	4	11	11	0	
Intellectual curiosity	7	9	7	3	
Reading	4	18	3	1	
Sources of information	1	8	15	2	
Types of information	14	8	1	3	
Judging information	16	6	1	3	
Argumentation	16	8	0	2	
Use of evidence	22	0	3	1	
Places information in context	7	11	8	0	
	Excellent	Good	Moderate	Fair	Poor
Knows subject matter	8	13	4	1	0
Lab techniques	12	12	1	1	0
Understands research process	6	14	5	1	0
Able to carry out research	12	9	4	1	0

Note: The first 10 items were adapted from the rubric shown in Figure 3.4.

To further examine the role of previous experience, we need to examine the experiences of introductory students who are encountering scientific research for the first time. The authors are continuing research in this direction.

Plans for future careers and learning style may be factors influencing student learning. Students who are oriented toward a career in science may find research courses instrumental to their plans, and thus show high motivation to succeed. Learning style may also influence student performance, or even the decision to engage in science (Romero et al., 1992). A surprising finding of the present study was that students representing diverse learning styles, classified on dimensions of concrete-abstract learning and reflective-active learning, were represented in these courses. According to conventional wisdom, students scoring on the concrete side of the concrete-abstract learning style dimension favor studies in humanities, fine arts, and business. In the current study, over half (14 of 26) of the students who provided learning style data scored on the concrete side of the concrete-abstract dimension.

Figure 3.4. A research skills evaluation form developed by the authors. Course instructors or supervisors use the form to evaluate individual students.

For *each student* who completed the course, please choose one statement for each item below that best describes the current (end of course) level of the student's abilities.

1. Independence
   1. Student is dependent, follows instructions.
   2. Student works independently without supervision.
   3. Student has independent ideas.
   4. Student takes ownership of the project, works as a colleague.

2. Research design
   1. Student does not know how to proceed.
   2. Student can work within a structured plan.
   3. Student can propose several methods but cannot judge between them.
   4. Student can make reasonable decisions about design and methodology.

3. Intellectual curiosity
   1. Student is passive.
   2. Student asks questions for clarification.
   3. Student asks questions that expand the topic.
   4. Student asks creative questions.

4. Reading
   1. Student has trouble understanding content.
   2. Student can summarize material but cannot place it in context.
   3. Student can place material in context but does not think independently.
   4. Student thinks independently about the material.

5. Sources of information
   1. Student does not search for information.
   2. Student relies on summaries and secondary sources.
   3. Student does partial search, finds some primary sources.
   4. Student does comprehensive search for primary sources.

6. Types of information
   1. Student cannot tell which information is relevant.
   2. Student uses only one kind of information.
   3. Student can use several modes of information but does not link them.
   4. Student links several modes of information to present a coherent argument.

7. Judging information
   1. Student believes what she/he reads or hears.
   2. Student responds to conflictive information by saying that everything is relative.
   3. Student takes a position but does not make a supported argument.
   4. Student makes an argument based on evidence.

8. Argumentation
   1. Student reports on a topic without reference to an argument.
   2. Student reports on arguments in the field but takes no position.
   3. Student makes an assertion but does not make an argument.
   4. Student makes a well-reasoned argument.

9. Evidence
   1. Student does not use evidence.
   2. Student uses evidence without judging its quality.
   3. Student selects or manipulates evidence to support his/her preconceptions.
   4. Student considers relevant evidence fairly.

10. Factual and theoretical context
    1. Student does not relate findings to their appropriate disciplinary context.
    2. Student attempts to relate findings to their context, but does so in an incomplete or flawed way.
    3. Student usually relates findings to their appropriate disciplinary context.
    4. Student consistently relates findings to their appropriate context as a means of analysis.

The present study, being an exploration of the means by which research-oriented courses might be characterized, does not qualify as an experiment. Students self-selected into the courses, and there was no control group. Therefore, while we can speculate about the role of experience, career orientation, and learning style, we cannot make any causal conclusions regarding student learning. Nevertheless, we find it encouraging that both students and instructors reported learning gains, and that dimensions of this learning in many instances resemble those resulting from a full-time summer research experience.

ACKNOWLEDGMENTS

We thank April Bednarski for preparation of Figure 1. Special thanks to Professors Douglas Chalker and Dewey Holten, to other faculty and staff who support the research lab courses, and to the Washington University students who participated in this study. Development of Bio 4342 Research Explorations in Genomics has been supported by a Howard Hughes Medical Institute (HHMI) Professorship awarded to Washington University for SCRE (Grant 52003904). This study was supported by Grant 52003842 from the HHMI Undergraduate Biological Sciences Education Program to Washington University.

REFERENCES

Astin, A. (1993). *What matters in college?* San Francisco: Jossey-Bass.

Fortenberry, N. L. (1998). Integration of the research curriculum. *Council on Undergraduate Research Quarterly, 18*, 54–61.

Katkin, W. (2004). *Integrating Research into Undergraduate Education: The Value Added.* Retrieved January 1, 2008, from http://www.reinventioncenter.miami.edu/Conference_04/proceedings.htm

Lopatto, D. (2003). The essential features of undergraduate research. *Council on Undergraduate Research Quarterly, 24*, 139–142.

Lopatto, D. (2004). Survey of undergraduate research experiences (SURE): First findings. *Cell Biology Education, 3*, 270–277.

Lopatto, D. (2006). Undergraduate research as a catalyst for liberal learning. *Peer Review, 8*, 22–25.

Lopatto, D., & Trosset, C. (2001). The utility of learning style data for learning outcomes assessment. *A Collection of Papers on Self-Study and Institutional Improvement.* Chicago: The Higher Learning Commission.

Roe, A. (1952). A psychologist examines 64 eminent scientists. *Scientific American, 187*, 21–25.

Romero, J. E., Tepper, B. J., & Tetrault, L. A. (1992). Development and validation of new scales to measure Kolb's (1985) learning style dimensions. *Educational and Psychological Measurement, 52*, 171–180.

Seymour, E., Hunter, A.-B., Laursen, S., & DeAntoni, T. (2004). Establishing the benefits of research experiences for undergraduates: First findings from a three-year study. *Science Education, 88,* 493–594.

Slawson, E. E., Shaffer, C. D., Malone, C. D., Kellmann, E., Shevchek, R. B., Craig, C. A., Bloom, S., Bogenpohl, J., II, Dee, J., Morimoto, E. T. A., Myoung, J., Nett, A. S., Ozsolak, F., Tittiger, M. E., Zeug, A., Pardue, M. L., Buhler, J., Mardis, E., & Elgin, S. C. R. (2006). Comparison of dot chromosome sequences from *D. melanogaster* and *D. virilis* reveals an enrichment of DNA transposon sequences in heterochromatic domains. *Genome Biology, 7,* R15.

Assessments of Undergraduate Research Experiences

Undergraduate Research Opportunities: Facilitating and Encouraging the Transition from Student to Scientist

Susan H. Russell

BETWEEN 2003 AND 2005, SRI International conducted four Web-based surveys designed to assess undergraduate research opportunities (UROs). The surveys were conducted under contract to the National Science Foundation (NSF) and involved almost 15,000 respondents. Survey respondents were participants in undergraduate research programs sponsored by NSF and recent graduates in a so-called hard science, technology, engineering, or mathematics (STEM), or in a social, behavioral, or economic science (SBES). Despite the differences in the populations surveyed, the surveys produced remarkably consistent results. We found strongly positive effects of UROs on participants' understanding of the research process, confidence in their research-related abilities, and awareness of academic and career options in STEM/SBES; changes in interest in STEM/SBES careers; and expectations of obtaining a PhD. Participation in undergraduate research seemed most likely to have positive outcomes when it was done voluntarily and out of a genuine interest; research that was done because it was required was less likely to lead to positive outcomes. Specific activities appeared to be less important than a long-term, multifaceted experience that drew the undergraduate into the culture and process of research. It is likely that talented mentors played a central role in making this happen. We found no evidence that UROs should be structured differently depending on the race/ethnicity or gender of participants.

There have been a number of other studies assessing UROs, but these are either dated—such as NSF's 1990 assessment of the Research Experiences for Undergraduates (REU) Program[1]—or relatively small-scale studies, generally focused on one or a few institutions, a single program, or even a single researcher's experiences. NSF has also funded a study of UROs at four liberal arts institutions that used both qualitative and quantitative approaches to assess the impact of "effective" undergraduate research experiences on learning, attitude, and career choice.[2]

SRI's study differs from these other studies in a number of ways, but most importantly in its greater comprehensiveness in terms of the NSF programs included and the survey sample sizes, and, correspondingly, in the numbers and diversity of institutions included. The study addressed six major questions:

- What are the activities and characteristics that comprise undergraduate "research experiences"?
- For what reasons do faculty and students choose to participate in these experiences?
- What criteria do faculty use in selecting undergraduates for research activities?
- What effects do research experiences have on undergraduates' academic and career decisions?
- What are the key variables that influence the effects of research experiences? In particular, do the effects differ by whether the experience took place during the summer versus the academic year (fall through spring), the NSF program sponsoring the experience, the academic field of research, or the student's race/ethnicity or sex?
- Are different kinds of research experiences more effective with some types of students than with others? In particular, are the characteristics of the optimal experience different for minorities versus nonminorities or for men versus women?

URO SURVEYS

The study included the following surveys:

- An initial NSF-program participant survey (undergraduates, graduate students, postdocs, and faculty), conducted in 2003.
- A follow-up survey of undergraduate participants in the NSF survey, conducted in 2005.
- A nationally representative survey of individuals ages 22 to 35 who have received a bachelor's degree in ("hard") science, technology, engineering, or mathematics (STEM), conducted in 2003.
- A nationally representative survey of individuals ages 22 to 35 who have received a bachelor's degree in a social, behavioral, or economic science (SBES), conducted in 2004.

The NSF initial survey focused primarily on respondents' undergraduate research experiences during summer 2002 or the 2002–03 academic year. The other three surveys asked about research experiences throughout the respondent's undergraduate years. To the extent feasible, given the different survey populations and time frames of interest, survey questions were identical across the four surveys. Each survey is described briefly below.[3]

Initial NSF-Program Participant Survey

This survey was actually a set of surveys, involving approximately 8,000 students and faculty participants in more than 1,000 awards in the following NSF programs:

- Research Experiences for Undergraduates (REU) Sites and Supplements
- NSF-sponsored research centers that include a significant undergraduate research component, identified by NSF as all Engineering Research Centers ($n = 18$), all Materials Research Science and Engineering Centers ($n = 25$), and 16 other centers, laboratories, and observatories
- Research in Undergraduate Institutions (RUI)
- Historically Black Colleges and Universities Undergraduate Program (HBCU-UP)
- Tribal Colleges and Universities Program (TCUP)
- Louis Stokes Alliance for Minority Participation (LSAMP) Program
- Cooperative Activity with Department of Energy's Education Programs (DOE)
- Grants for Vertical Integration of Research and Education in the Mathematical Sciences (VIGRE).

Generally speaking, the sampling strategy was to obtain a diverse group of awards across the NSF programs. For REU sites (459 awards), REU supplements (1,155 awards), and RUI (338 awards), awards were randomly sampled, with stratifications by whether the institution was a primarily undergraduate institution (PUI) and by NSF directorate/division. For the other programs (each of which had fewer than 60 awards), all awards that were active as of September 2002 were included. Within each sampled award, all participants involved with undergraduate research—undergraduates, graduate-student and postdoc mentors, principal investigators (PIs), and other faculty mentors—were included.

Prior to the questionnaire administration, contact information was obtained from the PI of each award. In addition, for each individual named, the PI was asked to specify the time period (summer 2002, 2002–03 academic year, or both) during which the individual had participated in undergraduate research. Participants were then contacted by e-mail and directed to a Web site to complete the appropriate questionnaire. (Participants for whom an e-mail address was not available were surveyed by postal mail.) As an incentive, undergraduates were offered a $20 Amazon.com gift certificate in return for their participation, and all respondents were promised a summary of the survey results. Reminders to complete the questionnaire were sent at approximately weekly intervals over an 8-week period between April and June 2003. Ultimately, completed questionnaires were obtained from 76% of the undergraduates ($n = 4,560$), 80% of the graduate students and postdocs ($n = 822$), 81% of the faculty mentors ($n = 2,140$), and 95% of the PIs ($n = 616$).

NSF Undergraduates Follow-up Survey

The sample for this survey comprised all undergraduate respondents to the initial NSF-program participant survey (henceforth, the initial survey). In the initial survey, we told undergraduate respondents that we would be conducting a follow-up survey in 2005, and we asked them to provide information to help us locate them at that time: their own personal e-mail address and the name and contact information for someone who would be likely to know how to reach them in 2005. One or more of these pieces of information were provided by 4,367 respondents (96%). Late in 2004, we began a series of contact attempts by e-mail, postal mail, and telephone to confirm or update respondent contact information. These efforts focused mostly on attempting to obtain correct addresses for e-mails that bounced.

Survey data collection began in early May 2005. Procedures were the same as those used for the initial survey. Seven reminders were e-mailed to nonrespondents over the course of the next 3½ months. Ultimately, we received responses from 3,354 individuals, representing 74% of all undergraduates who responded to the initial survey and 80% of those for whom (as far as we knew) we were able to find a valid address.

Surveys of STEM and SBES Graduates

The STEM and SBES surveys involved nationwide samples of approximately 3,400 and 3,200 individuals, respectively. SRI subcontracted with NFO WorldGroup—now TNS NFO—to provide the sample and do the data collection.

For each survey, NFO selected the sample from its Interactive Panel, which comprises 1.2 million households and 3.6 million individuals. The starting samples were composed of individuals ages 22 to 35 with a bachelor's degree or higher. To ensure that the samples were representative, they were balanced to U.S. Census profiles for adults of the specified age and education, with an added oversample of Hispanics/Latinos and Blacks. Survey sample members were screened to confirm that they met the age and education requirements.

STEM/SBES graduates were identified as those who indicated that they had received their bachelor's degree in a STEM/SBES field. Only those who met all eligibility criteria completed the remainder of the questionnaire and are included in the final data file.

For both surveys, the response rate was 40%. In spite of the low response rates, this approach was preferable to one using institution-based lists of past URO participants because the latter approach tends to produce respondent groups with disproportionately high numbers of individuals who are employed in academia. In a study of the effects of UROs on career and academic decisions, such a bias would have seriously damaged the validity of the results.

PROFILE OF UNDERGRADUATE RESEARCHERS

Overall, 53% of STEM graduates and 52% of SBES graduates reported that they participated in hands-on research while they were undergraduates. This section provides a general description of the demographic and academic characteristics of these individuals and their counterparts in the NSF surveys.

Key Survey Subgroups

Across the four surveys, four groups of undergraduates proved to have distinctive characteristics for a wide range of study variables.

- *NSF researchers.* These were the individuals who were undergraduate respondents to the NSF initial survey and who participated in the NSF follow-up survey.
- *Sponsored researchers.* These were respondents to the STEM and SBES surveys who reported that at least some of their research, as far as they knew, was sponsored by NSF, the National Aeronautics and Space Administration (NASA), or the National Institutes of Health (NIH). Sponsored researchers, especially those in STEM fields, tended to be more similar to the NSF researchers than to their nonsponsored counterparts. Sponsored researchers comprised 7% of STEM graduates and 5% of SBES graduates.
- *Nonsponsored researchers.* These were respondents to the STEM and SBES surveys whose research was not (as far as they knew) sponsored by NSF, NASA, or NIH. Nonsponsored researchers comprised 46% of STEM graduates and 47% of SBES graduates.
- *Nonresearchers.* These were respondents to the STEM and SBES surveys who did not participate in undergraduate research. Nonresearchers comprised 47% of STEM graduates and 48% of SBES graduates.

Demographic Characteristics

Findings from all four surveys indicated that women and traditionally under-represented minorities were well represented in undergraduate research opportunities (UROs). In the STEM and SBES surveys, Hispanic/Latino and Black participation rates were equivalent to or slightly higher than those of non-Hispanic Whites, and participation rates for men and women were almost identical. Minorities and women were similarly well represented among NSF undergraduate researchers in 2002–03. Similar percentages of participants were men (47%) and women (53%), 10% were Black, and 17% were Hispanic/Latino. By comparison, excluding nonresident aliens, 9% of STEM bachelor's degrees in the United States in 1999–2000 were awarded to Blacks and 5% to Hispanics/Latinos.[4]

Academic Characteristics

NSF researchers' academic class level. Undergraduate researchers were disproportionately juniors and seniors. In the NSF initial survey, more than 60% of the undergraduate researchers were seniors.[5] Another 27% were juniors, 8% were sophomores, and 1% were freshmen. Among SBES graduates who participated in research, 52% said that they participated as seniors, 54% participated as juniors, 22% as sophomores, and 9% as freshmen. (STEM survey respondents were not asked this question.)

Academic major. There were substantial differences in research participation rates across the various academic majors, especially in STEM fields. Rates ranged from a high of 74% of those who majored in environmental sciences and 72% of those in chemistry to a low of 28% of those who majored in STEM education. Other majors with relatively low research participation were computer sciences (37%) and mathematics (34%)—fields in which research activities tend to be atypical. In SBES fields, participation rates ranged from 63% of psychology majors to 38% to 40% of majors in criminology/criminal justice, economics, and political science.

Undergraduate grade point averages (GPAs). In both the STEM and SBES surveys, we found that researchers' self-reported GPAs tended to be higher than those of nonresearchers, and the GPAs of sponsored and NSF researchers were especially high (see Figure 4.1).

Precollege/preresearch degree expectations. STEM and SBES researchers were twice as likely as nonresearchers to have precollege or preresearch expectations of obtaining a PhD. (That is, they reported that before they attended college

Figure 4.1. Mean self-reported GPAs.

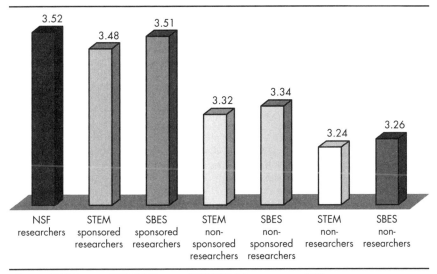

Sources: STEM survey, 2003; SBES survey, 2004; NSF follow-up survey, 2005.

or participated in any undergraduate research, they expected to obtain a PhD.) Overall, 14% of both STEM and SBES researchers had such expectations, compared with 7% of the nonresearchers in each survey. Early PhD expectations were related to both research sponsorship and total duration of undergraduate research experiences. For example, 37% of NSF researchers, 26% of STEM sponsored researchers, and 21% of STEM nonsponsored researchers who participated in more than 12 months of undergraduate research had early expectations of obtaining a PhD.

Type of school. Rather surprisingly, the STEM and SBES surveys found that research participation rates were not very different across the major types of 4-year institutions, ranging from a low of 49% among STEM graduates of master's institutions to a high of 57% among STEM graduates of doctoral/research-extensive universities and baccalaureate colleges. Similarly, rates of participation in sponsored research were lowest at master's institutions (11% of STEM graduates and 5% of SBES graduates) and highest at doctoral/research-extensive universities (17% of STEM graduates and 13% of SBES graduates). Students who had started their undergraduate education at a 2-year college (17% of STEM graduates and 18% of SBES graduates) were as likely to have participated in research as those who had started at a 4-year institution.

Origins of Interest in STEM/SBES

For STEM and NSF researchers, interest in STEM was likely to have begun in childhood. About 60% of STEM and NSF researchers, reported that they had been interested in science/ math/engineering "ever since I was a kid," and only 8% to 10% became interested in college. In contrast, only about 25% of SBES researchers said they had become interested in SBES in childhood, about the same percentage as became interested during college (see Figure 4.2). We suspect that the percentage interested in STEM/SBES since childhood is lower for SBES majors than for STEM majors in part because SBES topics are less likely than STEM topics to be covered in elementary school, so awareness of SBES among elementary school students is relatively low. The low percentage of STEM majors who became interested during college also may reflect the steep learning curve required (or at least perceived to be required) of someone who waits until college to take up a STEM field.

Within the STEM and SBES groups, sponsored researchers were more likely than their nonsponsored counterparts to have developed an early interest in STEM/SBES, and nonsponsored researchers were more likely than nonresearchers to have

Figure 4.2. Origins of researchers' interest in STEM/SBES.

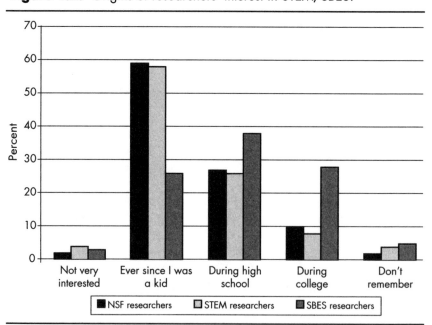

Sources: NSF initial survey, 2003; STEM survey, 2003; SBES survey, 2004.

developed an early interest. Overall, the large percentages who developed early interest in STEM suggest that the most effective time to attract students to STEM may well be while they are in grammar school; it would appear that waiting until college is too late for many.

REASONS FOR PARTICIPATING OR NOT PARTICIPATING IN UNDERGRADUATE RESEARCH

Undergraduates' Perceptions

Reasons for research participation. During site visits conducted early in the study,[6] we talked with undergraduates about why they were interested in doing research. From these interviews and a review of other surveys about undergraduate research, we developed a list of nine potential reasons for participating in research. We asked undergraduates in the NSF initial survey and STEM and SBES survey respondents to rate the importance of each reason. The percentages of NSF respondents and STEM/SBES sponsored and nonsponsored researchers who rated each reason as extremely important are presented in Table 4.1.

There was considerable variation in the five groups' responses. The only reason that close to half or more of each group rated as extremely important was wanting hands-on experiences to reinforce what had been learned in class. On most of the items, NSF researchers had relatively high ratings, and STEM/SBES sponsored researchers were more like NSF respondents than like their nonsponsored STEM/SBES counterparts. However, there were two rather dramatic exceptions. STEM and, especially, SBES researchers were much more likely than NSF researchers to rate need for academic credit and need to fulfill academic requirements for research as extremely important.

Reasons for not participating in research. STEM and SBES respondents who indicated that they had not participated in undergraduate research were asked to select from a list of options to describe why they had not participated. Among both groups, responses reflecting a choice not to participate (not interested, didn't have time, never occurred to me, research opportunities weren't interesting, research didn't pay enough/at all) were much more common than those reflecting an inability to participate (wasn't aware of research opportunities, no research at my school, grades not good enough, was turned down).

Mentor Perceptions

Benefits of undergraduate research. During the site visits, we talked with faculty and graduate students about why they chose to involve undergraduates in their

Table 4.1. Undergraduates' motivations for participating in research: Percentage of each group who rated each reason as "Extremely important" (percent of respondents).

	NSF Initial Survey	STEM Sponsored	SBES Sponsored	STEM Non-sponsored	SBES Non-sponsored
I wanted to learn more about what it's like to be a researcher.	**62**	44	47	*18*	29
I wanted hands-on experiences to reinforce what I learned in class.	**57**	52	49	*43*	46
I wanted to know if going to grad school in science or engineering [a social/behavioral science] was for me.	**50**	45	43	*17*	29
I thought it would be fun.	**48**	39	42	*31*	36
I thought it would help me get into graduate/medical school [graduate/law/business school] or get a job.	45	**49**	**49**	*29*	40
Doing research was more appealing than other kinds of jobs.	**45**	42	45	24	22
I wanted to know if science or engineering [a social/behavioral science] was for me.	28	34	**35**	*16*	30
I needed/wanted the academic credit I could get from doing research.	*8*	21	37	24	**43**
I needed to fulfill my school's/my scholarship's requirements for research.	*6*	15	**31**	20	28
	(*n* = 4541)	(*n* = 246)	(*n* = 163)	(*n* = 1542)	(*n* = 1459)

Notes: Boldface indicates the group with the highest percentage in that row; italics indicate the group with the lowest percentage. Percentages are listed in descending order of the "NSF Initial Survey." *Sources:* NSF initial survey, 2003; STEM survey, 2003; SBES survey, 2004.

research and what the benefits and drawbacks were. From these interviews, we developed a number of agree-disagree items reflecting many of the views that were expressed. Overall, responses to these items suggest that it was personal satisfaction much more than career, political, or research factors that was the driving force for most mentors. Three of the four most commonly agreed-to items related to personal motivation. For example, 80% of PIs, 73% of other faculty mentors, and 64% of graduate-student/postdoc mentors agreed or agreed somewhat that "I get a lot of personal satisfaction out of working with undergraduates doing research." Other factors appeared to be weighted somewhat against undergraduate research. For instance, among those to whom the items applied, fewer than half of PIs and other faculty mentors agreed or agreed somewhat that mentoring undergraduates enables them to expand their research avenues (45%), is viewed favorably in their department's tenure/promotion review process (38%), or is a good way to recruit the undergraduates to be graduate students in their lab/department (35%).

Potential barriers to increased undergraduate research. NSF-center and REU-site PIs were asked their perceptions of a variety of potential barriers to increasing the number of undergraduates involved in their center/site. The most commonly perceived barriers were related to financial support. Seventy-five percent agreed or agreed somewhat that they would include more undergraduates if they had financial support for more undergraduates. The only other factor perceived to be a barrier by more than half of the respondents was insufficient faculty or researchers available/willing to be mentors (60% agreed or agreed somewhat).

CHARACTERISTICS AND ACTIVITIES OF UNDERGRADUATE RESEARCH EXPERIENCES

In this section, we summarize the characteristics of undergraduate research experiences and the activities that comprised those experiences. The relationships between research activities/characteristics and URO effects are discussed in subsequent sections.

Types of Research Experiences

The surveys focused on four major types of undergraduate research experiences, described in the questionnaires as follows:

1. Summer research, other than intern or co-op program. A full-time hands-on research project for the summer with a professor or researcher.
2. Hands-on research with a professor during one or more academic terms, while enrolled in classes.

3. Intern or co-op program that involves hands-on research as its *main* component. Usually, a company or other organization pays you for working on a research project at their site. Sometimes you receive academic credit at your school for this research. May happen any time of year.
4. A junior or senior thesis that involves hands-on research (other than library research) as its *main* component.

Figure 4.3 shows the various rates of participation in these types of research. Respondents to the NSF follow-up survey were considerably more likely than STEM and SBES sponsored researchers and much more likely than STEM and SBES nonsponsored researchers to have participated in summer research. NSF and STEM/SBES sponsored researchers also were more likely than nonsponsored researchers to have participated in academic-year research, but the differences were not nearly as large. There were only small differences in rates of participation in intern/co-op programs and junior/senior thesis research.

Figure 4.3. Rates of participation in major types of undergraduate research.

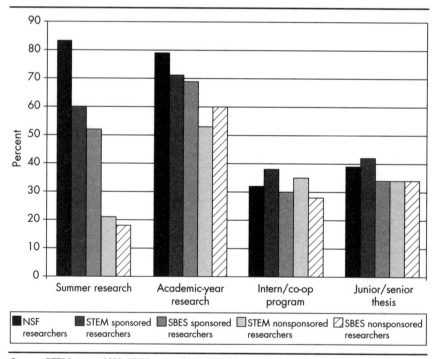

Sources: STEM survey, 2003; SBES survey, 2004; NSF follow-up survey, 2005.

Research Duration

NSF and STEM sponsored researchers tended to spend considerably more time engaged in undergraduate research than did STEM nonsponsored or SBES researchers (see Figure 4.4). Among SBES researchers, the sponsored group averaged more time in research than those who were not sponsored, but the difference was not nearly as large as that between STEM sponsored and nonsponsored students. In all of these groups, those who reported that they either had a PhD or expected that they would have one in 10 years tended to have more research experience than those without PhD expectations. For example, among NSF follow-up survey respondents who had received their bachelor's degree, 40% of current graduate students expecting a PhD participated in research for at least 24 months, compared with 28% of other graduates.

Research Locations

By far the most common location of undergraduate research was the respondent's own college or university. Among each of the five researcher groups that we have been discussing, 80–90% of respondents participated in research at their own school.

Figure 4.4. Median months of undergraduate research.

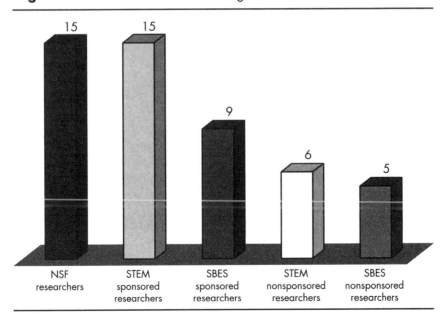

Sources: STEM survey, 2003; SBES survey, 2004; NSF follow-up survey, 2005.

Rates of research participation at some other college or university were highest among NSF researchers, at 41%; 18% of STEM and 13% of SBES sponsored researchers did so; only 6% of STEM and 4% of SBES nonsponsored researchers did so. The five groups' rates of participation at other types of entities—for-profit companies, nonprofit organizations, and government facilities—ranged between 6% and 22%.

Research Activities

Table 4.2 shows the percentage of each of the five researcher groups who reported engaging in each of 19 research-related activities and experiences. Only five activities were reported by more than 50% of all groups:

- Collected and/or analyzed data or information to try to answer a research question
- Had input to or responsibility for decisions about what to do next
- Had a choice of projects to work on
- Had input to or responsibility for decisions about research techniques/ materials
- Was able to complete my project.

There was considerable variation among the five groups in the percentages who engaged in the various activities, but NSF researchers tended to have relatively high participation rates and SBES researchers tended to have relatively low rates. Activities with the largest differences among the groups were preparation of a poster presentation (64% of NSF researchers versus 18% of SBES nonsponsored researchers), delivery of an oral presentation (73% of NSF researchers versus 35% of SBES sponsored researchers), and having gained increasing independence (69% of NSF researchers versus 35% of SBES nonsponsored researchers). Differences between sponsored and nonsponsored groups tended to be larger and were more consistent among STEM researchers than among SBES researchers. Sponsored versus nonsponsored differences probably were due in large part to the fact that sponsored researchers tended to participate in research longer than did nonsponsored researchers.

PERCEPTIONS AND OUTCOMES

The questionnaires included a variety of topics related to the respondents' opinions of their research experiences, as well as their academic and employment characteristics. All four surveys included questions about perceptions of gains made on various dimensions, perceptions of effects of their experiences on their interest in several STEM/SBES-related careers, and academic degree expectations. Other outcome-related topics were covered in only some surveys.

Table 4.2. Undergraduate research activities and experiences reported in the NSF follow-up, STEM, and SBES surveys (percent of respondents).

	NSF Follow-up Survey	STEM Sponsored	SBES Sponsored	STEM Non-sponsored	SBES Non-sponsored
Collected and/or analyzed data or information to try to answer a research question	**88**	84	*61*	79	81
Understood how my work contributed to the "bigger picture" of research in that field	**76**	66	52	57	*49*
Had input to or responsibility for decisions about what to do next	76	**81**	77	71	*68*
Delivered an oral presentation describing my research and results	**73**	59	*35*	44	39
Had a choice of projects to work on	72	76	**78**	*65*	67
Prepared a final written research report describing my research and results	**70**	63	*47*	58	60
Gained increasing independence over the course of the research	**69**	59	45	43	*35*
Had input to or responsibility for decisions about research techniques/materials	65	73	**76**	64	*63*
Prepared/presented a poster presentation describing my research and results	**64**	44	27	21	*18*
Was able to complete my project	58	65	*51*	66	**67**
Provided input to designing my project	58	**64**	53	47	*41*
Attended student conference(s) that included students from other colleges	**44**	36	21	14	*13*
Wrote a proposal describing the research I planned to do	*41*	52	**53**	42	47
Went on research-related field trip(s)[a]	37	**39**		*21*	
Attended professional conference(s)	**36**	32	21	*15*	16
Had primary responsibility for designing the project that I worked on	*33*	40	**41**	37	38
Authored or coauthored a paper that was submitted for publication in a professional journal	**30**	29	13	10	*8*
Mentored other students conducting research or led a student research team[b]	24				
Did little or nothing that seemed to me to be real research	*6*	7	**13**	7	6
	(*n* = 3278)	(*n* = 246)	(*n* = 163)	(*n* = 1542)	(*n* = 1459)

Notes: Boldface indicates the group with the highest percentage in that row; italics indicate the group with the lowest percentage. Percentages are listed in descending order of the "NSF Follow-up Survey." *Sources:* NSF follow-up survey, 2003; STEM survey, 2003; SBES survey, 2004.

[a] NSF and STEM surveys only.

[b] NSF survey only.

Satisfaction with Undergraduate Research

Satisfaction with undergraduate research experiences overall (assessed in the NSF surveys) tended to be high: 64% of NSF follow-up survey respondents said they were very satisfied; 48% said it was "one of the best experiences of my life"; a mere 2% said they wished they had done less undergraduate research, whereas 43% wished they had done more.

In contrast with the high levels of satisfaction with conducting undergraduate research, NSF follow-up survey respondents tended to be only moderately satisfied with how well informed they were about the UROs at their own college or university (36% were very satisfied, 38% somewhat satisfied) and less so with how well informed they were about UROs at places other than their own school (23% were very satisfied, 36% somewhat satisfied). A number of respondents' suggestions for how to improve UROs related to more effective dissemination of information about UROs.

Perceptions of Increased Understanding, Confidence, and Awareness

All surveys assessed perceived gains by asking respondents to rate how much they thought they had gained in each of a number of areas as a result of their research experiences. Variables that correlated with one another were aggregated into indices, which we labeled *understanding*, *confidence*, and *awareness*. The components of each index are listed below.

INCREASED UNDERSTANDING ABOUT

How to formulate a research question
How to plan/conduct a research project
How to deal with setbacks, negative results, and so on
How STEM knowledge is built
The nature of the job of a researcher (in index only in NSF surveys)

INCREASED CONFIDENCE IN

Research skills
Ability to succeed in grad school
Qualifications for jobs in related fields

INCREASED AWARENESS OF

What graduate school is like
STEM/SBES career options
Variety of STEM/SBES fields available
Faculty career paths.

In all surveys, most respondents reported gains of "a fair amount" or "a great deal" on all three dimensions, although more so on understanding and confidence than on awareness (see Figure 4.5). Overall, NSF researchers tended to have the highest scores, followed by SBES researchers and then STEM researchers. Among SBES and STEM researchers, those who were sponsored tended to have higher scores than those who were not.

In the NSF initial survey, graduate-student/postdoc and faculty mentors and PIs were asked how much they thought that the undergraduates they mentored during summer 2002 (or the 2002–03 academic year) developed on each of the dimensions that the students were asked about. For the most part, faculty tended to believe that undergraduate gains were greater than the undergraduates themselves believed, and principal investigators tended to have somewhat more positive perceptions than mentors. The particularly positive ratings by PIs probably reflect the fact that they are the ones who obtained the grants to involve undergraduates and whose responsibility it is to show positive effects.

Figure 4.5. Mean percentage of each group who rated gains as "a fair amount" or "a great deal."

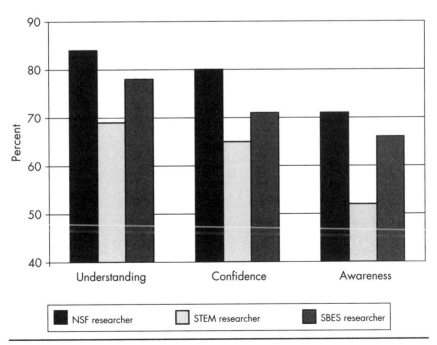

Sources: STEM survey, 2003; SBES survey, 2004; NSF follow-up survey, 2005.

Importance of Undergraduate Research in Academic and Career Decisions and Interests

Choice of baccalaureate school. As noted previously, the vast majority of undergraduate researchers participated in undergraduate research at their own college/university. The NSF follow-up survey found that, when these researchers first enrolled as undergraduates, only half were aware that the school offered undergraduate research. Of those who were aware, 55% said that UROs were fairly or extremely important in their decision to enroll. Thus, overall, UROs were important in the decision to enroll for only a fourth of the respondents.

Graduate school decisions. Although undergraduate research was unlikely to play a role in decisions about undergraduate schools, it did help inform graduate school decisions. About 8 in 10 graduate students who expected to obtain a PhD reported that their undergraduate research experiences were fairly or extremely important in their decision to attend graduate school, their decision about what field to study in graduate school, and their acceptance into graduate school. Six in 10 also indicated that their undergraduate research experiences were important in helping them decide where to apply.

Career decisions. Regardless of whether they expected to obtain a PhD, almost all follow-up survey respondents (90%) reported that their undergraduate research experiences were fairly or extremely important to their career decision. Sponsored researchers in the STEM and SBES surveys gave similar ratings; nonsponsored researchers' ratings were lower (70% of STEM and 62% of SBES nonsponsored researchers said their undergraduate research experiences were fairly or extremely important).

Changes in interest in various careers. In all surveys, about half or more of the respondents reported that their undergraduate research experiences increased their interest at least somewhat in careers in STEM/SBES and in research. In the NSF follow-up survey, 67% said their interest in a research career increased, and 21% said it decreased (see Figure 4.6). Percentages whose interest increased were somewhat lower among STEM and SBES researchers than among NSF researchers, but STEM and SBES sponsored researchers' responses were equivalent to those of the NSF follow-up respondents.

Interestingly, among all groups, larger percentages reported a decreased interest in a career in research than in a career in STEM/SBES. For example, the 21% of NSF follow-up survey respondents who reported a decreased interest in a research career compares with only 7% who reported a decreased interest in a STEM career. Similarly, 17% of follow-up survey respondents reported that one

Figure 4.6. Change in interest in a career in research as a result of undergraduate research experiences among NSF follow-up survey respondents.

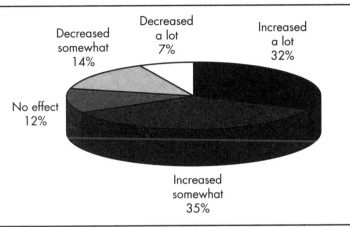

Source: NSF follow-up survey, 2005.

of the things they learned from their undergraduate research was that "research is not for me." Thus the surveys found support for the anecdotal reports many have heard of how undergraduate research participation shows some students that research is not what they want to do after all.

Use of STEM knowledge in jobs. The use of STEM knowledge in one's job is not limited to those with PhDs. Eight in 10 NSF follow-up survey respondents who were no longer students reported that their job was at least somewhat related to their (STEM) undergraduate major, 75% said that they used skills learned doing undergraduate research in their job, and 64% said that their job involved science/math research or engineering.

Highest degree expectations and attainment. We reported above that undergraduate research tends to attract those with high degree expectations. We found that it also encourages such expectations. In both the STEM and SBES surveys, researchers were more likely than nonresearchers to have obtained a PhD, to have current expectations that they would have a PhD in 10 years (that is, at the time of the survey, they expected they would obtain one), and to have new expectations of obtaining a PhD (that is, before they started college or did undergraduate research, they did not expect to obtain one, but now they did have such expectations). Consistent with other findings, sponsored researchers and NSF researchers were especially likely to have or expect to obtain a PhD (see Figure 4.7).

CORRELATES OF UNDERGRADUATE RESEARCH OUTCOMES

The preceding section discussed a number of outcome measures. In this section, we focus mostly on three of those measures: gains in confidence, increased interest in a career in research, and current expectations of obtaining a PhD. These

Figure 4.7. Percentage of each group who have or expect to have a PhD.

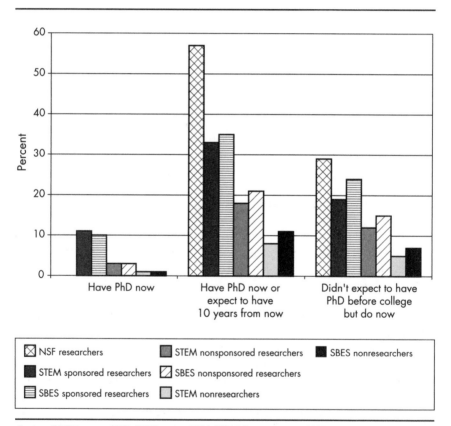

Sources: STEM survey, 2003; SBES survey, 2004; NSF follow-up survey, 2005.

measures were quite strongly related to some motivations for participating in re-search and to some of the characteristics of research experiences. They also were related to one another to varying degrees. However, there were only small differ-ences in outcomes among racial/ethnic groups and essentially no differences be-tween men and women. Each group of relationships is discussed below.

Relationships Between Outcomes and Reasons for Participating in Research

Respondents for whom needing help with an academic or career decision and personal enthusiasm/interest were important reasons for participating in research[7] tended to report higher gains, be more likely to have an increased interest in a research career, and be more likely to expect to obtain a PhD than did those for whom these were not important motivations. The results for STEM researchers reflect this report:

- 59% of those for whom needing help with an academic or career decision was very important were "high gainers"[8] on the confidence index, com-pared with 16% of those for whom needing help with a decision was not important.
- 47% of those for whom needing help with a decision was very important said their interest in a research career increased a lot, compared with 5% of those for whom needing help with a decision was not important.
- 37% of those for whom needing help with a decision was very important expected to obtain a PhD, compared with 12% of those for whom needing help with a decision was not important.

In contrast, engaging in undergraduate research to meet academic require-ments tended not to be as strongly related to the outcome measures and was actu-ally slightly negatively related to expectations of obtaining a PhD. These findings suggest that research participation is most likely to be an effective motivator when it is done voluntarily and out of a genuine interest, whereas requiring research experiences for undergraduates may be counterproductive.

All research motivations were less strongly related to expectations of obtaining a PhD than they were to increased interest in a research career or to gains in confidence. Also, in most cases, the relationships between motivations and outcomes were much stronger among STEM and SBES respondents than among NSF respondents, probably because the motivation questions were struc-tured somewhat differently in the STEM and SBES surveys than in the NSF survey rather than because of any substantive difference among the survey groups.[9]

Relationships Between Outcomes and Research Experience Characteristics

With the exception of duration of the research experience and number of research activities, research experience characteristics were not related as strongly to research outcomes as research motivations were, at least among STEM and SBES respondents. Those that were the most strongly related to research outcome measures are listed below, in approximate descending order of the strength of their relationship with outcome measures in the several surveys:

> Total duration of the research experience (see Figure 4.8)
> Number of research activities
> Having gained increasing independence
> Having mentored other student researchers or led a student research team (asked in NSF follow-up survey only)
> Having attended professional or student conferences
> Having authored/coauthored a paper that was submitted for publication in a professional journal

Figure 4.8. Percentage of stem graduates who expect to obtain a PhD, by duration of undergraduate research experience.

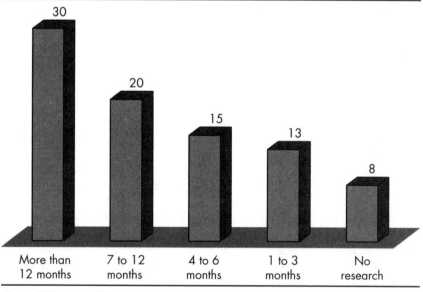

More than 12 months	7 to 12 months	4 to 6 months	1 to 3 months	No research
30	20	15	13	8

Source: STEM survey, 2003.

The following characteristics of the research experiences (again, in approximate descending order of the strength of their relationship with outcome measures) tended to be only weakly related (if at all) to outcomes:

Involvement in project decision making
Ability to complete any of one's projects
Having collected/analyzed data to try to answer a research question
Having delivered an oral presentation about one's research
Having had a choice of projects
Having prepared a final written report about one's research

It appears to us that the central difference between the two lists is that the activities that were more strongly related to outcome measures tend to connote a more substantive involvement with the process and culture of research. Together with the finding that research seems most effective if it is done voluntarily, these findings suggest that it is not research activities per se that draw students into STEM/SBES careers. Rather, it is the development of interest and curiosity followed by an acculturation process that appears most likely to succeed.

As with research motivations, research activities tended to be more strongly related to perceived gains in confidence and understanding and increased interest in research and STEM careers than to PhD expectations, and almost all variables were more strongly related to current PhD expectations than to new PhD expectations. For instance, 36% of NSF follow-up survey respondents who reported that they gained increasing independence over the course of their undergraduate research experiences were high gainers on the confidence index, compared with only 15% who did not report increasing independence—a difference of 21 percentage points. By comparison, 60% of those who reported increasing independence expected to obtain a PhD, compared with 49% of those who did not report increasing independence—a difference of only 11 percentage points.

Relationships Among Outcome Measures

As one might expect, current and new expectations of obtaining a PhD were strongly related to increased interest in STEM and research careers. The relationship was particularly strong among NSF follow-up survey respondents: 83% of those whose interest in a research career increased a lot expected to obtain a PhD, compared with only 14% of those whose interest in a research career decreased a lot (Figure 4.9). Increased interest in STEM-related careers also was strongly related to gains in confidence and understanding: among STEM researchers, 70% of those whose interest in a research career increased a lot were high gainers on the confidence index, compared with a mere 9% of those whose interest in a research career decreased. In

Figure 4.9. Percentage who expect to obtain a PhD by effect of UROs on respondent's interest in a career in research among NSF follow-up survey respondents.

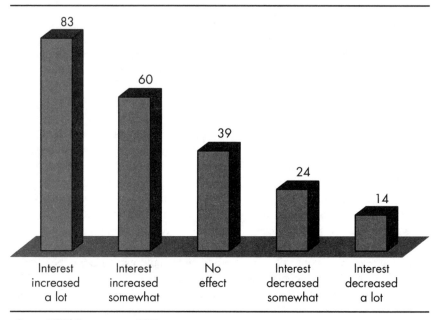

Source: NSF follow-up survey, 2005.

contrast, gains in understanding, confidence, and awareness were only moderately related to PhD expectations.

Relationships Between Outcomes and Respondents' Demographic Characteristics

The relationships between outcomes and respondents' race/ethnicity varied somewhat across the several outcome measures and surveys, but broadly speaking, the differences tended to be small (typically, less than 10 percentage points difference between high and low groups). Where there were differences, most often it was Hispanics/Latinos who showed the greatest gains and non-Hispanic Whites who showed the smallest gains.

Differences between men and women on the several outcome measures were even smaller than those among the racial/ethnic groups. On most measures, the two sexes' ratings were almost identical.

Role of Mentors in Undergraduate Research Outcomes

The NSF surveys included several items assessing amount of undergraduate researchers' interaction with mentors and perceptions of the mentors' supportiveness, technical guidance, and so on. None of these items was appreciably related to our research outcome measures. We believe that the absence of strong relationships on these items reflects the complexity of the mentor's role rather than its unimportance. That is, because the role is complex, unidimensional survey items are unable to capture it. As evidence of the centrality of the mentor's role, in response to an open-ended question about how to improve undergraduate research programs, follow-up survey respondents' most common suggestions—by a considerable margin—related to increased and more effective faculty guidance. One respondent's comment summarized the suggestions nicely: "Finding faculty who are not only bright people and good researchers but who also have excellent interpersonal skills is the most crucial aspect to making these programs successful."

Differential Group Needs in Undergraduate Research

One of the initial study questions was whether different types of students—in particular, different racial/ethnic groups or men versus women—benefit differentially from different kinds of mentoring or different research environments. Our analyses found no patterns of differential relationships among research characteristics and outcomes across the racial/ethnic groups or between men and women. Similarly, in our survey of PIs and mentors, only 4% identified differences in needs between men and women, and a mere 2% specified differences by racial/ethnic group. Thus, from the perspective of mentors, the answer to whether there should be different mentoring approaches or research environments for different types of students appears to be a resounding no.

Some participants and observers of undergraduate research believe that it is important for students, especially for women and minorities, to have mentors who are like themselves, and some studies of targeted programs have supported these beliefs.[10] We explored this hypothesis in the initial and follow-up NSF surveys, not by asking students what they thought about it, but by comparing research outcomes for those who had different types of mentors. We found that women who had some female mentors or all female mentors were no more likely than those who had no female mentors to expect to obtain a PhD or to have new expectations of obtaining a PhD, and the findings with regard to targeted minorities (Blacks and Hispanics/Latinos) were parallel. Not only were none of the differences statistically significant, but those that did exist were not in the hypothesized direction.

Overall, on more than 100 comparisons made with regard to the various respondent groups, types of mentors, and outcome measures, there were statistically significant differences in outcomes on only about half. Where there were statistically significant differences, respondents who had both male and female mentors or both same- and different-race/ethnicity mentors tended to have slightly "better" outcomes (e.g., higher confidence gains) than did those who had either only same or only different mentors. However, statistically significant differences were as common among men as among women and more common with non-Hispanic Whites than with minorities. Thus, in brief, our findings suggest that having a mix of mentors (in terms of their sex and race/ethnicity) has a mildly beneficial effect across all students, not just women and minorities.

SUMMARY AND CONCLUSIONS

About half of STEM and SBES graduates reported that they participated in hands-on research while they were undergraduates. Rates of participation varied substantially across the various STEM and SBES academic majors, but they were not very different across types of institutions.

Undergraduate researchers were demographically diverse but less diverse in terms of their academic characteristics. They were disproportionately juniors and seniors, had relatively high GPAs, and were considerably more likely than non-researchers to have precollege or preresearch expectations of obtaining a PhD. Among SBES and STEM graduates, those who participated in research sponsored by NSF, NASA, or NIH were especially likely to have high GPAs and early expectations of obtaining a PhD.

For STEM and NSF researchers, interest in STEM was likely to have begun in childhood; very few became interested when they were in college. These findings suggest that the most effective time to attract students to STEM may well be while they are in elementary school; it would appear that waiting until college is too late for many. In contrast, only about a fourth of SBES researchers said they had become interested in SBES in childhood.

Undergraduates' reasons for participating in research differed considerably among NSF, STEM, and SBES respondents and between the sponsored and non-sponsored groups in the STEM and SBES surveys. Across all groups, wanting hands-on experiences to reinforce what had been learned in class was important. STEM and SBES graduates who did not participate in undergraduate research were much more likely to have chosen not to participate than to have been unable to participate.

For mentors, personal satisfaction—much more than career, political, or research factors—appeared to be the driving force in their inclusion of undergraduates in their research. The most commonly perceived barriers to including undergraduates were related to financial support.

NSF researchers were the most likely, and nonsponsored researchers by far the least likely, to have participated in UROs during the summer and at locations other than their own college or university. NSF and STEM/SBES sponsored researchers tended to spend more time in UROs than did nonsponsored researchers and to have participated in a greater variety of activities.

Overall satisfaction with undergraduate research experiences tended to be high, and most respondents reported gains of a fair amount or a great deal on their understanding of the research process, confidence in their abilities, and awareness of academic and career options in STEM. Most researchers also reported that their research experiences were important to their career decision and that their interest in STEM- or SBES-related careers increased as a result of their research participation.

Researchers were more likely than nonresearchers to expect to obtain a PhD and to have new expectations of obtaining a PhD (that is, before they started college or did undergraduate research, they did not expect to obtain one, but now they did have such expectations). Among NSF follow-up survey respondents who were in graduate school and expecting a PhD, a large majority reported that their undergraduate research experiences were fairly or extremely important in their decision to attend graduate school, their decision about what field to study in graduate school, and their acceptance into graduate school.

In contrast to their very positive reports of the research experiences themselves, researchers tended to believe that they were not very well informed about UROs, especially those at places other than their own school. Also, when they first enrolled as undergraduates, only half were aware that the school offered undergraduate research; of those who were aware, only about half said that UROs were fairly or extremely important in their decision to enroll. Together, these findings suggest that the major shortcoming in UROs is not in how they are run but in the paucity of information that is disseminated about them.

Participation in undergraduate research seems most likely to have positive outcomes (e.g., increased confidence in one's abilities, interest in a STEM-related career, expectations of obtaining a PhD) if it is done voluntarily and out of a genuine interest; research that is done because it is required is less likely to lead to positive outcomes. Specific activities appear to be less important than a long-term, multifaceted experience that draws the undergraduate into the culture and process of research. It is likely that talented mentors play a central role in making this happen.

We found no patterns of differential relationships among research characteristics and outcomes across the racial/ethnic groups or between men and women. There also was no evidence that minorities benefited more from same-race/ethnicity mentors than from those of a different race/ethnicity or that women benefited more from female than from male mentors. However, having a diverse group of mentors (in terms of their race/ethnicity and sex) appeared to be mildly beneficial to all respondents.

This study was unique in the large number and variety of individuals, academic fields, colleges, universities that were represented. It provides strong confirmation of the positive effects of UROs on students' interests in STEM/SBES careers and in obtaining PhDs.

NOTES

The data collection, analysis, and reporting of this material were conducted by SRI International under contracts numbered REC-9912172 and GS-10F-0554N, which gave the National Science Foundation the right to place the material into the public domain. This research was conducted in accordance with OMB No. 3145-0121. Any opinions, conclusions, or recommendations expressed in this material are those of the author and do not necessarily reflect the views of the United States Government.

1. National Science Foundation, *NSF's Research Experiences for Undergraduates (REU) Program: An Assessment of the First Three Years* (Washington, DC: Author, 1990).

2. David Lopatto and Elaine Seymour, *Pilot Study to Establish the Nature and Impact of Effective Undergraduate Research Experiences on Learning, Attitude, and Career Choice*, http://www.ehr.nsf.gov/rec/programs/research/proposal/Lopatto/Lopatto_proposal_final.pdf (accessed October 29, 2007).

3. Detailed reports on the several URO surveys, including survey questionnaires and data tables, are available on SRI's Web site (http://www.sri.com/policy/csted/reports/university/index.html#uro).

4. National Center for Education Statistics, *Digest of Education Statistics, 2002*, Data table 266, http://nces.ed.gov/programs/digest/d02/dt266.asp (accessed October 29, 2007). The relatively high percentage of Hispanics/Latinos in the NSF survey was due partly to the 185 Puerto Rican respondents (most were LSAMP participants), who comprised 30% of all Hispanic/Latino respondents. Mainland U.S. Hispanics/Latinos comprised 10% of undergraduate researchers.

5. Academic class participation in research includes those who participated in the summer preceding the specified class level. For example, "seniors" includes rising seniors.

6. Primarily to help guide development of the survey questionnaires, SRI conducted site visits to a diverse group of 20 institutions in the United States that provide research opportunities to undergraduates.

7. These were indices created from questions in the NSF initial, STEM, and SBES surveys that asked respondents to rate the importance of each of various factors in their decision to participate in undergraduate research. The NSF initial survey covered 17 to 23 factors (some factors related only to summer research). The STEM and SBES surveys included only 9 of the factors that were asked in the NSF survey. (The other factors dealt with why a specific project was chosen.)

8. For each index, respondents were grouped into four approximately equally sized categories on the basis of their mean ratings in that index. "High gainers" are those with scores in the top category.

9. We asked STEM/SBES respondents why they participated in undergraduate research, whereas we asked NSF respondents why they participated in research last summer/last year.

10. See, for example, Baine Alexander and Julie Foertsch, *The Impact of the EOT/PACI Program on Partners, Projects, and Participants: A Summative Evaluation*, (Madison: University of Wisconsin, LEAD Center, 2003). (available at http://www.eot.org/Summative.pdf)

Evaluation of the Undergraduate Research Program at the University of Delaware: A Multifaceted Design

Karen Webber Bauer and Joan S. Bennett

DURING THE PAST decade, undergraduate research has gained increasing prominence as a feature of the American college experience, especially in engineering and the sciences. The National Science Foundation (NSF) named undergraduate research as a critical component of its core strategy for integrating research and education (NSF, 2000). An article in the Kaplan/Newsweek *How to Get into College* guide suggested that its readers could expect to "learn like Ph.D. candidates" by conducting research during their undergraduate careers (Halpert, 2002). *USA Today* reported that "[undergraduate] research accelerates learning" (Marklein, 2002, p. D06). The most recent national report of the Carnegie Commission urged research-intensive universities to reform undergraduate education by making "research-based learning the standard" (Boyer Commission, 1998); and in the commission's follow-up survey of 123 universities in 2001, the majority of institutions claimed increased student participation in research as their most noteworthy achievement in reforming undergraduate education (Boyer Commission, 2001). Given the high value accorded the undergraduate research experience, it is desirable to document the educational outcomes of this experience. The present study used a multifaceted design to document student outcomes from a campuswide initiative designed to promote the undergraduate research experience. There were four major components: (1) a content analysis of student evaluations; (2) a survey to examine faculty perceptions of students' learning through participation in undergraduate research; (3) a survey of alumni, some with and some without undergraduate research experience, to examine perceived skills and abilities acquired through baccalaureate education; and (4) a longitudinal study with a group of approximately 200 students from first through senior years.

THE VALUE OF VIEWING MULTIPLE FACETS

When undergraduate research is defined as undergraduates' direct involvement in faculty research projects, often as part of a team that includes graduate and postdoctoral students as well as other research scientists, faculty mentors of these undergraduates believe that their students gain significant educational benefits from the research experience (Gates, 1999; Kardash, 2000; Zydney, Bennett, Shahid, & Bauer, 2002). Student participants themselves report high levels of satisfaction with their learning through the undergraduate research experience (Hakim, 1998; Kardash, 2000; Kremer & Bringle, 1990; Mabrouk & Peters, 2000; Manduca, 1997). However, self-report data alone can be problematic. First, it is theoretically possible that students and faculty who know their responses are related to program evaluation may provide biased or incomplete answers in an attempt to cast the program in as favorable a light as possible. Second, a survey completed only by program participants lacks a comparison or control group.

One way to eliminate possible respondent bias and at the same time obtain a comparison group is to survey alumni, matching a set of program participants to a set of individuals who resemble the participants except for the fact that they did not participate in the program. A recent study that was part of this evaluation compared responses from alumni who participated in undergraduate research with a comparable group of alumni with no research involvement (Bauer & Bennett, 2003). Unaware that their responses would be used to assess the impact of undergraduate research, alumni with undergraduate research experience reported the enhancement of important skills and abilities to a greater extent than did alumni with no research experience. The skills and abilities in which significantly greater gains were perceived included developing intellectual curiosity and increasing the ability to acquire information independently, knowing literature of merit in the field, understanding scientific findings, analyzing literature critically, carrying out research, speaking effectively and possessing clear career goals. In the same study, a principal components factor analysis showed alumni of the institution's undergraduate research program reporting greater gains in problem-solving skills, literature and language skills, and personal initiative/communication skills than comparison alumni with no undergraduate research involvement.

In addition to studying the perceptions of alumni, another important way to examine student skill enhancement is by studying a cohort of currently enrolled students over a period of time when that cohort includes students with and without research experience and when the study participants are kept unaware that the study is related to undergraduate research. Longitudinal or cohort studies are most helpful for examining individual variations in characteristics or traits, offer the opportunity to examine growth curves, and may enable the researcher to determine a causal relationship between variables (Bauer, 2004). The research presented here includes a 4-year longitudinal study of the academic experiences of a cohort of science and engineering undergraduates, some of whom were involved in undergraduate research and some of whom were not. The study sought to determine whether students with undergraduate research experience perceived greater academic and psychosocial gains from their education than did students who had no undergraduate research experience. The study also sought to determine whether standardized tests of critical thinking and reasoning could measure directly some of the growth in educational outcomes previously reported by faculty and self-reported by students. No standard instrument has been developed to measure directly student- and faculty-reported gains in such abilities as "carry out research," "acquire information needed for problem solving," or "analyze literature critically." However, since many of the skills believed to be developed are general ones, not tied to particular scientific or technical content knowledge, it was decided to examine results from two different measures of general critical thinking and reasoning, to see whether changes in scores or entering level of ability are associated with participation in undergraduate research.

Cognitive Development and Social Processes

Researchers generally acknowledge an interrelationship between cognitive complexity and social processes (Love & Guthrie, 1999). Rogoff (2003) views cognitive development as a form of "apprenticeship" in that one must learn through observation and participation. Chickering and Reisser (1993) note that relationships provide powerful learning experiences and opportunities to increase cognitive development. The development of social cognition is also two-directional, according to Rubin and Henzel (1984), as cognitively complex persons are more skilled at taking others' perspectives and can thus be more skilled communicators. Therefore, it was decided to examine students' growth in psychosocial behaviors as well as in cognitive skills.

The attempt to identify instruments that could measure both cognitive and behavioral growth for the students in the longitudinal study was influenced by faculty members' belief that participation in faculty research develops students' psychosocial behavioral skills as well as their cognitive abilities. For instance, faculty who take undergraduate collaborators into their research programs believe not only that the students gain the ability to think logically about complex materials and understand scientific findings but also that they develop intellectual curiosity and openness to new ideas and that they gain the self-confidence necessary both to solve problems independently and to work effectively as part of a team (Zydney et al., 2002).

Critical Thinking

Higher level cognition is often described by the term *critical thinking*. While critical thinking skills are desired outcomes of college education (Facione, Sanchez, Facione, & Gainen, 1995; Pascarella, 1989; Pascarella & Terenzini, 1991), the term *critical thinking* has different shades of meaning. Commonly, it describes an ability to analyze statements for logical consistency and to make logically valid inferences, abstractions, and generalizations from the statements. The "well-structured" problems included on standardized tests such as the verbal section of the SAT or ACT, used in the educational setting, or the Watson-Glaser Critical Thinking Appraisal (Watson & Glaser, 1994), used often in the workplace as well as in education, are tests of this kind of critical thinking. As can be seen by a comparison of the verbal sections of the SAT and GRE exams, it is not expected that a large amount of growth will occur in this ability over the 4 years of college; however, some measurable change is likely.

Recently, educators have become interested in examining how students learn to reason effectively about "ill-structured" questions, that is, open-ended problems for which there cannot be one correct answer because logic is not the only interpretive principle required (Simon, 1973, 1978; Wood, 1997a; Wood, Kitchener, & Jensen, 2002). In contrast to well-structured problems in which all procedures for organizing and evaluating information are agreed upon, ill-structured problems require one actively to organize and structure information which is incomplete and at times conflicting in order to arrive at a solution. As Simon notes (1973, p. 187), more real problem-solving effort is actually directed to structuring problems and only a fraction of it to solving problems once they are structured. The American Association of Colleges commission report *The Challenge of Connecting Learning* (1990) discussed the importance of teaching reasoning about the ill-structured questions involved in real-world issues as a means of "empowering individuals to know that the world is far more complex than it first appears and that they must make interpretive arguments and decision-judgments that entail real consequences for which they must take responsibility and from which they may not flee by disclaiming expertise" (American Association of Colleges, 1990).

In addition to honing logical skills, then, college students are believed by some scholars to develop increasingly sophisticated epistemological skill. King and Kitchener (1994), Wood (1997b), Widick (1977), Baxter-Magolda (1987), and Baxter-Magolda and Porterfield (1985) have adapted Perry's (1970) theory of ethical and intellectual development to college students and have demonstrated that it is possible to measure change from first to senior year in students' ability to reason complexly about ill-structured problems. In a series of studies of particular interest to the present investigation, Kitchener and King (1981), along with colleagues Parker (in Welfel, 1982), Lawson (1980), Strange (Strange & King,

1982), and Wood (King, Kitchener, & Wood, 1994), developed and examined a seven-stage epistemological theory of *reflective judgment*, a term that refers to reasoning about ill-structured problems. The semi-structured interview, the reflective judgment interview (RJI), and the paper-and-pencil instrument reasoning about current issues (RCI) have established a positive correlation between college students' educational level and reflective judgment score (Wood, 1997b). Welfel (1982) notes in addition that higher stages of reflective judgment cannot be explained by maturation alone, and although verbal ability is closely associated with critical thinking about well-structured problems, verbal ability does not account fully for differences between groups' judgments about ill-structured problems. Thus testing for epistemological thinking about open-ended problems seems possible.

Personality

The decision to include personality as a variable in one part of the present study was prompted by a desire to see whether students with certain personality types tend to seek the undergraduate research experience. Such information might contribute to current discussions concerning the use of personality type to understand college student success. Introversion, for instance, has been associated with academic achievement as measured by grades (Entwistle, 1972) and has been assumed to lead to good study habits (Kunderewicz, Michener, & Chambliss, 2001) and academic success (O'Connor, 1993) that requires collaboration. Neuroticism has also been positively associated with higher ability (Austin, Gibson, & Deary, 1997); however, neuroticism may not encourage behaviors helpful to research collaborations. On the other hand, conscientiousness has been strongly linked to achievement of high grades (Digman & Takemoto-Chock, 1981; Tross, Harper, Osher, & Kneidinger, 2000) and to success in future life (Soldz & Vaillant, 1999). Finally, Soldz and Vaillant's 45-year longitudinal study of 63 men found that openness to experience was strongly related to creativity, a trait highly valued in researchers.

DEFINITION OF UNDERGRADUATE RESEARCH:
THE INSTITUTIONAL CONTEXT

Undergraduate research at the university in this study was defined as collaboration between the undergraduate and his or her faculty research sponsor(s). Related experiences common in the undergraduate curriculum such as research methods courses, design courses, or independent studies were *not* included in this definition of undergraduate research; undergraduate researchers worked with their faculty mentors, often as part of a team including graduate and postdoctoral students and research scientists, on problems for which there were no known or agreed-upon answers. Although research students were not exempted from performing the relatively low-skilled tasks of technician in such investigations, they were required to experience a steady progression in their abilities to develop a research hypothesis, design and carry out an investigation and analysis of results, contextualize their work within the scholarly literature, and present their work orally and in writing.

Over 90% of the faculty in engineering and science at the university in this study regularly sponsored undergraduate researchers. In an academic support unit, the Undergraduate Research Program (URP), staff members worked with departmental faculty liaisons to help students identify potential research mentors, provided summer research scholarships as well as limited supply-and-expense funding for undergraduate research, and gave students numerous opportunities to present ongoing work. The URP coordinated summer research programs targeted at specific research areas; for instance, the program for science and engineering provided funds for students who had completed the sophomore year. The URP also facilitated a university-wide senior thesis program through which students prepared a research proposal, made oral presentations of research-in-progress to other students and faculty, established a formal thesis committee, and gave oral defenses of their theses.

Students could begin research at any point in their undergraduate careers; however, normal starting time was mid-sophomore year. In order for faculty research to benefit as much as possible from the training that faculty gave their undergraduates, students were advised by the URP that they should plan to be involved in research for at least one year even though their commitment was made one term at a time. The average length of a student's involvement in research was about three terms (1.5 years) as reported in the alumni survey. During the academic year, students usually registered for academic credit for research although those with financial need could earn work-study money doing research. During the summers, about 125 full scholarships and about 25 partial scholarships were provided to students in science and engineering to enable them to work full-time on research. Additional stipends were provided by faculty research grants.

RESEARCH QUESTIONS GUIDING STUDY

A primary goal for this study was to evaluate the benefits and outcomes of participation in undergraduate research. Because no one measure or method would adequately address this question, a multifaceted design was employed to examine different aspects of the undergraduate research experience from alumni, faculty, graduate student, and undergraduate student perspectives.

The following questions guided this study:

1. Over the course of their undergraduate careers, do undergraduate research participants believe that they develop greater intellectual curiosity, expend greater academic effort, gain greater scientific skills and understanding, and enhance leadership skills to a greater extent than do comparable undergraduates who do not have the research experience?
2. Over the course of undergraduate careers, do changes in critical thinking and reasoning scores differ for students who do and do not participate in undergraduate research, and are there differences by gender and major? Does personality typology affect students' critical thinking or reasoning scores or the change in these scores from first to senior year?
3. When reflecting back on their undergraduate experience, what skills and abilities do alumni report having achieved and is there a difference in the type or level of skills achieved for those who participated in undergraduate research?
4. Why do faculty members participate in undergraduate research (UR)? What benefits do they perceive for themselves, graduate students, and undergraduate students from the UR experience?

METHODOLOGY

Procedure and Participants

After Human Subjects Committee approval was granted, researchers set out to obtain information on four major components.

1. *Summative content analysis of student evaluations available at Undergraduate Research Program office.* A random sample of approximately 200 student evaluations completed between 1982 and 1996 by summer Science and Engineering Scholars was analyzed to indicate level of satisfaction, self-reported gains, and the perceived difficulties and drawbacks of their experience with the URP. Seventeen categories of responses were established in this content analysis, including increased technical skills, working with others, increased desire to learn, and overall satisfaction with this research experience.
2. *Analysis of impact for faculty.* Through an institutionally developed questionnaire, data were gathered from faculty who supervise undergraduate research students to examine their satisfaction, benefits, and challenges faced from involvement in undergraduate research.

3. *Survey of alumni who were involved with URP as a student.* A University of Delaware (UD) alumni survey was mailed to 2,444 alumni from the graduating classes of 1982 through 1997, approximately half of whom participated in undergraduate research. The purposes of this survey were to gauge alumni perceptions of the benefits gained and level of satisfaction with their undergraduate experience and specifically to examine differences in perceived benefits between those alumni who were involved in undergraduate research and those who were not.

4. *Analysis of impact for current undergraduate students.* Beginning in the spring of 1998, full-time first-year students majoring in science and engineering departments at UD were invited to participate in a 4-year longitudinal study of undergraduate academic experiences called the University of Delaware Academic Experiences Study (UDAES). Of the students contacted, 266 agreed to participate. Each participant signed a consent form that contained permission for researchers to examine demographic data (i.e., SAT scores, high school GPA, college major, and college grades) from the student records system. Each spring, the cohort of students completed a battery of instruments to monitor level of critical thinking, college satisfaction, and level of educational engagement. Because no one or two instruments were able to capture the information we hoped to gather, we sought to examine changes in academic skills and perceptions of students' research experiences through several instruments and interview methods.

Instruments

Information about the participants in this longitudinal study was collected from the university's student records database and from participants' responses on the following published measures: the College Student Experiences Questionnaire (Pace, 1984), the Watson-Glaser Critical Thinking Appraisal (Watson & Glaser, 1994), the Reasoning About Current Issues Test (Wood, 1997b), and the NEO Five Factor Inventory (Costa & McCrae, 1991).

College Student Experiences Questionnaire (CSEQ). The *CSEQ* (Pace, 1984) examines students' responses to items in 14 scales that measure the quality of effort (defined as time and energy) put forth each year in various activities that are empirically linked to the outcomes of college (Kuh, Pace, & Vesper, 1997) and to 23 academic and personal items in which students estimate their level of improvement over the past academic year. As specified in the manual, Quality of Effort items can be grouped into two factors: Academic-Intellectual and Personal-Social. Gains items can be grouped into five factors: Academic-Intellectual, Science and Technology, Vocational Preparation, General Education, and Personal-Social. The CSEQ was administered to the study's participants in the spring of each academic year. Internal consistency estimates of the Quality of Effort scales ranged from 0.75 to 0.91 with an average of 0.85.

Watson Glaser Critical Thinking Appraisal (WGCTA). The WGCTA Form S consists of 40 items measuring five subtests of critical thinking about well-structured problems: (1) inference, (2) recognition of unstated assumptions, (3) deduction, (4) interpretation—weighing evidence and deciding if generalizations or conclusions based on given data are warranted—and (5) evaluation of arguments (Watson & Glaser, 1994, pp. 9–10). The WGCTA is the measure of critical thinking most commonly used with postsecondary students (Pascarella, 1989) and has been used in both cross-section and longitudinal studies. Coefficient alpha for the composite score was 0.77 for this sample, based on subtests. Students in this study completed the WGCTA in the spring of their first and senior years.

Reasoning About Current Issues Test (RCI). The RCI is a paper-and-pencil test designed to measure the epistemological construct "reflective judgment." Reflective judgment research seeks to document progressive sophistication in the way that individuals reason about ill-structured problems (King & Kitchener, 1994; Wood, 1997b); thus tests of reflective judgment are usually used longitudinally. The RCI paper-and-pencil test is based upon the structured interviews developed by King and Kitchener and, for the period of this study, was itself being refined and studied to evaluate whether it could be used to detect age and educational differences in reasoning in a way that is comparable to the reflective judgment interview (Kitchener, Wood, & Jensen, 2001). It is composed of two parts: (1) Student Essay Discrimination Measure, in which participants were presented with pairs of very brief real-world current-events topics and are asked to judge which essay in each pair is reasoning about the issue in a more complex or sophisticated fashion; and (2) RCI Dilemmas: Student Endorsement of Justifications, in which participants were given five brief real-world issues along with a set of statements written at varying levels of sophistication according to the reflective judgment model. For this section of the test, participants were asked to indicate how similar each statement was to their own thinking about the issue and to rank the three statements that were most similar to their own reasoning. When the evaluation of the RCI instrument was completed in 2001, it was found that the instrument's overall alphas, although moderate, were comparable to alphas for other paper-and-pencil measures of epistemological development (Wood & Kardash, 2002); overall alphas for the Discrimination score ranged from .75 to .83 while the overall alpha for the Endorsement score was .65 (Kitchener et al., 2001). The RCI was completed three times by the participants in the present study, in the spring of the students' sophomore, junior, and senior years. The Reflective Judgment Interview (King & Kitchener, 1994) is a complementary method to the RCI, but in individual interview format as opposed to paper and pencil. The RJI was employed only once, in students' third year (spring 1999).

NEO Five Factor Inventory (NEO-FFI). As a broad measure of personality, this short form consists of five subtests, each composed of twelve items (Costa & McCrae, 1991). The subtests are: (1) NEO-Neuroticism, a measure of adjustment and emotional stability; (2) NEO-Extroversion, a measure of sociability and consequent behaviors; (3) NEO–Openness to Experiences, a measure of imagination, aesthetic sensitivity, attentiveness to inner feelings, preference for variety, intellectual curiosity, and independence of judgment; (4) NEO-Agreeableness, a measure of sympathy toward others and altruism, eagerness to help; and (5) NEO-Conscientiousness, a measure of ability to manage impulses and desires as well as organizing and carrying out tasks. Reported alpha coefficients ranged from 0.73 to 0.86. Participants in this study completed the personality inventory at the end of their first and senior years.

Reflective Judgment Interview (RJI). The reflective judgment model was developed jointly by Patricia King and Karen Kitchener (1994) as one way to document the gains in complex reasoning that students demonstrate during the undergraduate and graduate years. The research seeks to document progressive sophistication in the way that individuals reason about a particular type of problem through an ill-structured problem. The RJI was administered one time to a sample of 27 students. Because RJ interview scores for these students paralleled scores for the RCI, we did not continue the use of the RJI or report the scores in this report.

STUDY FINDINGS

Summative Content Analysis of Student Evaluations Available at Undergraduate Research Program Office

To examine the educational effectiveness of the undergraduate research experience, a content analysis was conducted on 183 randomly selected free-form evaluation letters (one to four pages long) written during the period 1985 to 1995 by undergraduate research students who participated in a 10-week summer program for engineering and science scholars. This content analysis determined 17 categories of responses, including increased technical skills, increased general self-confidence, insight into the value of teamwork, and deepened understanding of where knowledge comes from. Interrater reliability between the two scorers was .65. Table 5.1 shows the number and percentage of students in this sample who indicated an increase in academic-related skills and abilities.

Of the 183 responses, 113 students (62%) felt that they had learned more through the research experience than in standard courses. Some students felt liberated by the realism of their research experience; for instance, an electrical engineering student reported, "My research experience allows me to be independent,

Table 5.1. Students who indicated that summer research experience increased their academic skills and abilities.

Skill/Ability	n	%
Increased technical skills	176	96
Increased ability to act independently	107	57
Insight into graduate school	82	45
Insight into value of teamwork	78	43
Ability to work with ambiguities/obstacles	67	37
Ability to think creatively/synthetically	59	32
Increased desire to learn	59	32
Increased general self-confidence	51	28
Improved communication skills	44	24
Deepened understanding of where knowledge comes from	44	24

flexible, creative, etc. It truly presents a challenge to myself that I have yet to find in any standard course." In addition to those students who reported they learned more through research, another 39 students felt that their learning in research was as valuable as that in courses but of a different kind; the students making this comment represented 21% of the total evaluation letters and 25% of those commenting on the comparison. Two individuals, representing 1% both of the total and of the students commenting on the comparison, felt that they learned more through course work than through research.

Almost all of the students (96%) described the advanced technical skills they had learned through their research assistance. These skills were what many of the students expected to gain when they sought the research experience, and they were proud to report that they had measured up to or exceeded their own expectations in this area. The reported gains were sometimes accompanied by a statement describing increased general self-confidence, as in the following comment by a physiology student, which was coded for two comment categories, increased technical skill and increased general self-confidence: "Of greatest importance to me was the training in and performance of delicate small animal surgery. At the onset of the program I thought these skills were beyond the scope of my abilities; however, through careful supervision, my confidence and ability have grown tremendously." Overall, 28% of the students commented directly on their generalized increased self-confidence.

Nearly half of the responses (45%) indicated that the research experience had given the students important insight into the world of graduate study, thus aiding their own career decision. Forty-three percent of the respondents also commented on a new understanding of the importance of collaboration in research, not only with graduate students and their faculty sponsors, but also with technicians, industrial scientists and engineers, and others. About a quarter of the evaluations (24%) mentioned improved communications skills gained from professional presentation of research. For instance, "I have learned how to speak at the professional and technical levels with my peers as well as my superiors, and I feel confident discussing the various aspects of the research" with both faculty and industry professionals. A quarter (24%) also said they had gained a new understanding of where ideas and theories in their field came from and recognition of the tentativeness of scientific findings. For the full report on the content analysis, please go to: http://www.udel.edu/RAIRE/Content.pdf.

Analysis of Impact for Faculty

An institutionally developed UD Faculty Survey was completed by 156 science and engineering faculty (44% response rate) to examine satisfaction, benefits, and challenges faced from involvement in undergraduate research. For the analyses, respondents were grouped into five disciplines: agricultural sciences, natural sciences, engineering, mathematics, and psychology. Of the faculty who responded, 86% said they have supervised one or more undergraduate research assistants (URAs) in the past 5 years. On average, faculty respondents who supervised URAs had worked with seven URAs and eight graduate or postdoctoral research assistants (GRAs) in the past 5 years. About one quarter of the respondents involved undergraduates as coauthors on papers or presentations, and about two thirds had some or all undergraduates complete a senior thesis. According to responses, there was a significant relationship between completion of the senior thesis and/or professional research presentations and perceived cognitive gains for students. Correlation analyses yielded significant relationships between these two activities (thesis and presentations) and students' ability to solve problems independently, synthesize and use information, think logically about complex material, approach problems creatively, maintain openness to new ideas, and develop intellectual curiosity. Table 5.2 shows responses to select survey questions. As shown, faculty respondents said they believed the research experience contributed substantially to cognitive and affective development including intellectual curiosity, understanding scientific findings, thinking logically about complex material, and synthesizing information from diverse sources.

Nearly half of the faculty respondents (46%) who supervised URAs said they designed their research program to accommodate undergraduates, and half (50%) said that participation of research assistants was important or very important in contributing to their research program. Accommodations for URAs include sav-

Table 5.2. Faculty responses to "importance of research" question.

"When you think of the undergraduates who have done research with you at UD, how important do you think their research experience was to their intellectual and personal development in the following areas?"

Skill/Ability	"Important" or "Very Important" (%)
Develop intellectual curiosity	80
Think logically about complex materials	77
Understand scientific findings	77
Synthesize and use information from diverse sources	69
Solve problems independently, without supervision	66
Approach problems creatively	65
Work as part of a team	63
Maintain openness to new ideas	63
Possess clear career goals	55
Adapt to rapidly changing technology	37
Understand ethical implications of issues	30

ing small or shorter projects, designing simpler projects, providing extra money or time, and expanding exploratory research. Results from this faculty survey showed a significant correlation between number of GRAs and URAs,[1] indicating that faculty who have a higher number of GRAs are more likely to have a higher number of URAs. Examining this question by discipline, we found this relationship to be strongest in engineering. Survey results also show a significant relationship between the number of GRAs and faculty members' involvement in supervision of the research assistants.[2] Faculty respondents also indicated some barriers to the undergraduate research experience. Fifty-seven percent of the respondents said that the cost in terms of time was "important" to "very important" and 41% said the financial cost was great. Thirty-nine of the respondents said they would accommodate more URAs if additional funds were available. For additional information on the UD Faculty Survey, see Zydney and colleagues (2002).

Survey of Alumni Who Were Involved with URP as a Student

Responses to the UD Alumni Survey were received from 996 individuals, for a final response rate of 42%. Ten respondents did not include identifying information and thus were omitted from the analysis. The remaining 986 respondents fell into three groups of alumni: (1) those respondents who had participated in research and were in UD's Undergraduate Research Program database; (2) those who were not in the URP database but who identified themselves as having participated in research as an undergraduate; and (3) those with no research participation at UD. Thus we decided to analyze survey results using a three-way comparison. Initial analysis of the three groups revealed a difference in cumulative grade point average (GPA); therefore, GPA was included as a covariate in all subsequent analyses.

Of the 986 identifiable respondents, 418 were alumni who had participated in research through the Undergraduate Research Program (the "URP" respondents), 213 responded to survey questions about research and were thus self-identified alumni with research experience (the "self-report" respondents), and 355 had had no undergraduate research experience (the "no-research" respondents). Of the total sample, nearly half (46%) had enrolled in at least one honors course, 428 (44%) were men and 558 (56%) were women. Approximately 95% of the respondents were Caucasian.

As a total group, respondents spent, on average, one semester in study abroad, two semesters in internships, and three to five semesters participating in intercollegiate and/or intramural sports, clubs/performing arts, and employment. The alumni who had not participated in research had worked significantly more hours off campus than had the alumni with self-reported research involvement. The URP alumni reported having lived on campus longer as well as having participated to a greater extent in student government than the alumni with no research participation (overall number of respondents who participated in student government was small). URP alumni reported having spent more semesters conducting research than did self-report research respondents. Alumni respondents also indicated the level of benefit they received from the activities included on the survey. Involvement in undergraduate research, completion of a senior thesis, study abroad, and internship related to major were rated as most beneficial for the total group of respondents. URP alumni reported greater benefit from honors classes than did self-report and non-research alumni. Benefit received from participation in undergraduate research was significantly higher for alumni who participated in formal research than for those who self-reported research participation. Furthermore, perceived benefit from participation in undergraduate research was even stronger for those URP respondents who completed a senior thesis compared to the research alumni who did not complete a thesis. Alumni were also asked the extent to which skills and abilities had been enhanced by their baccalaureate studies. Not surprisingly, both groups of alumni with research experience reported significantly greater enhancement of their ability to carry out research than did alumni who had done no research beyond that required for courses. Furthermore, alumni whose undergraduate research had been facilitated by the URP reported significantly higher growth in their ability to carry out research than did the alumni with self-reported research experience. Alumni with formal undergraduate research experience reported greater increases than non-research alumni for seven additional items, including the ability to develop intellectual curiosity, acquire information independently, understand scientific findings, analyze literature critically, speak effectively, act as a leader, and possess clear career goals. While alumni perceived even one semester's experience in undergraduate research to be very beneficial, responses indicated that, in general, the longer one had participated in research, the greater the perceived benefit.[3] Of the total respondent sample, 70% reported pursuing graduate education. Graduate school attendance rates differed by research participation: 80% of the URP alumni, 71% of the alumni with self-reported research experience, and 59% of the alumni with no research experience pursued graduate education. A final question asked respondents to indicate their overall satisfaction with their baccalaureate experience. Although alumni in all three research groups reported high overall growth and satisfaction, results showed that, compared to alumni with no research, URP alumni reported significantly greater overall satisfaction. Additional information about the UD Alumni Survey can be found in Bauer and Bennett (2003).

Analysis of Impact for Current Undergraduate Students

Identifying the undergraduate research students. In spring 1998, full-time first-year students majoring in science and engineering departments at UD were invited to participate in the University of Delaware Academic Experiences Study, a 4-year longitudinal study of undergraduate academic experiences. As with the alumni survey, participants did not know that this study specifically concerned undergraduate research. Of the students contacted, 266 agreed to participate. Each spring, students who volunteered to participate in this study gathered to complete the paper-and-pencil instruments. Study participants were informed that four randomly drawn prizes would be awarded to participants, and at the end of their testing session study participants were included in a random drawing for one of four $100 prizes in "purchasing points," usable at any campus store or restaurant. In addition, upon completion of the survey instruments, students were offered refreshments and a small monetary incentive. The cash incentive was $5 in spring 1997; $10 in spring 1998; $15 in spring 1999 and $20 in spring 2000. As a further reminder, at the beginning of each year, participants were also sent small gifts, such as pens, floppy disk holders, and mugs, all imprinted with the study's logo.

At the start of this longitudinal study, it was anticipated that some of the study's participants would become involved in undergraduate research, leaving the remaining study participants to serve as a comparison group coming from the same class and set of academic majors. The initial participants were first-year students from 10 science or engineering majors. They included 155 females (58%) and 111 males (42%). They were 202 White (76%), 35 African American (13%), 17 Asian American (6%), 5 Hispanic (2%), 7 other (3%). By the time the participants graduated, those still participating in the study had declared 47 different majors. These students were grouped into four major disciplinary groups: biological sciences, physical sciences and chemical engineering, all other engineering disciplines, and social sciences.[4] Nonscience majors ($N = 24$) were excluded from analyses presented herein. By spring 2000, the number of participants who had completed the instruments was 215, including 191 science and engineering majors, yielding an overall subject retention rate of 81%. It turned out that about half of the students undertook undergraduate research, leaving the other half to serve as a comparison group. The number of participants who were racial minorities completing all tests was too small to allow for statistical significance in analyses of results by race.

Each spring, when students completed the instruments listed above, they also reported the approximate average number of hours per week they had been involved in a variety of college activities, including undergraduate research. Student self-reports of research involvement were verified with faculty and then summed to reveal the approximate total number of hours over the 4 baccalaureate years each student had participated in undergraduate research. Total number of hours for participation in research over the course of the baccalaureate years ranged from 0 to 3,342. Mean number of hours for those who participated in research was 626 hours (standard deviation = 596). Students were grouped into three levels of research intensity; those with (1) no research involvement ($N = 109$), (2) a moderate research involvement (1 to 500 hours; $N = 45$), and (3) intensive research involvement (501 or more hours; $N = 52$). Students who participated in research for one summer and one academic year spent about 700 hours of time in this activity. However, the median of research hours for participating students for this sample was 500 hours, thus the rationale to divide research students in this way. Based on a scatter plot of research hours of participants' belonging to four science and engineering groups, two outliers were omitted, leaving a final sample of 206 students.

Demographics of the sample. Table 5.3 shows descriptive statistics and Table 5.4 highlights the correlation matrix for the measures used in this study. In addition, overall CSEQ scores for this population were either consistent with or higher than the norm for doctorate-granting institutions. Based on normative scores presented in the respective manuals, NEO and WGCTA scores are generally consistent with those obtained from other baccalaureate students. RCI scores were slightly above norms for sophomores, consistent with norms at the junior year, and slightly below norms at the senior year (Wood, 2001).

Although WGCTA scores were significantly correlated with SAT verbal scores, when repeated measures analyses were run both with SAT total as a covariate and without, findings did not differ substantially. RCI scores were not highly correlated with SAT since, even though the correlation coefficients were significant, the values, which were between 0.21 and 0.29, did not reveal strong rela-

Table 5.3. UDAES mean scores by level of research participation.

	No Research			Moderate Research (1–500 hours)			High Research (> 500 hours)			Total, All Students		
	M	n	SD	M	n	SD	M	n	SD	M	N	SD
SAT math score[a]	605.47	106	84.17	618.67	45	65.77	646.35	52	78.39	618.87	203	80.40
SAT verbal score[a]	593.33	105	73.57	612.44	45	75.86	632.50	52	85.26	607.67	202	78.59
Yr2 RCI	5.18	97	0.65	5.34	42	0.58	5.34	51	0.59	5.26	190	0.62
Yr3 RCI	5.26	87	0.67	5.34	38	0.64	5.41	49	0.68	5.32	174	0.67
Yr4 RCI	5.24	90	0.68	5.30	43	0.65	5.38	49	0.77	5.29	182	0.70
Yr1 WGCTA	28.89	107	4.99	29.27	45	4.97	30.88	52	5.25	29.48	204	5.10
Yr4 WGCTA[a]	29.52	95	5.10	29.48	42	5.00	31.92	48	5.28	30.13	185	5.21
Yr1: NEO-N 1997[a]	20.19	106	7.83	22.64	45	6.84	24.69	52	8.94	21.89	203	8.12
Yr4: NEO-N 2000[a]	18.79	97	8.01	18.91	43	8.40	22.88	50	9.96	19.89	190	8.78
Yr1: NEO-E 1997[b]	31.37	106	6.29	32.24	45	5.68	27.58	52	5.83	30.59	203	6.28
Yr4: NEO-E 2000[c]	31.00	97	7.13	32.51	43	6.03	28.54	50	6.68	30.69	190	6.89
Yr1: NEO-O 1997	29.22	106	5.51	31.16	45	6.35	31.17	52	5.90	30.15	203	5.86
Yr4: NEO-O 2000[a]	29.93	97	5.70	30.81	43	6.10	32.90	50	5.43	30.91	190	5.83
Yr1: NEO-A 1997	32.58	106	6.07	31.93	45	5.09	32.15	52	6.97	32.33	203	6.10
Yr4: NEO-A 2000	29.93	97	5.70	30.81	43	6.10	32.90	50	5.43	30.91	190	5.83
Yr1: NEO-C 1997	33.08	106	6.80	32.42	45	6.79	34.25	52	6.66	33.23	203	6.76
Yr4: NEO-C 2000	32.26	97	6.99	33.37	43	7.04	34.28	50	5.54	33.04	190	6.67

[a] No research group significantly different from high research group.
[b] Mean score for this group significantly different from other two groups.
[c] Mean score for this group significantly different from small research group.

Table 5.4. UDAES correlation matrix.

	1	2	3	4	5	6	7	8	9	10	11	12	13	14	15	16
1. SAT math																
2. SAT verbal	0.534** (202)															
3. RCI: Yr 2	0.007 (187)	0.245** (186)														
4. RCI: Yr 3	0.135 (171)	0.324** (170)	0.526** (174)													
5. RCI: Yr 4	0.089 (181)	0.267** (180)	0.476** (172)	0.694** (159)												
6. WGCTA: Yr 1	0.475** (201)	0.553** (200)	0.123 (188)	0.311** (172)	0.224** (180)											
7. WGCTA: Yr 4	0.578** (182)	0.565** (181)	0.204** (173)	0.320** (160)	0.263** (176)	0.661** (183)										
8. NEO-N: Yr 1	-0.095 (200)	-0.025 (199)	-0.052 (187)	-0.054 (171)	-0.124 (179)	-0.037 (203)	0.003 (182)									
9. NEO-E: Yr 1	-0.168** (200)	-0.160* (199)	0.051 (187)	0.049 (171)	0.020 (179)	-0.189** (203)	-0.153* (182)	-0.392** (203)								
10. NEO-O: Yr 1	-0.039 (200)	0.116 (199)	0.311** (187)	0.202** (171)	0.193** (179)	0.147* (203)	0.063 (182)	-0.060 (203)	0.097 (203)							
11. NEO-A: Yr 1	-0.151* (200)	0.002 (199)	0.198** (187)	0.208** (171)	0.193** (179)	0.109 (203)	0.093 (182)	-0.116 (203)	0.258** (203)	0.138* (203)						
12. NEO-C: Yr 1	-0.200** (200)	-0.185** (199)	-0.045 (187)	-0.135 (171)	-0.049 (179)	-0.292** (203)	-0.344** (182)	-0.258** (203)	0.262** (203)	0.050 (203)	0.079 (203)					
13. NEO-N: Yr 4	-0.068 (187)	-0.030 (186)	-0.066 (179)	-0.083 (166)	-0.121 (182)	-0.012 (188)	0.004 (184)	0.687** (187)	-0.324** (187)	-0.041 (187)	-0.158* (187)	-0.151 (187)				
14. NEO-E: Yr 4	-0.153* (187)	-0.100 (186)	0.107 (179)	0.146 (166)	0.098 (182)	-0.145 (188)	-0.116 (184)	-0.295** (187)	0.786** (187)	0.131 (187)	0.240** (187)	0.194** (187)	-0.409** (190)			
15. NEO-O: Yr 4	-0.010 (187)	0.149* (186)	0.201** (179)	0.324** (166)	0.257** (182)	0.183* (188)	0.107 (184)	-0.017 (187)	0.037 (187)	0.704** (187)	0.129 (187)	0.026 (187)	-0.090 (190)	0.128 (190)		
16. NEO-A: Yr 4	-0.063 (187)	0.037 (186)	0.130 (179)	0.053 (166)	0.081 (182)	0.039 (188)	0.034 (184)	-0.037 (187)	0.205** (187)	0.079 (187)	0.697** (187)	0.047 (187)	-0.253** (190)	0.305** (190)	0.145 (190)	
17. NEO-C: Yr 4	-0.120 (187)	-0.070 (186)	0.081 (179)	0.054 (166)	0.113 (182)	-0.165* (188)	-0.214** (184)	-0.085 (187)	0.268** (187)	0.132 (187)	0.093 (187)	0.610** (187)	-0.171* (190)	0.307** (190)	0.084 (190)	0.169 (190)

Note: Numbers in parentheses indicate the number of observations.

* $p < .05$, two-tailed. ** $p < .01$, two-tailed.

tionships. Correlations for each measure were moderately to highly correlated across time (e.g., correlation between RCI score in Year 3 and Year 4 is .70). Because SAT did not affect results for either test, even though the three research groups have mean SAT scores that are significantly different from each other, except where noted, SAT as a covariate was not included in our analysis of repeated measures in the models presented below.

Changes in self-reported Quality of Effort and perceived gains.
Responses to items on the CSEQ provided consistent data on perceived Quality of Effort (QE) and gains in academic and psychosocial skills. Preliminary analyses used repeated measures analyses of variance (Tabachnick & Fidell, 1996) and specified a 4 (year) by 3 (levels of research) by 4 (major groups) by 2 (gender) design. All models were checked for good fit by "lack of fit" test; and, except where noted below, each analysis was based on a model that fitted the data well. In accordance with factor groupings presented in the CSEQ manual (1987), and individual items within each factor described in each section below, repeated measures ANOVAs were completed to examine overall differences in Quality of Effort scores and difference in gains scores for each year by three independent variables: participation in research, sex, and major discipline.

Quality of Effort in Academic-Intellectual activities.
Self-reported actions that comprise this factor included such experiences as writing and speaking; use made of libraries; use of material learned in courses; interactions with faculty; becoming informed and discussing current events; and issues and ideas in the arts, history, philosophy, social problems, science, and technology.

Analyses showed no significant differences in reported Quality of Effort in Academic-Intellectual activities by major or gender, although undergraduate research students, both those with moderate research experience and those with intensive research experience, reported greater Academic-Intellectual (AI) effort in all 4 years than did students who did not participate in research,[5] as shown in Figure 5.1. Academic-Intellectual effort reported by students with intensive research experience was significantly higher than AI effort reported by those with no research. Thus, as shown in Figure 5.1, students who devoted more time to undergraduate research perceived themselves from the beginning to be harder workers academically and more self-directed intellectually than those who did no research perceived themselves to be. Although the interaction by year was not significant, it is interesting to note that over time, AI effort scores became even higher for students involved in intensive research but decreased for students who were not participating in research and who spent 500 hours or less in research (see Figure 5.1).

Some evidence that research involvement was associated with an increased desire of students to learn was provided by the students' course selection. When

Figure 5.1. CSEQ academic-intellectual scores by level of undergraduate research.

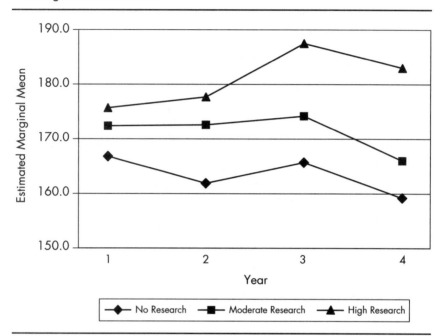

study participants' enrollment in upper-level and graduate-level courses was examined in a related but separate analysis, and with SAT verbal score used as a covariate, students with no research involvement enrolled in significantly fewer upper-level courses during their 4 years of college than did students with research experience. In addition, students with intensive research experience enrolled in significantly more upper-level and graduate-level courses than students with moderate research experience[6] (Bauer, 2001).

Quality of Effort in Personal-Social activities. A separate repeated measures ANOVA revealed significant findings for Quality of Effort invested in Personal-Social activities. Although no significant effects for major group or gender were found, there was a strong main effect by undergraduate research.[7] As shown in Figure 5.2, scores for all three groups declined each year; yet this score for moderate research students declined more precipitously in the third year and remained lower than it did for intensive research students.

Gains in Science and Technology skills. The Science and Technology gains factor included perceived gains in understanding new scientific and technical devel-

Figure 5.2. CSEQ personal-social scores by level of undergraduate research.

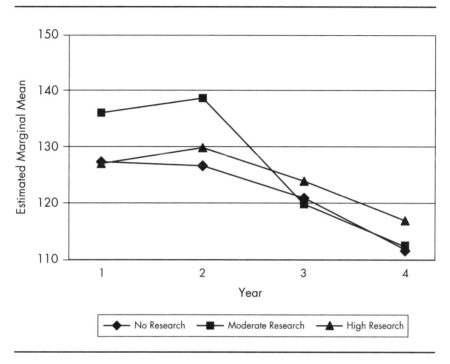

opments, understanding the nature of science and experimentation, and becoming aware of consequences of new applications in science and technology. Along with a significant main effect, effects of undergraduate research experience in the repeated measures ANOVA for perceived gains in Science and Technology approached significance.[8] As shown in Figure 5.3, all groups reported gains in science and technology from the first through third years, then all three groups declined in Year Four. Regardless of the decline in Year Four, students who participated in an intense level of research consistently reported greater gains than all other students.

Gains in Intellectual, Personal-Social, and Vocational Preparation. Three additional repeated measures ANOVAs examined effects for perceived gains in Intellectual, Personal-Social, and Vocational Preparation; findings revealed a significant main effect for each of these factors over time (year) but did not reveal an effect for undergraduate research, major, or gender.

Changes in critical thinking and reflective judgment. Two additional repeated measures analyses of variance were performed to examine the effect of research

Figure 5.3. CSEQ science and technology gains by level of undergraduate research.

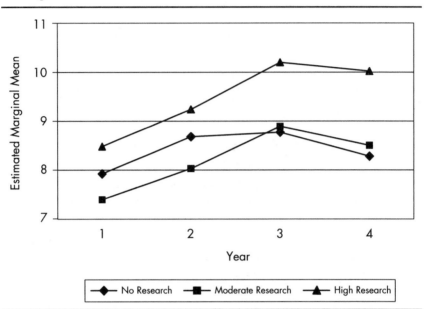

participation on changes in critical thinking as measured by the WGCTA and reflective judgment as measured by the RCI. The WGCTA was administered at the end of first and senior years. The RCI was administered at the end of the sophomore, junior, and senior years. A repeated measures ANOVA for WGCTA found a significant increase from first to senior year for the total group of students,[9] but no significant effect for level of research involvement (none, moderate, intensive), the four major groups, or gender. For RCI, although we attempted several iterations using the same factors, all repeated measures ANOVAs revealed an ill-fitting model; thus findings indicate increases but no significant main or interaction effects for increase in RCI over time.

Change in personality from first to senior year. To examine relationships between personality type and participation in research, academic discipline, and gender, we originally planned to include the five NEO typology scores as covariates. However, means for the five NEO typology scores (N, E, O, A, C) differed for the three research groups, so we decided to not use NEO scores as covariates for the analyses. Instead, we decided to examine the changes in each of the five typologies from first to senior year by research, major, and gender.

Repeated measures findings revealed a significant main effect decrease (by year) in Neuroticism from first to senior year,[10] but no significant differences by research, major, or gender (see Figure 5.4).

The analysis for openness to experience revealed a significant main effect increase by year from first to senior year,[11] yet no differences by research, major, or gender were found. Analyses for extraversion, agreeableness, and conscientiousness revealed no significant changes from the first to senior years.

DISCUSSION

Because we believed that no one instrument or method would adequately evaluate the Undergraduate Research Program, a multifaceted design was developed

Figure 5.4. NEO-neuroticism score change by major group.

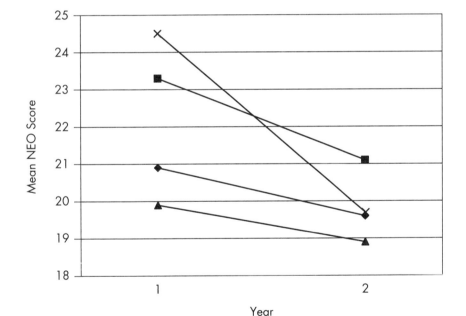

and implemented. Overall, the content analysis of summer Science and Engineering Scholars indicated high satisfaction and positive academic progress as a result of scholars' undergraduate research experience. Similarly, alumni who participated in undergraduate research as students reported significantly higher skills and abilities as a result of their undergraduate experiences. Alumni who participated in UR also participated in other college experiences, such as study abroad, and more alumni with UR experience went on to graduate school. Based on results from the faculty survey, science and engineering faculty members also reported personal benefits from involvement in UR (Zydney et al., 2002), and they believed that students who participated in UR achieved benefits such as intellectual curiosity, an understanding of scientific findings, thinking logically about complex material, and synthesizing information from diverse sources. On several items, faculty perceptions about gains were consistent with those of the alumni, and the finding that significantly more research students progressed to graduate school appears to indicate UR benefits for students. In addition, the finding that, for both faculty members and alumni, completion of a senior thesis correlates with higher levels of critical thinking and other cognitive skills may reflect the fact that the design senior thesis typically builds upon three to six semesters of research experience prior to the senior year. Further, the senior thesis course helps to ensure that all candidates are taught systematically to develop a research hypothesis, design and carry out an investigation, analyze the results within a context of the scholarly literature, and present their work to specialist and nonspecialist audiences, including a formal defense before a faculty committee.

In attempting to complement and enhance evidence from student, alumni, and faculty on the value added to an undergraduate education by the undergraduate research experience, the design of a 4-year study allowed for an examination of both self-reported and objective measures of academic growth, providing the benefit of perspectives on growth from several vantage points and incorporating a consideration of personality typology. Like the alumni study, the longitudinal study design minimized the possibility of respondent bias because the students had no way of knowing that the study of "academic experiences" in which they were participating had any direct relationship to undergraduate research. CSEQ results did show that in general, regardless of major discipline or sex, students with undergraduate research experience report an increase in their academic efforts overall and gain scientific and technical understanding and skill to a greater extent than comparable students who had not undertaken research. Thus CSEQ measures of academic effort and gains in currently enrolled students match the perceptions of alumni.

However, undergraduate research experience did not influence the perceived social effort and gains measured by the CSEQ, even though faculty who supervise undergraduate researchers believe that the students' ability to assume leadership roles and work collaboratively improve through the research experience and alumni with research experience report greater confidence in these abilities than do comparable alumni with no research experience (Zydney et al., 2002). This difference may suggest that social effort, as measured by the CSEQ, is a different phenomenon from effort in research collaboration.

Differences in Critical Thinking Gains by Major and Research Involvement

Although just below the level of significance, WGCTA results showed Biological Sciences and Physical Sciences/Chemical Engineering majors who were involved in an intense level of research achieved a larger increase from first to senior year in critical thinking skills, that is, the ability to reason logically about well-structured problems, than was achieved by comparable students in these majors who did not participate in research. In addition, students majoring in Biological and Social Sciences reported CSEQ gains in general education results that approached significance, possibly indicating an emphasis placed on gaining a stronger philosophy of life, valuing general education, and lifelong learning for students in these disciplines.

Although results only approached significance, students with intensive research experience showed higher gains in reflective judgment, that is, the ability to reason effectively about open-ended problems, than did comparable students who did not participate in research. Thus the WGCTA and RCI scores indicate that the research experience made a difference in critical thinking for some students (see Table 5.3).

Although differences did not reach statistical significance, it is notable that gains in both areas of critical thinking were related most strongly to research experience in the biological sciences, possibly suggesting that research experiences for biological science students may make a particularly strong addition to classroom learning. Further testing with larger numbers of biology majors would be needed to see whether differences could be related to the biology research experience or just to the specific individuals in this study.

Differences in Critical Thinking Gains by Gender and Research Involvement

Although RCI changes did not reach significance, findings showed that women with intensive research experience achieved higher RCI scores and a higher increase in scores for reflective judgment than women with no or moderate levels of research experience. However, for WGCTA results, while women and men grew at about the same rate from first to senior year with no measurable effects due to level of research experience, the men's scores began and remained somewhat (but not statistically significantly) higher than the women's. From this set of observations, it might be inferred that intensive research experience was particularly beneficial for women students, causing them to grow noticeably in their ability to reason well about open-ended, real-world problems. If so, this finding suggests that intensive research experience could be a vehicle for encouraging women in science and engineering.

Limitations

Several limitations in this study are noted. First, since the students and faculty in most of these studies were only from the sciences and engineering, results cannot necessarily be generalized to other disciplines. The UD Faculty and Alumni Surveys were institutionally developed and were designed to address unique aspects of the UD Undergraduate Research Program and thus may not generalize to faculty and alumni at other institutions. For the UDAES study, based on a one-sample t-test using SAT scores, all students who volunteered to participate in this study except those in animal science, civil engineering, and psychology were representative of majors in their departments at this university. Although the total number of participants gave sufficient power for main effect analyses, the power to detect statistically significant interactions was quite low (Wood & Conner, 1999).

It is also possible, for all the studies, that students' voluntary decision to participate in undergraduate research may have caused some bias in the results. Mean SAT math and verbal scores of UR students indicate their overall ability, and it is possible that high-achieving students are drawn to undergraduate research more than lower ability students. Similarly, perhaps students who choose to explore undergraduate research hold a different level of internal motivation that may affect academic or cognitive change. The inclusion of a measure of motivation would be valuable in a future study.

The lack of abundant significant findings for RCI by research groups may have been due to the small sample size. In addition, the RCI items may not have resonated for the science and engineering students in this particular sample. RCI item questions were developed using a preponderance of social science students as subjects. A study comparing the effectiveness of RCI in capturing reflective judgment when compared to the effectiveness of the RJ interviews found that students achieved much better scores when the ill-structured problems posed to them were related to their major (P. K. Wood, personal communication, May 2002). The RCI test dilemmas are reasonably related to the interests of students of psychology and of medically significant biological sciences but may not be of interest to most of the engineering and physical science students. It is possible that if the latter were given a set of RCI dilemmas dealing with complex technical questions, their epistemological scores would be higher because they would be more engaged intellectually with the problem described.

SUGGESTIONS FOR FUTURE RESEARCH

Because there are many facets to an undergraduate research program, evaluation via a multifaceted design is appropriate and more likely to yield a fuller and more detailed description of the program and its outcomes. A multifaceted evaluation design, however, requires substantial time, personnel, and dollar resources. Surveying graduate students and postdoctoral students who supervise undergraduate research assistants would be beneficial.

Because the longitudinal design can provide highly reliable information on change over time, we believe this methodology to be valuable; however, we would recommend increasing the sample size. If possible, a random assignment of students between the research and no research conditions may be useful to examine motivation or other inherent conditions that could affect change results. In addition, although it was desirable to see what could be learned from instruments with already proven reliability, we believe that in order to develop the most useful method for assessing student learning through the undergraduate research experience or any similar curricular or cocurricular innovation, it might be worthwhile to pilot and establish reliability for an inventory of general cognitive and psychosocial skills and abilities that could replace the CSEQ with fewer items, and in a paper-and-pencil test format, at the end of each academic year. In addition to eliminating items from the lengthy CSEQ that are not of direct interest to a study of academic development (e.g., perceptions of the environment), items on such an inventory could parallel those on the survey of general skills and abilities included on the alumni survey referenced earlier in this article and could make possible a follow-up survey with the same skills items to be given to the longitudinal subjects when they become alumni.

The cognitive skill closely related to gains that undergraduate research is strongly positioned to develop is reasoning about open-ended questions. Therefore, for studying effects of the undergraduate research experience in engineering and the sciences, it might be valuable to develop engineering and science content for the RCI test dilemmas. We recommend administering such a version of the RCI at the beginning of the first year and at the end of each of the four academic years if possible. It might also be the case, however, that the skills gained from a research experience, even though identified by participants in terms that sound like reflective judgment, actually represent a different set of skills than those assessed by the RCI. Finally, we also recommend the inclusion of a measure of motivation. Although personality traits were not shown to correlate with the decision to undertake undergraduate research, a motivation measure, used both for alumni and for current students, might provide insight into whether students' general motivation level accounts for their decision to undertake research and for any of the perceived educational effort and gains found to correlate with the intensive research experience.

ACKNOWLEDGMENTS

This research was sponsored by National Science Foundation Awards #9620082 and #9902000. The authors wish to thank Drs. Phil Wood, Abdus Shahid, Christine Ward, Sarah Fine, and Hye-Sook Park for assistance with portions of data collection or analysis for this project.

NOTES

1. $r = .40, p < .01$.
2. $r = .33, p < .01$.
3. $r = .33, p < .01$.
4. The 10 original majors were animal science, biology, chemical engineering, chemistry and biochemistry, civil engineering, computer and information science, electrical and computer engineering, mechanical engineering, physics, and psychology.
5. Wilk's Lambda $F (6,318) = 2.81, p = .011$; Hotelling's Trace $F (6,316) = 2.827$, $p = .011$; Roy's Largest Root $F (3,160) = 4.95, p = .003$.
6. $F (6,318) = 12.654, p < .000$.
7. Wilk's Lambda $F (6,318) = 2.361, p = .03$; Hotelling's Trace F $(6,318) = 2.376$, $p = .029$; Roy's Largest Root $F (3,160) = 4.23, p = .007$.
8. Wilk's Lambda $F (6,310) = 2.047, p = .059$; Hotelling's Trace $F (3,157) = 2.07$ $p = .056$; Roy's Largest Root $F (3,157) = 4.12, p = .008$.
9. $F (1,182) = 4.72, p = .031$.
10. $F (1,213) = 15.889, p < .001$.
11. $F (1,213) = 6.391, p = .012$.

REFERENCES

American Association of Colleges. (1990). *The challenge of connecting learning: Liberal learning and the arts and science major.* Washington, DC: Author.

Austin, E. J., Gibson, G. J., & Deary, I. J. (1997). Relationship between ability and personality: Three hypotheses tested. *Intelligence, 25,* 49–70.

Bauer, K. W. (2001). *Enrollment in upper level undergraduate and graduate level courses for UDAES students.* Unpublished report, University of Delaware, Office of Undergraduate Research, Newark, DE.

Bauer, K. W. (2004). Conducting longitudinal studies. In S. Porter (Ed.), Overcoming survey research problems [Special issue]. *New Directions for Institutional Research* [On line], No. 121, 75–90.

Bauer, K. W., & Bennett, J. S. (2003). Alumni perceptions used to assess the undergraduate research experience. *Journal of Higher Education, 72,* 210–230.

Baxter-Magolda, M. B. (1987). Comparing open-ended interviews and standard measures of intellectual development. *Journal of College Student Development, 28,* 443–448.

Baxter-Magolda, M. B., & Porterfield, W. D. (1985). A new approach to assessing intellectual development on the Perry scheme. *Journal of College Student Development, 26,* 343–351.

Boyer Commission on Educating Undergraduates in the Research University. (1998). *Reinventing undergraduate education: A blueprint for America's research universities.* New York: Author.

Boyer Commission on Educating Undergraduates in the Research University. (2001). *Reinventing undergraduate education: Three years after the Boyer report.* Retrieved December 15, 2003, from http://www.sunysb.edu/pres/pdfs/0210066-Boyer%20 Report%20Final.pdf

Chickering, A. W., & Reisser, L. (1993). *Education and identity.* San Francisco: Jossey-Bass.

Costa, P., & McCrae, R. R. (1991). *The NEO Five Factor Inventory.* Odessa, FL: Psychological Assessment Resources.

Digman, J. M., & Takemoto-Chock, N. K. (1981). Factors in the natural language of personality: Re-analysis, comparison and interpretation of six major studies. *Multivariate Behavioral Research, 16,* 149–170.

Entwistle, N. J. (1972). Personality and academic attainment. *British Journal of Educational Psychology, 42,* 137–151.

Facione, P. A., Sanchez, C. A., Facione, N. C., & Gainen, J. (1995). The disposition toward critical thinking. *Journal of General Education, 44,* 1–25.

Gates, A. Q. (1999). Explaining participation in undergraduate research using the affinity group model. *Journal of Engineering Education, 88,* 409–414.

Hakim, T. (1998). Soft assessment of undergraduate research: Reactions and student perspectives. *Council on Undergraduate Research Quarterly, 18,* 189–192.

Halpert, J. (2002). Yes, you can do real research. In Kaplan/Newsweek, *How to get into college, 2003 edition* (p. 67). New York: Kaplan/Newsweek.

Kardash, C. A. (2000). Evaluation of an undergraduate research experience: Perceptions of undergraduate interns and their faculty mentors. *Journal of Educational Psychology, 92,* 191–201.

King, P. M., & Kitchener, K. S. (1994). *Developing reflective judgment: Understanding and promoting intellectual growth and critical thinking in adolescents and adults.* San Francisco: Jossey-Bass.

King, P. M., Kitchener, K. S., & Wood, P. K. (1994). Research on the reflective judgment model. In P. M. King & K. S. Kitchener, *Developing Reflective Judgment: Understanding and promoting intellectual growth and critical thinking in adolescents and adults* (pp. 124–128). San Francisco: Jossey-Bass.

Kitchener, K. S., & King, P. M. (1981). Reflective judgment: Concepts of justification and their relationship to age and education. *Journal of Applied Developmental Psychology, 2,* 89–116.

Kitchener, K. S., Wood, P. K., & Jensen, L. (2001). *The development and assessment of complex problem solving in college students.* Final Report–Executive Summary for OERI award. Unpublished manuscript.

Kremer, J. F., & Bringle, R. G. (1990). The effects of an intensive research experience on the careers of talented undergraduates. *Journal of Research and Development in Education, 24,* 1–5.

Kuh, G., Pace, C. R., & Vesper, N. (1997). The development of process indicators to estimate student gains associated with good practice in undergraduate education. *Research in Higher Education, 38*, 435–454.

Kunderewicz, L., Michener, S., & Chambliss, C. (2001). *The educational impact of e-mail: Extraverted versus introverted students.* (ERIC No. ED449411).

Lawson, J. M. (1980). The relationship between graduate education and development of reflective judgment: A function of age or educational experience. *Dissertation Abstracts International, 41*, 4655A.

Love, P. G., & Guthrie, V. L. (1999). Perry's Intellectual Scheme. *New Directions for Student Services, 88*, 5–15. (ERIC No. EJ604548).

Mabrouk, P. A., & Peters, K. (2000). *Student perspectives on undergraduate research (UR) experiences in chemistry and biology.* Retrieved on December 10, 2003, from http://www.chem.vt.edu/confchem/2000/a/mabrouk/mabrouk.htm

Manduca, C. (1997). Broadly defined goals for undergraduate research projects: A basis for program evaluation. *Council on Undergraduate Research Quarterly, 18*, 64–69.

Marklein, M. B. (2002, April 8). Research accelerates learning: Students gain much. *USA Today*, pp. D06.

National Science Foundation (NSF). (2000). *NSF GPRA Strategic Plan, FY 2001–2006* (NSF Publication 0104). Washington, DC: Author. Retrieved on October 25, 2007, from http://www.nsf.gov/pubs/2001/nsf0104/start.htm

O'Connor, J. C. (1993). *Use of the MBTI as a predictor of successful academic and military performance at the United States Coast Guard Academy* (Report 10-93). (ERIC No. ED367672).

Pace, C. R. (1984). *College Student Experiences Questionnaire* (3rd ed.). Los Angeles: University of California, Center for the Study of Evaluation. Now available through the Center for Postsecondary Research, Indiana University, Bloomington.

Pascarella, E. T. (1989). The development of critical thinking: Does college make a difference. *Journal of College Student Development, 30*, 19–26.

Pascarella, E. T., & Terenzini, P. T. (1991). *How college affects students.* San Francisco: Jossey-Bass.

Perry, W. G., Jr. (1970). *Forms of intellectual and ethical development in the college years.* New York: Holt, Rhinehart & Winston.

Rogoff, B. (2003). *The cultural nature of human development.* London: Oxford University Press.

Rubin, R. B., & Henzel, S. A. (1984). Cognitive complexity, communication competence, and verbal ability. *Communication Quarterly, 32*, 263–70.

Simon, H. A. (1973). The structure of ill-structured problems. *Artificial Intelligence, 4*, 181–201.

Simon, H. A. (1978). Information-processing theory of human problem solving. In W. Estes (Ed.), *Handbook of learning and cognitive processes* (Vol. 5, pp. 291–295). Hillsdale, NJ: Erlbaum.

Soldz, S., & Vaillant, G. E. (1999). The Big Five personality traits and the life course: A 45-year longitudinal study. *Journal of Research in Personality, 33*, 208–232.

Strange, C. C., & King, P. M. (1982). Intellectual development and its relationship to maturation during the college years. *Journal of Applied Developmental Psychology, 2*, 281–295.

Tabachnick, B., & Fidell, L. (1996). *Using multivariate statistics.* New York: Harper Collins.

Tross, S. A., Harper, J. P., Osher, L. W., & Kneidinger, L. M. (2000). Not just the usual cast of characteristics: Using personality to predict college performance and retention. *Journal of College Student Development, 41*(3), 323–334.

Watson, G. B., & Glaser, E. M. (1994). *The Watson-Glaser critical thinking appraisal, Form S.* San Antonio, TX: Psychological Corporation.

Welfel, E. R. (1982). How students make judgments: Do educational level and academic major make a difference? *Journal of College Student Personnel, 23,* 490–497.

Widick, C. (1977). The Perry scheme: A foundation for developmental practice. *Counseling Psychologist, 64*(4), 35–38.

Wood, P. K. (1997a). Development of assessment measures of epistemic cognition: How do students think about real-world ill-structured problems? *Assessment Update, 9,* 11–13, 16.

Wood, P. K. (1997b). A secondary analysis of claims regarding the reflective judgment interview: Internal consistency, sequentiality, and intra-individual differences in ill-structured problem solving. In J. C. Smart (Ed.), *Higher education: Handbook of theory and research* (pp. 245–314). Edison, NJ: Agathon.

Wood, P. K., & Conner, J. (1999). Assessment measures: Deciding how many participants to use in assessment research. *Assessment Update, 11*(4), 8–11.

Wood, P. K., Kitchener, K., & Jensen, L. (2002). Considerations in the design and evaluation of a paper-and-pencil measure of epistemic cognition. In B. K. Hofer & P. R. Pintrich (Eds.), *Personal epistemology: The psychology of beliefs about knowledge and knowing* (pp. 277–295). Mahwah, NJ: Erlbaum.

Wood, P. K., & Kardash, C. (2002). Critical elements in the design and analysis of studies of epistemology. In B. K. Hofer & P. R. Pintrich (Eds.), *Personal epistemology: The psychology of beliefs about knowledge and knowing* (pp. 231–260). Mahwah, NJ: Erlbaum.

Zydney, A. L., Bennett, J. S., Shahid, A., & Bauer, K. W. (2002). Faculty perspectives regarding the undergraduate research experience in science and engineering. *Journal of Engineering Education, 91,* 291–297.

Exploring the Benefits of Undergraduate Research Experiences: The SURE Survey

David Lopatto

UNDERGRADUATE RESEARCH is a popular vehicle for science education and science career planning. The efficacy of undergraduate research as a vehicle for both professional and liberal learning is endorsed by national associations such as the Association of American Colleges and Universities, the Council on Undergraduate Research, and the National Conference on Undergraduate Research. Opportunities for undergraduate research have been funded by the National Science Foundation and the Howard Hughes Medical Institute (HHMI), among others (Lopatto, 2006). As popular as the concept seems to be, however, credible reports of the outcomes of undergraduate research have only recently emerged (Lopatto, 2004; Seymour, Hunter, Laursen, & DeAntoni, 2004). The purpose of the present report is to describe the utility of the SURE survey for assessing the benefits of undergraduate research experiences. The report begins by describing the development of instruments used to assess the benefits of undergraduate research experiences. It then describes the successful corroboration of earlier research and extends the findings by describing the results of follow-up surveys. The data support the hypothesis that the undergraduate research experience fosters gains in skills, self-confidence, professional plans, and active learning.

Research in science, technology, engineering and mathematics (STEM) is generally described as an investigation that is at once systematic and original. Scientific research progresses according to conventional rules of scientific epistemology and at the same time moves toward new knowledge. A related concept is the undergraduate research experience, a concept that integrates the authenticity of research with the education of novice scientists. Science educators generally believe that the experience of doing authentic research, by conjoining the learning of the epistemology of science with the excitement of discovery, benefits the student in a manner that reading texts or listening to lectures does not. Although science educators continue to refine "research-like" or "inquiry-based" experiences within the undergraduate science curriculum, these experiences are not established as equivalent to authentic research (but see Trosset, Lopatto, & Elgin, Chapter 3). As Fortenberry (1998) put it, "the fundamental difference between research and inquiry-based learning is the prior state of knowledge of the broader community. In research it is unknown by all; in inquiry it is only unknown by the learner" (p. 54).

The essential features of undergraduate research experiences are difficult to identify (Lopatto, 2003). It is an apprentice experience in which the student devotes most or all of his or her work time to an original project, working with a mentor and often, though not always, with a team of peers. Some undergraduate research experiences are brief while others span a summer, a semester, or a year. In some instances the student initiates the research idea while in others the faculty mentor does. In some programs the student is a direct apprentice to the faculty mentor while in others the student becomes a member of a team that includes faculty, graduate students, postdoctoral students, and others.

The undergraduate research experience is widely touted as an effective educational tool (Mogk, 1993; Tomovic, 1994) with multiple benefits (Lopatto, 2003), the most instrumental of which is an increased interest in a career in the STEM workforce (Fitzsimmons, Carlson, Kerpelman, & Stoner, 1990; Zydney, Bennett, Shahid, & Bauer, 2002). Seymour and colleagues (2004) reported a comprehensive review of the literature on the benefits of undergraduate research experiences in science. Reviewing 54 published accounts of the benefits of undergraduate research experiences in the sciences, they divided the literature into two major types: those in which hypothesized benefits are both claimed and supported (Type I) and those in which the hypothesized benefits are simply stated or claimed (Type II). Type II accounts outnumbered Type I accounts by 45 to 9, and in the latter category only 4 accounts were described as research articles (Kardash, 2000; Kremer & Bringle, 1990; Rauckhorst, Czaja, & Baxter-Magolda, 2001; Ryder, Leach, & Driver, 1999).

The present report originates from a qualitative and quantitative effort to clarify the benefits of good undergraduate research experiences in the sciences at four undergraduate liberal arts colleges. The leading edge of the project was an intensive effort by Seymour and colleagues (2004) to interview 76 undergraduates in the science disciplines and to extract from these interviews the reported benefits of the undergraduate research experience. By coding the transcribed responses of the 76 respondents, they were able to describe seven categories of benefits. The seven categories, listed in Table 6.1 in order of highest to lowest in frequency of relevant responses, suggest a broad range of benefits across cognitive, behavioral, and attitudinal domains. Personal/professional benefits, exemplified by a growth in self-confidence, were among the most frequently reported

Table 6.1. Factors associated with the seven benefit categories identified by Seymour and colleagues.

Benefit Category	Factors
Personal/professional (e.g., increased confidence in ability to do research)	Personal development (e.g., self-confidence)
Thinking and working like a scientist (e.g., application of knowledge and skills)	Knowledge synthesis (e.g., learning a topic in depth)
Skills (e.g., improved communication)	Interaction and communication (e.g., skill at oral communication) Data collection and interpretation Design and hypothesis skills Information literacy Computer skills
Clarification, confirmation, and refinement of career/education (e.g., validation of disciplinary interests)	Professional development (e.g., understanding professional behavior)
Enhanced career/graduate school preparation (e.g., authentic research experience)	Professional advancement (e.g., enhancement of professional or academic credentials)
Changes in attitude toward learning (e.g., undertaking greater responsibility)	Responsibility (e.g., learning ethical standards)
Other benefits (e.g., summer job)	

Note: The first column summarizes the seven benefit categories set forth by Seymour, Hunter, Laursen, and DeAntoni (2004) in their qualitative analysis of interview data from undergraduate researchers at four liberal arts colleges. The second column shows the results of an exploratory factor analysis of quantitative survey data from undergraduate researchers at the same four colleges.

by the undergraduate respondents. Benefits related to thinking and working like a scientist, which include the application of knowledge and skills, were also frequently reported. References to specific skills ranked third among the responses, and references to career ranked below skills. This pattern of responses suggests that matters of personal development, or maturity, may be at least as important a benefit from undergraduate research as career choice.

Conjointly with the qualitative work of Seymour et al., I constructed a survey (called the Research On Learning and Education, or ROLE survey) that required quantitative rating of each of 45 potential benefits of undergraduate research for students. Over a period of 2 years, 384 students from the same four liberal arts colleges studied by Seymour et al. responded to the survey. An exploratory factor analysis on complete data sets yielded a set of 10 factors accounting for 66% of the variance in the data. The names of these factors are listed in Table 6.1. They revealed a set of research benefits similar to those suggested by the qualitative research. Triangulation of findings through two methodologies argues for the validity of the findings; however, it remained to be seen if the findings could be generalized beyond these four liberal arts colleges.

SURE SURVEY

The opportunity for a more extended study was presented by the Howard Hughes Medical Institute, which funds grant activity for undergraduate science education at a variety of institutions. The new survey effort, called the Summer Undergraduate Research Experiences (SURE), was constructed to offer student researchers a common assessment tool for evaluating intensive summer research experiences in the sciences.

The SURE survey, in addition to serving as a replication and extension of the earlier work, was motivated by three research questions, primarily concerning, but not limited to, HHMI-funded undergraduate research experiences in the sciences. These questions were:

1. Is the educational experience of undergraduates being enhanced by undergraduate research?
2. Are undergraduate research programs attracting and supporting talented students interested in a career involving scientific research?
3. Are undergraduate research programs retaining minority students in the "pathway" to a scientific career?

HHMI program directors were contacted to solicit interest in the use of the survey for their undergraduates. Participant program directors were sent a form with a list of 50 possible benefits of undergraduate research for students. Program directors were instructed to indicate if each benefit was taught implicitly or explicitly in the undergraduate research program. *Teaching implicitly* was defined as: "Your program relies on individual mentors (or the program's general ethos) to have the expertise to teach, train, model, or encourage this goal without an actual programmed event." *Teaching explicitly* was defined as: "Your program explicitly teaches, trains, models, or encourages this goal for students. For example, on the topic of research ethics place a check if you can point to a specific seminar or workshop that covers research ethics in your field." Program director responses were employed in an examination of implicit versus explicit teaching in undergraduate research. More specifically, program director responses were used as a grouping variable with which to examine student learning gains. In addition to whatever differences may occur between implicit and explicit teaching strategies, the data were examined for interactions with institutional type.

The online survey was first employed in the summer of 2003. Students were provided with a name and password for access to the survey. Within the survey, students identified their institution and provided ethnographic information but anonymity was maintained. Student respondents were presented with 20 learning gains items, and these items were supplemented by general demographic and satisfaction measures. Student names were collected for a raffle that awarded gift certificates to the winners, but the names were separated from the survey material. The name file also retained the students' e-mail address, if offered, for a later invitation to complete the follow-up survey. The target date for completing the main survey was immediately after the end-of-program symposium or other "summing-up" activity. Two weeks after that date, program directors were informed how many students had participated. Program directors were given the option of contacting their students to remind them to participate in the survey.

In its first year of use 1,135 undergraduate researchers from 41 institutions provided data concerning undergraduate research experiences (Lopatto, 2004). Requests were made to program directors for estimates of the maximum number of undergraduates who could have responded to the survey. Based on their information, the response rate for the summer of 2003 was estimated at 74%. Of the 1,135 respondents, 1041 identified their institution. Of these, 742 (71%) respondents attended research universities, 243 (23%) attended colleges, and 56 (5%) attended master's institutions.

The sample included 618 women and 423 men, with ethnic representation including Caucasian (57%), Asian American (16%), African American (9%), Hispanic (5%), and Foreign National (7%) respondents. Figure 6.1 shows the distribution of students by gender and research fields. As HHMI funds science education primarily in the biological sciences it is not surprising that over two thirds (68.5%) of the respondents identified their research field in the biological sciences.

Results for SURE Survey

Because increased interest and preparation for a STEM career are seen as a major goal of undergraduate research experiences, respondents were asked to report their plans for science education beyond the undergraduate degree. Most respondents reported some plan for further education; approximately 84% indicated interest in further science education, including medicine (see Figure 6.2). Respondents were also asked to reflect on how their undergraduate research experience influenced these plans. Almost 91% reported that their research experience maintained or increased their interest in further science education (see Figure 6.3). An interesting finding from the survey was that a small group of students (4.7%) indicated that they had not decided on a science career prior to their research experience but were now inclined to science. An almost equally sized group (3.7%) indicated that they had been planning on a science career until their research experience

Figure 6.1. Research fields represented in the data, categorized by gender.

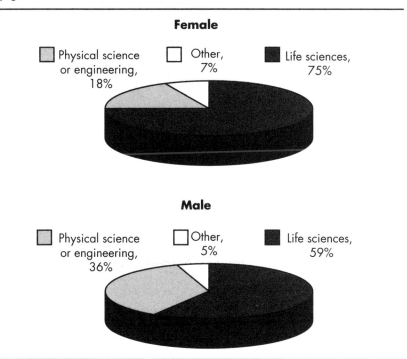

but were now no longer inclined to science. Neither of these groups was characterized by a specific demographic variable such as gender, ethnicity, or type of institution. Because these two groups are composed of students who actually changed their plans following an undergraduate research experience, it is useful to break out their perceived learning gains from the overall cohort and examine the results for evidence of differences in their experiences.

The educational experience of the students was evaluated through 20 learning gain items. Students were asked to evaluate their gain in each of the items on a scale of 1 (no or little gain) to 5 (very large gain). The means of the reported gains for the overall cohort, for the students who changed their career plans to include postgraduate education in science, and for the students who changed their career plans away from postgraduate education in science are shown in Figure 6.4. The highest rated item was "Understanding the research process in your field," followed by "Readiness for more demanding research," "Understanding how scientists work on real problems," and "Learning laboratory techniques." The lowest

Figure 6.2. Plans for further education reported by SURE survey respondents.

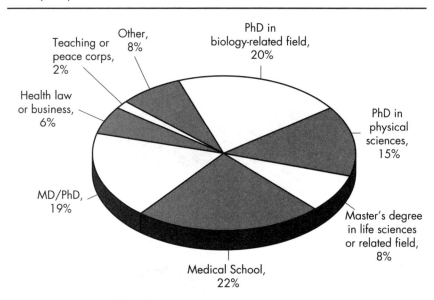

rated items were "Learning ethical conduct in your field," followed by "Skill in science writing," and "Skill in how to give an effective oral presentation." As reported in Lopatto (2004), the items showed a high degree of interitem consistency (Cronbach's Alpha = .92). Because these items had been featured in the earlier ROLE survey, it was of interest to look at the results of the two surveys. A correlation was computed between the means of the identical ROLE and SURE items, yielding a high consistency of means ($r = 0.90$).[1]

Data were collected from 19 research universities, 7 master's level institutions, and 15 colleges. Representation from the master's institutions was small, therefore in the following analysis this group of respondents was set aside. The remaining data on the 20 learning gain items was categorized by institutional type and by the program director's data indicating if the item was taught implicitly or explicitly. A multivariate analysis of variance (2 institution types by 2 types of teaching by 20 learning gains) found no significant differences between research university students and college students on learning gains.[2] Turning to the implicit/explicit teaching distinction, the analysis found no significant differences between implicit teaching and explicit teaching on learning gains. While no main effects resulted from these comparisons, visual inspection of the data (see Fig-

Figure 6.3. Self-reported influence of research experience on respondents' plans for further education.

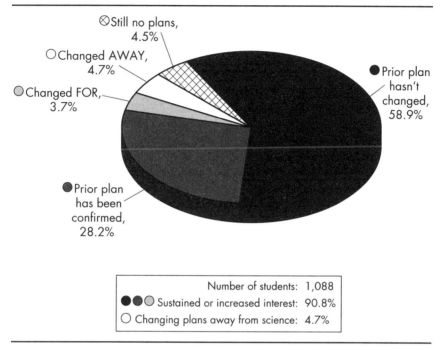

⊗Still no plans, 4.5%

○Changed AWAY, 4.7%

◎Changed FOR, 3.7%

●Prior plan hasn't changed, 58.9%

●Prior plan has been confirmed, 28.2%

| Number of students: 1,088 |
| ●◎○ Sustained or increased interest: 90.8% |
| ○ Changing plans away from science: 4.7% |

ure 6.5) suggested some interactions between type of institution and teaching type. Of the 20 learning gains, three could not be analyzed for the joint effect of institution type and teaching type due to missing cells. No college program director claimed to teach "Clarification of career path" explicitly; no research university program director claimed to teach "Understanding how knowledge is constructed" explicitly; and neither college nor university program directors claimed to teach "Self-confidence" explicitly. Of the remaining 17 learning gains, student data yielded eight statistically significant interactions between institution type and teaching type. These interactions were analyzed by independent groups ANOVA (2 institution types × 2 teaching types) on each variable separately. This strategy was followed because the membership of the implicit or explicit group changed with every item. Data from 15 college program directors and 16 university program directors were used in the analysis (three university program directors did not respond). All of the interactions follow the same pattern: college students report higher learning gains for items taught implicitly, while university students report higher learning gains for items taught explicitly (Figure 6.5). These results should

Figure 6.4. Comparative mean ratings of respondents who changed in the direction of further science education and respondents who changed away from further science education following their research experience. The overall means are shown for comparison.

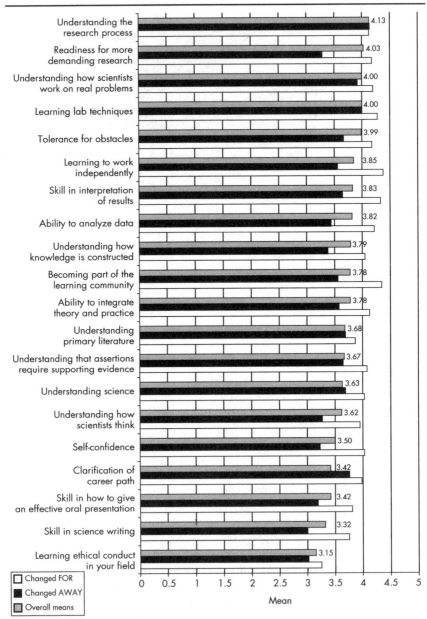

Figure 6.5. Mean gains in eight learning benefits classified by type of institution (college and university) and by implicit or explicit teaching. Data from 15 college program directors and 16 university program directors were used for the classification of data. The number of observations in each group is printed across the bar.

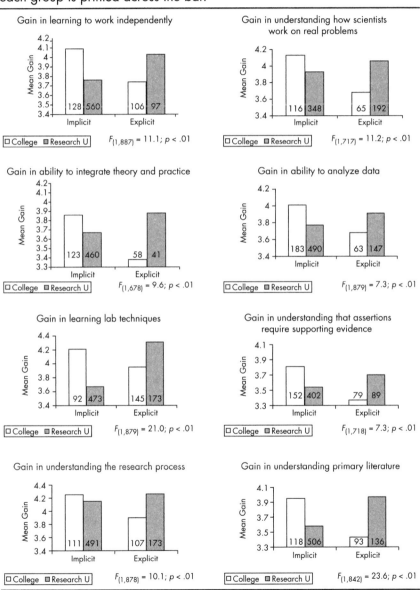

be viewed with caution; there are a number of statistical challenges to the analysis, including shifting membership of the implicit/explicit groups, varying sample sizes, departures from normal distributions, and so on. Nevertheless, the pattern is striking enough to call to the reader's attention. The results suggest that generalizations about the superiority of the type of institution or the manner of teaching for student learning gains cannot be defended. There may be, however, a difference in the teaching and learning culture across institutions that permits several routes to success.

The survey results did generally support an affirmative answer to each of three research questions listed at the beginning of this section (Lopatto, 2004). The answer to these questions was yes. A large majority of the students reported learning gains and high satisfaction with their experience. Most students reported continuing with a plan for postgraduate education in science, and there were few differences in career plans or learning gains between genders or among ethnic groups (Lopatto, 2004). Career plans, learning gains, and overall satisfaction with the research experience did not differ among research universities and colleges. The general results were also consistent with the earlier ROLE survey work, providing evidence that the earlier findings from four liberal arts colleges were robust.

FOLLOW-UP SURVEY

The SURE survey afforded an opportunity to follow up with the summer 2003 respondents to gauge how opinions of the experience may have changed with the passage of time. A follow-up survey including learning items was offered to survey respondents in May of 2004. In addition to repeating the estimates of learning gains, the survey asked several exploratory questions concerning the student's behavior in regular course work during the intervening time period. Of the original 1,135 respondents, 782 supplied e-mail addresses at the time of the first survey. Of these 782, 405 responded to the follow-up survey. The follow-up sample was fairly consistent with the demographic characteristics of the original cohort, and was representative of the original cohort with respect to fields and career plans.

Results for Follow-Up Survey

The follow-up learning gains items showed a high level of interitem consistency (Cronbach's Alpha = .93). Because the surveys were anonymous, specific comparisons across individual data taken from the original survey and the follow-up could not be analyzed. To assess reliability, the means of the 20 evaluative questions were computed for the original survey and again for the follow-up survey. These two sets of means were then correlated, yielding a correlation of $r = .95$.[3] The SURE survey asked students for influence of the research experience on their plans for postgraduate education. The follow-up survey asked the same question. The proportion of students answering in each category is nearly identical to the proportions in Figure 6.3 for the original cohort. The pattern of results is very similar. The SURE survey asked students to give an overall sense of their summer research as a learning experience. Over 86% of the cohort gave the research a positive rating, either "learned a lot" or "fantastic." In the follow-up, about 83% of the sample gave these positive ratings. Because the response options were best viewed as an ordinal scale, nonparametric inferential statistics were employed to analyze the data. There were no statistically significant differences among institutional types, gender, or ethnicity on this variable.[4]

The SURE survey analysis included a comparison of responses from those students who had changed their plans in the direction of postgraduate education with responses from those students who had changed their plans in a direction away from postgraduate education. In the follow-up, 11 students reported changing to postgraduate education and 27 reported changing away. The patterns of the means are similar across the two surveys. In both cases, the students who began planning for postgraduate education report higher mean gains than the students not planning for postgraduate education. There was a tendency for female respondents to rate the gains higher than male respondents. This result is consistent with the results of the original survey and other previous surveys (Lopatto, 2004).

The follow-up survey asked if the student had completed his or her summer research project. There were 190 students who reported that they finished, while 215 students reported that they did not finish. Of this latter group, 190 students reported that they continued to work on the project after the summer program ended. Forty-five members of this group worked on the project for one semester, while 116 worked for two semesters. Thirty-seven students wrote a comment in an optional text box, adding statements such as "still at it," "it's still going on," "plan to finish this summer," and "one month while new people were trained." The follow-up survey asked students to mark which of 10 opportunities for scientific communication they engaged in. Table 6.2 shows the frequencies of the kinds of communication students engaged in. In some cases students gave multiple responses. Posters and talks were more frequent vehicles for communication than papers written for the research mentor. Manuscripts prepared for professional journals were relatively less common.

Taking advantage of the passage of time since the summer research experience, the survey asked if the students had subsequently taken courses in the same department as their summer research; 305 students answered yes and 98 answered no. A second question asked if the students' research experience had affected their behavior in these courses. A few students who had answered the previous question in the negative nevertheless answered this question in the affirmative, yielding 310 responses: 241 yes and 69 nos. (Despite answering no, 11 students responded to the three behavior questions.) The three specific ways in which behavior may

Table 6.2. Frequency of the modes of communication of summer research.

Communication	Frequency
An academic paper read by your research mentor	191
A poster on campus	244
A poster at a conference or professional meeting	119
A talk or colloquium on campus	220
A talk or colloquium at a conference or professional meeting	49
A manuscript intended for a professional journal	79
A manuscript intended for a technical report	23
A manuscript intended for a student scientific journal	17
A performance or demonstration	46
A Web site or Internet presentation	13

have changed—greater independence, greater intrinsic motivation, and greater active learning—were rated on a scale of 1 (no change) to 5 (very large change). The results of these questions are shown in Figure 6.6. Slightly more than 87% of the 252 students who answered the question reported at least a moderate improvement in independence, 79% reported at least a moderate improvement in intrinsic motivation, and 85% reported at least a moderate improvement in active learning. Analysis of variance on the two grouping variables of gender and ethnicity yielded no significant differences in gender or ethnicity on the course behavior questions.[5]

Student respondents were supplied with a text box for any additional comments they wished to make about their experience. Comments were offered by 196 respondents, or 48% of the sample. Many comments were brief or uninformative. The majority of the meaningful comments were positive and echoed some of the gains tested in the survey. For example, the following comments allude to confidence, discovery of a community, and communication.

> My summer research helped me gain confidence in conducting independent work. I now feel like I know how to do research like "real scientists" do. I learned new techniques that have helped me better visualize information and research regarding genetics. And, I gained a new family in the Biology Department.

Figure 6.6. Percentage of respondents who reported their behavior in courses in their own fields after completion of a summer undergraduate research experience. The three items were, "I feel that I have become better able to think independently and formulate my own ideas," "I feel that I have become more intrinsically motivated to learn," and "I feel that I have become a more active learner."

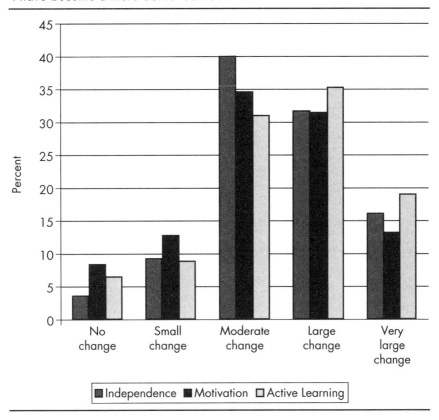

Most important to me in my research experience, was the sense of fellowship I experienced in my lab, among my mentor, the lab technician, the postdocs, and myself. There was always someone to turn to if I had a question, someone who was enquiring about my well-being (both in the lab and outside of it), and someone to share a laugh with. This experience also extends to people in other labs, who are always quick to share a few words with me.

The summer research experience allowed me to learn how to communicate complex theoretical computing and mathematical concepts basic to computer science but to explain [them] clearly to biologists.

Some students also volunteered comments on the influence of their research experience on subsequent course behavior.

I had a very positive summer research experience. Although the study I worked on was a learning experience in itself, I benefited most by becoming part of a research team and feeling like I was more connected to my department, including relationships with grad students and professor. This gave me a better understanding of academia and gave me greater confidence and interest in my classes this year.

It was a great experience, away from the textbooks and problem sets of school. By applying the knowledge I had gained, I became more motivated in certain classes, since I knew the value of what I was learning. I am continuing my research again this summer and look forward to it even more than last year.

The student comments not only testify to the effectiveness of the undergraduate research experience as a learning experience, they convey the significant impact this experience has on students:

I value my research experience not only for laboratory techniques acquired but also for the ability to think critically about my research and advance significant hypotheses. On a personal level, my research has taught me patience, perseverance, and self-analysis, qualities that are important in my development as a research scientist. Finally, the HHMI's financial commitment to my future gave me the confidence to pursue my academic interests in biomedical research.

The most important part of my summer research experience was the ability to engage in cutting edge work with my own [two] hands. It was a great feeling moving from a relatively dependent stage to an independent one. I look forward to learning more and becoming more independent.

WHAT SURE TELLS US ABOUT SUMMER RESEARCH EXPERIENCES

The SURE survey has demonstrated its utility in describing the benefits of undergraduate research. It provides a quantitative index of learning gains, documents the intent of the student to continue with a science education, and exposes the different experiences of students who are enthusiastic about further work in science compared to students who are discouraged. Taken together with data collected from program directors, it suggests that universities and colleges may be achieving comparable levels of support through different—implicit or explicit—contexts. The pattern of reported learning gains is consistent with previous work and remains consistent in a follow-up survey. Responses to the follow-up survey indicate that the summer undergraduate research experience has a positive influence on independence, motivation, and active learning in the classroom.

The pattern of learning gains found with the SURE survey is consistent with previous findings, both from qualitative and quantitative research. The gains reflect cognitive, personal, and vocational (career) dimensions. Gains in items such as "Understanding the research process" and "Learning lab techniques" may seem to be obvious outcomes among a cohort of science researchers; however, previous efforts to intuit these outcomes are corroborated here with quantitative data. Undergraduate research experiences have been associated in the literature with a variety of cognitive gains. Gains in the domains of observation, data collection, data analysis, problem solving, and communication have been found in studies of research interns (Kardash, 2000; Kardash et al., Chapter 9), biology and chemistry undergraduate researchers (Mabrouk & Peters, 2000), and university alumni who had participated in research while undergraduates (Bauer & Bennett, 2003; Bauer & Bennett, Chapter 2). While some gains may be described as narrow quantitative, analytic, or communication skills, the current results also indicate gains in a broader set of metacognitive skills. Gains in items such as "Understanding how scientists think," "Understanding that assertions require supporting evidence," and "Understanding how scientists work on real problems" may reflect the learning of how to think and act like a scientist and set the occasion for satisfaction from acting in this role. Similar gains are reported by Seymour et al. (2004) using primarily interview methodology (see also Taraban et al., Chapter 8). This higher level learning may be related to career planning; however, the relation is not clear.

The cognitive gains resulting from an undergraduate research experience may be characterized as a growth or developmental process. Baxter-Magolda (Baxter-Magolda, Boes, Hollis, & Jaramillo, 1998) interviewed undergraduate researchers before and after their research experience. Baxter-Magolda has developed a rubric for characterizing epistemological reflection—the Measure of Epistemological Reflection (Baxter-Magolda & Porterfield, 1985). The MER yields data that permit the classification of epistemological reflection into one of four progressively sophisticated domains, ranging from Absolute Knowing (reliance on authority) through two levels of greater independence to Contextual Knowing (perspective requiring supporting evidence). Baxter-Magolda found that undergraduate researchers working over the course of one summer demonstrated movement to the more sophisticated domains while control participants showed little movement. Thus the cognitive gains stemming from undergraduate research experiences may be much broader than narrow research skills. (See also Bauer & Bennett, Chapter 5.)

While some features of the experience and their correlation with student satisfaction are reported, there is no attempt here to define the causes of a successful undergraduate research experience or to assert that a successful undergraduate research experience leads directly to an increase in the STEM workforce. Although continuation of education into graduate work in the sciences is cited as a goal of many undergraduate research opportunities (Fitzsimmons et al., 1990), many students who apply for graduate school in the sciences may have decided on this course of action prior to their undergraduate research experience (see Russell, Chapter 4). Most of the participants in the SURE survey research indicated that they intended to go on in science and that the research experience did not change their plans. It is likely that some undergraduates pursue an undergraduate research experience precisely because it fits their plans for graduate school or careers. Early work on the personalities and lives of scientists (Roe, 1952) had indicated that a research experience was compelling in choosing science as a career (see Blanton, Chapter 12). In describing the career choices of a cohort of scientists, Roe wrote, "What decided him (almost invariably) was a college project in which he had occasion to do some independent research—to find out things for himself. Once he discovered the pleasures of this kind of work, he never turned back" (p. 22) (see alumni narratives, Chapter 11). Despite the power attributed to the research experience to inspire a career in science, recent studies have been equivocal on the role of the undergraduate research in career clarification. As Seymour et al. (2004) wrote, "it is important to distinguish between claims that the undergraduate experiences can prompt undergraduates to *choose* a graduate school career path, and more qualified claims that the experience can *clarify*, *refine*, and *reinforce* such a choice" (p. 522). The present results provide some evidence that the decision to change one's previous plan can be affected by the undergraduate research experience—for good or ill. As reported, two small cohorts emerged from the data, one that changed in the direction of postgraduate science education and one that changed away from postgraduate science education. Comparisons of the average learning gains for these two groups (see Figure 6.4) show that the students changing toward science rated their learning gains generally higher than the other group. An intriguing result is that students who changed in favor of science rated their gains higher on a number of items that are more personal than professional, such as working independently and self-confidence. Both groups were aware of the effect of the experience on their plans, that is, both groups rated their gains on "Clarification of career path" higher than the overall cohort.

Despite the differences captured by the SURE survey results, the relation between the undergraduate experience and the decision to go into a science career remains refractory. One complication is that most undergraduate research opportunities favor student applicants who already plan a career in science and who are likely to enjoy the research experience. In their interview study of undergraduate researchers, Seymour et al. (2004) reported that only 4% of over 1,200 observations could be categorized as negative statements about the undergraduate research experience. In the present project only 2.2% of the respondents characterized their experience as dissatisfying. The bias toward positive experiences is not difficult to understand. The institutions studied here have worked hard to achieve successful undergraduate research programs. Most institutions have been the recipients of grant funds for undergraduate science education. Funded programs require peer-reviewed proposals and periodic reporting that help sustain the quality of the program. The programs are examples of "what works" (Project Kaleidoscope, 1991).

A second complication to the relation is that some students enjoy their undergraduate research experience, find it valuable, and achieve the insight that they do not wish to continue in science. This sentiment is expressed in the occasional text comments that appeared on the survey. The next two examples both appeared on surveys from the summer of 2003:

> The entire experience itself was most important. In my case it helped me realize that I do not want to pursue a postgraduate education in the natural sciences, which is an extremely important decision. The research experience was without a doubt worthwhile.

> The greatest benefit that I derived from summer research was the knowledge that science research is not for me. Despite the fact that I disliked research, I found the experience very rewarding. Without such a comprehensive and accessible research program, I might have made the mistake of going on to grad school for science.

Thus the relation between the undergraduate research experience and the decision to go on in science is not entirely predictable. But if an undergraduate research experience can be characterized as successful, even if the student does not wish to continue in science, in what way is it successful? The first answer is that the student achieves an insight into his or her vocation based on experience. The second answer lies in the gains a student reports on a variety of personal qualities, including independence, self-confidence, tolerance for obstacles, and becoming part of a learning community. Gains in these personal qualities are ubiquitous. The student may employ his or her maturation in a wide variety of careers. Undergraduate research experiences in the sciences set the occasion for rapid personal maturity. In this sense, the undergraduate research experience delivers more than it promises.

The present study does not include a control group and does not sort out all the influences, including precollege career intentions, general academic achievement, and family influence, that might account for the choices students make to pursue careers in science. Thus the interpretations of the results of the SURE survey stop short of making the claim for uncovering the causal component variables that account for the success of the undergraduate research experience.

A standard experimental design is difficult to achieve in the study of undergraduate research programs. The requirements for a randomized experimental design include random selection, random assignment, a control group, and a means of preventing experimenter's expectations or behaviors from confounding the experiment. Even a cursory review of authentic undergraduate research programs leads to the conclusion that such design requirements are difficult to meet. It is neither practical nor ethical to randomly select students for an undergraduate science research program. Universities and colleges seldom have enough control over student behavior to engineer a random selection into a research program, nor should they. The pursuit of disciplines, science or not, rests on the student's inclination to do this activity. To include uninterested students and exclude interested students would undercut a program and reduce student morale. Random assignment to groups, assuming there is a control group, would also be technically difficult and ethically dubious. An appropriate control group for an undergraduate research program is difficult to specify. One solution—to use as controls applicants who were not selected for the program—is undermined by the possibility of confounding due to preexisting differences between the selected applicants and rejected applicants. Another solution, to employ nonresearch students as controls, leads to questions regarding differential experience and motivation. Finally, while experimental design may require that subjects behave while observers do nothing but observe (Sidman, 1960), the research experience includes frequent interactions and adjustments in the behavior of students, peers, and mentors over the duration of the experiment. The mentor's behavior may change with regard to structuring the experience and providing consideration to the student as the experience progresses, influencing the behavior of the student (Lopatto, 2003).

The lack of experimental design, however, does not preclude finding results that are useful in understanding the benefits of the undergraduate research experience. The SURE data enumerates the benefits of the research experience and demonstrates the generalizability of findings to a large sample of diverse institutions. A potential next step in the study of these benefits might be to isolate features of the experience in a more controlled context so as to make causal inferences about the components of the molar effect. Campbell (1986) describes a molar effect as including possible interactions among more basic component variables. These variables may be more easily isolated for experimental control than the molar effect itself.

ACKNOWLEDGMENTS

The ROLE survey research was supported by National Science Foundation Grant REC0087611. The SURE survey was supported by HHMI grant 52003953 to Professor Sarah Elgin of Washington University. I am grateful to Marti Schafer and Frances Thuet for their contributions to the project.

NOTES

1. Degrees of freedom $(df) = 18$; $p < .01$.
2. $F_{(20,721)} = .766$; $p > .05$.
3. $df = 18$; $p < .01$.
4. Three institutional types were compared via a Kruskal-Wallis test yielding a chi square of 1.29 for 2 df $(p > .05)$. Genders (chi square = .75, 1 df, $p > .05$) and eight categories of ethnicity (chi square = 10.7; 7 df; $p > .05$) were evaluated in the same manner.
5. The comparison of gender on the three course behavior questions yielded the following results: For independence, $F_{(1,248)} = 1.38$, $p > .05$; for intrinsic motivation, $F_{(1,249)} = 1.64$, $p > .05$; for active learning, $F_{(1,246)} = 3.24$, $p > .05$. The comparison of ethnic categories yielded for independence, $F_{(7,243)} = 1.1.$, $p > .05$; for intrinsic motivation, $F_{(7,244)} = 1.15$, $p > .05$; for active learning, $F_{(7,241)} = 1.19$, $p > .05$.

REFERENCES

Bauer, K. W., & Bennett, J. S. (2003). Alumni perceptions used to assess undergraduate research experience. *Journal of Higher Education, 74*, 210–230.

Baxter-Magolda, M. B., Boes, L., Hollis, M. L., & Jaramillo, D. L. (1998). *Impact of the undergraduate summer scholar experience on epistemological development.* Unpublished manuscript, Miami University, Oxford, Ohio.

Baxter-Magolda, M. B., & Porterfield, W. D. (1985). A new approach to assess intellectual development on the Perry scheme. *Journal of College Student Personnel, 26*, 343–351.

Campbell, D. T. (1986). Relabeling internal and external validity for applied social scientists. In W. M. K. Trochim (Ed.), *Advances in quasi-experimental design and analysis.* New directions for program evaluation (no. 31, pp. 67–77). San Francisco: Jossey-Bass.

Fitzsimmons, S. J., Carlson, K., Kerpelman, L. C., & Stoner, D. (1990). *A preliminary evaluation of the Research Experiences for Undergraduates (REU) program of the National Science Foundation.* Washington, DC: National Science Foundation.

Fortenberry, N. L. (1998). Integration of research and curriculum. *Council on Undergraduate Research Quarterly, 19*, 54–61.

Kardash, C. M. (2000). Evaluation of an undergraduate research experience: Perceptions of undergraduate interns and their faculty mentors. *Journal of Educational Psychology, 92*, 191–201.

Kremer, J. F., & Bringle, R. G. (1990). The effects of an intensive research experience on the careers of talented undergraduates. *Journal of Research and Development in Education, 24,* 1–5.

Lopatto, D. (2003). The essential features of undergraduate research. *Council on Undergraduate Research Quarterly, 24,* 139–142.

Lopatto, D. (2004). Survey of Undergraduate Research Experiences (SURE): First findings. *Cell Biology Education, 3,* 270–277.

Lopatto, D. (2006). Undergraduate research as a catalyst for liberal learning. *Peer Review, 8,* 22–25.

Mabrouk, P. A., & Peters, K. (2000). *Student perspectives on undergraduate research (UR) experiences in chemistry and biology.* Retrieved December 1, 2001, from http://www.chem.vt.edu/confchem/2000/a/mabrouk/mabrouk.htm

Mogk, D. W. (1993). Undergraduate research experiences as preparation for graduate study in geology. *Journal of Geological Education, 41,* 126–128.

Project Kaleidoscope. (1991). *What works: Building natural science communities* (Vol. 1). Washington, DC: Author.

Rauckhorst, W. H., Czaja, J. A., & Baxter-Magolda, M. (2001, July). *Measuring the impact of the undergraduate research experience on student intellectual development.* Paper presented at Project Kaleidoscope Summer Institute, Snowbird, UT.

Roe, A. (1952). A psychologist examines 64 eminent scientists. *Scientific American, 187,* 21–25.

Ryder, J., Leach, J., & Driver, R. (1999). Undergraduate science students' images of science. *Journal of Research in Science Teaching, 36,* 201–219.

Seymour, E., Hunter, A.-B., Laursen, S. L., & DeAntoni, T. (2004). Establishing the benefits of research experiences for undergraduates in the sciences: First findings from a three-year study. *Science Education, 88,* 493–534.

Sidman, M. (1960). *Tactics of scientific research: Evaluating experimental data in psychology.* New York: Basic Books.

Tomovic, M. M. (1994). Undergraduate research: Prerequisite for successful lifelong learning. *ASEE Annual Conference Proceedings, 1,* 1469–1470.

Zydney, A. L., Bennett, J. S., Shahid, A., & Bauer, K. W. (2002). Impact of undergraduate research experience in engineering. *Journal of Engineering Education, 91,* 151–157.

The Experience of Science

Benefits of Participating in Undergraduate Research in Science: Comparing Faculty and Student Perceptions

Anne-Barrie Hunter, Sandra L. Laursen, and Elaine Seymour

FINDINGS FROM our study of undergraduate research (UR) demonstrate the multi-faceted benefits students take away from research experience in science, technology, engineering, and mathematics (STEM) fields and support many of faculty research advisors' anecdotal claims for UR (Seymour, Hunter, Laursen, & DeAntoni, 2004). Following a dearth of empirically based research on the outcomes of UR programs, it is gratifying to have data from several recent studies that have begun to establish the nature and extent of the many benefits long claimed for UR experiences (Adhikari & Nolan, 2002; Barlow & Villarejo, 2004; Bauer & Bennett, 2003; Hathaway, Nagda, & Gregerman, 2002; Lopatto, 2004; Nagda, Gregerman, Jonides, von Hippel, & Lerner, 1998; Russell, 2005; Seymour et al., 2004; Ward, Bennett, & Bauer, 2002; Zydney, Bennett, Shahid, & Bauer, 2002).

This chapter presents findings from our comparative analysis of faculty and student perceptions of the benefits of participating in UR in the sciences and illustrates the sometimes different ways in which faculty and their students view particular areas of gain and their significance. Results from the comparative analysis show that faculty advisors' observations largely match those of their students. As we will discuss, important distinctions emerged in the analysis in the ways in which each group perceives and values particular types of gains. Students emphasized the personal-professional transitions they experience as gains from UR. They reported shifts in their attitudes, practices, and levels of engagement as learners and apprentice researchers, and increased awareness of their temperamental aptitude for the risks and reversals inherent in authentic research. They defined these gains as having both personal and professional significance and regarded many of them as transferable to other areas of life. Faculty advisors agreed (to a greater or lesser extent) with their students' reports of the types and personal significance of their gains, but faculty also framed particular gains as evidence of their students' development as young professionals. Faculty advisors' added perspective on students' professional socialization suggests essential first steps in students' becoming scientists.

RESEARCH METHODS AND DESIGN

Our methods of data collection and analysis are ethnographic, rooted in theoretical work and methodological traditions from sociology, anthropology, and social psychology (Berger & Luckman, 1967; Blumer, 1969; Garfinkel, 1967; Mead, 1934; Schutz & Luckman, 1974). Classically, qualitative studies such as ethnographies precede survey or experimental work, particularly where existing knowledge is limited, because these methods of research can uncover and explore issues that shape informants' thinking and actions. Good software programs are now available to assist in text data analysis. They allow for the multiple, overlapping, and nested coding of a large volume of text data to a high degree of complexity, enabling ethnographers to disentangle patterns in large data sets and to report findings using descriptive statistics. Although conditions for statistical significance are rarely met, the results from analysis of text data gathered by careful sampling and consistency in data coding can be very powerful.

This qualitative study was designed to address fundamental questions about the benefits (and costs) of undergraduate engagement in faculty-mentored, authentic research undertaken outside of class work, about which the existing literature offers few findings and many untested hypotheses.[1] Longitudinal and comparative, this study explores the following aspects:

- What students identify as the benefits of UR—both following the experience and in the longer term (particularly career outcomes)
- What gains faculty advisors observe in their student researchers and how their view of gains converges with or diverges from those of their students
- What benefits and costs to faculty come from their engagement in UR
- What, if anything, is lost by students who do not participate in UR
- What processes generate the gains to students

This study was undertaken at four liberal arts colleges with a strong history of UR. All offer UR in three core sciences—physics, chemistry, and biology—with additional programs in other STEM fields, including (at different campuses) computer science, engineering, biochemistry, mathematics, and psychology. In the apprenticeship model of UR practiced at these colleges, faculty alone directed students in research; however, in the few instances where faculty conducted research at a nearby institution, some students did have contact with postdocs, graduate students, or senior lab technicians who assisted in the research as well.

We interviewed a cohort of (largely) rising seniors who were engaged in UR in summer 2000 on the four campuses ($N = 76$). They were interviewed for a second time shortly before their graduation in spring 2001 ($N = 69$), and a third time as graduates in 2003–04 ($N = 55$). The faculty advisors ($N = 55$) working with this cohort of students were also interviewed in summer 2000, as were nine administrators with long experience of UR programs at their schools.

We also interviewed a comparison group of students ($N = 62$) who had not done UR. They were interviewed as graduating seniors in spring 2001 and again as graduates in 2003–04 ($N = 25$). A comparison group ($N = 16$) of faculty who did not conduct UR in summer 2000 was also interviewed.

Interview protocols focused upon the nature, value, and career consequences of UR experiences, and the methods by which these were achieved.[2] After classifying the range of benefits claimed in the literature, we constructed a gains checklist to discuss with all participants of "what faculty think students may gain from undergraduate research." During the interview, UR students were asked to describe the gains from their research experience (or by other means). If, toward the end of the interview, a student had not mentioned a gain identified on our checklist, the student was queried as to whether he or she could claim to have gained the benefit and was invited to add further comment. Students also mentioned gains they had made that were not included in the list. With slight alterations in the protocol, we invited comments on the same list of possible gains from students who had not experienced UR, and solicited information about gains from other types of experience. All students were asked to expand on their answers, to highlight gains most significant to them, and to describe the sources of any benefits. Interviews took between 60 and 90 minutes and were tape-recorded with the interviewees' permission. Taped interviews and focus groups were transcribed verbatim into a word processing program and submitted to The Ethnograph (Seidel, 1998), a set of software programs to enable text data analysis.

In this type of qualitative analysis, each transcript—the text data—is searched for information bearing upon the research questions. Text segments referencing issues of different type are tagged by code names. Codes are not preconceived, but empirical: Each new code references a discrete idea not previously raised. Interviewees also offer information in spontaneous narratives and examples and may make several points in the same passage, each of which is separately coded. As transcripts are coded, both the codes and their associated passages are entered into The Ethnograph, creating a data set for each interview group. Code words and their definitions are concurrently collected in a codebook. Groups of codes that cluster around particular themes are given "parent" codes. Because an idea that is encapsulated by a code may relate to more than one theme, code words are often assigned multiple parent codes. Thus a branching and interconnected structure of codes and parents emerges from the text data, which at any point in time represents the state of the analysis.

As information is commonly embedded in speakers' accounts of their experience rather than offered in abstract statements, transcripts can be checked for internal consistency between the opinions or explanations offered by informants, their descriptions of events, and the reflections and feelings these evoke. Ongoing discussions between members of our research group continually reviewed the types of observations arising from the data sets to assess and refine category definitions and assure content validity.

The clustered codes and parents and their relationships define themes of the qualitative analysis. In addition, frequency of use can be counted for codes across a data set, and for important subsets (e.g., gender), using conservative counting conventions that are designed to avoid overestimating the weight of particular opinions. Together, these frequencies describe the relative weighting of issues in participants' collective report. As they are drawn from targeted, intentional samples, rather than from random samples, these frequencies are not subjected to tests for statistical significance. They hypothesize the strength of particular variables and their relationships that may later be tested by random sample surveys or by other means. However, the findings in this study are unusually strong because of near-complete participation by members of each group under study.

In the remainder of this chapter, we discuss in detail the six major gains categories listed in Table 7.1. Discussion of each of the gains categories is presented in rank order according to the number of faculty observations. In discussing each benefits category, we detail the various types of gains collected in each category and compare and contrast faculty advisors' and students' observations (Tables 7.2–7.7).

COMPARISON OF FACULTY AND STUDENT OBSERVATIONS ON GAINS FROM UNDERGRADUATE RESEARCH

Faculty and student reports of the positive outcomes of participating in UR describe a range of intellectual, personal and professional gains with multidimensional benefits for students. We describe these gains below and compare and contrast faculty and students' observations and the different ways in which faculty and students view particular gains and their significance.

Thinking and Working Like a Scientist

The largest number of gains observed by faculty referenced growth in students' intellectual and practical understanding of how science research is done; these

Table 7.1. Comparison of faculty and student observations on gains from UR.

Parent Categories: Grouping of Gain-Related Codes	Faculty-Observed Gains		Student-Observed Gains	
	%	n	%	n
Thinking and working like a scientist: Application of knowledge and skills: understanding science research through hands-on experience (gains in critical thinking/problem solving, analyzing and interpreting results); understanding the nature of scientific knowledge (open-ended, constantly constructed); understanding how to approach research problems/design. Increased knowledge and understanding of science and research work (theory/concepts/connections between and within sciences). Transfer between research and courses: increased relevance of course work.	23	527	24	294
Becoming a scientist: Demonstrated gains in behaviors and attitudes necessary to becoming a researcher (student takes "ownership" of project; shows responsibility, intellectual engagement, initiative; creative and independent approach in decision making). Greater understanding of the nature of research work and professional practice. Identification with and bonding to science.	20	450	12	150
Personal-professional gains: Increased confidence in ability to: do research, contribute to science, present/defend research and in "feeling like a scientist." Establishing collegial, working relationships with the faculty advisor and peers.	19	420	25	310
Clarification, confirmation, and refinement of career/ graduate school intentions: Increased interest/enthusiasm for field; validation of disciplinary interests and clarification of graduate school intentions (including increased likelihood of going to graduate school); greater knowledge of career/education options; clarification of which field to study; introduced to new field of study.	16	352	11	131
Enhanced career/graduate school preparation: Real-world work experience (students)/good graduate school/job preparation (faculty); opportunities for collaboration/ networking with faculty, peers, other scientists; new professional experiences; résumé enhanced.	10	228	10	120
Skills: Communication skills: presentation/oral argument; some writing/editing; lab/field techniques; work organization; computer; reading comprehension; working collaboratively; information retrieval.	8	174	17	214
Generalized and other gains: "Students learn a lot"; good summer job, access to good lab equipment, etc.	4	84	1	7
Working independently: Described as a skill, not linked to professional practice.	<1	8	<1	4
	(n = 2243)		(n = 1230)	

Note: Adapted from "Becoming a Scientist: The Role of Undergraduate Research in Students' Cognitive, Personal, and Professional Development," by A.-B. Hunter, S. L. Laursen, and E. Seymour, 2007, *Science Education, 91*(1), pp. 36–74. Copyright 2007 by John Wiley & Sons. Reprinted with permission of Wiley-Liss, Inc., a subsidiary of John Wiley & Sons, Inc.

benefits ranked second in student observations to those in the "Personal-professional gains" category by a difference of only 16 comments (see Table 7.1). Thus both faculty (23%) and students (24%) emphasized the benefits of learning how to "Think and work like a scientist." This category references benefits of two kinds: (1) the application of existing knowledge and skills to their research projects and (2) increases in knowledge. Table 7.2 shows the breakdown of observations in this category: A large majority (86%) of faculty observations in this category noted gains in students' abilities to apply their knowledge and skills to authentic research, while over half (58%) of students' comments discussed gains of this type. By contrast, one quarter (26%) of students' comments in this category reported gains in their knowledge, while only 15% of faculty comments cited this as a benefit. The remaining 16% of students' observations mentioned a benefit that faculty did not: deepening and consolidating knowledge through presenting or teaching others.

Gains in the application of knowledge and skills. The highest number of observations offered by faculty (42%) and students (24%) in this subset of intellectual gains discussed increases in students' understanding of the process of science research through direct, hands-on experience:

> If science is a way of knowing, and a particular mechanism for acquiring information by experimentation, as a way to extract information from the world, then [students] certainly see how that's done much more clearly in the summer experience than they would simply reading a textbook or taking part in a canned lab. I don't think there's any doubt that they get a better feel for how science is actually done. (Advisor)

> It's certainly very different from how it's taught. . . . It was definitely in doing research that I learned how science is done. . . . I've gained an experience of what doing science is really like, and doing it professionally in the sense of what it's really like to take data when you don't know what the answer's going to be beforehand, like in a laboratory course. And to test it against a model where you're not sure if you've accounted for everything and to really [learn] . . . what's acceptable for publication. . . . It's one thing to study science, but it's another to work on and solve problems. (Student)

One quarter (25%) of faculty observations in this category noted increases in students' abilities to apply their critical thinking and problem-solving skills to research, to analyze data, and to better understand the theory and concepts behind the science being studied. Nearly one quarter (22%) of student observations also mentioned these gains:

Table 7.2. Comparison of faculty and student observations on gains made in "thinking and working like a scientist" (share of observations).

Type of Observation	% Faculty Observations (n = 527)	% Student Observations (n = 294)
Gains in the application of knowledge and skills		
Understanding science research through hands-on, authentic experience	42	24
Gain in critical thinking and problem-solving skills related to research—using critical thinking and problem-solving skills in an authentic research experience; analyzing data within theoretical/conceptual frameworks	25	22
Understanding nature of scientific knowledge: its open-endedness, the nature of scientific "fact," science as "fallible," how scientific knowledge is built	17	3
Understanding how to frame research questions, develop/refine a research design	2	9
Subtotal	86	58
Gains in knowledge		
Increased knowledge; understanding in depth; understanding theory/concepts; making connections between and within science; solidifying knowledge	13	16
Increased appreciation of the relevance of course work to understanding science	2	10
Subtotal	15	26
Total comparable observations	100	84
Noncomparable student observations on gains in knowledge		
Consolidating and deepening knowledge through presentation and teaching		14
Critical thinking and problem-solving skills, generally (not linked to application/research)		2
Total noncomparable student observations		16

Note: Percentages do not sum to 100 due to rounding.

When they come in the lab they're not sure what to do. They don't know how to ask questions. . . . By the end of summer . . . they're able to bring me a graph of the data in final form with the statistical analysis and say, "Well, you know, you can see here that at one hour there was no significance, but at two hours there was," and, "Let's think about how that relates to that early experiment that you did. . . ." So they have this understanding, this ability to analyze the data. (Advisor)

It really does help you learn to detect your own dumb mistakes. Like, it's easy to think about something conceptually a little bit wrong, and go with that for about a week. But then you look at what you've got, and your spectra don't make any sense. . . . Then you realize what the problem is. You learn to recognize things like that quicker and quicker the more you do it. (Student)

Consistent with the reports of their students, as described in our earlier report, faculty offer fewer observations on student gains in understanding the nature of scientific knowledge. Nonetheless, from their experience of directing UR, 17% of faculty observations in this category indicate that some students do acquire greater insight into how scientific knowledge is built, including the understanding that researchers can never be sure what the outcome of the experiment will be. Just 3% of student observations mentioned gains in developing a more complex understanding of the nature of scientific knowledge, showing that a few students do make a shift from seeing science as facts to science as process:

They learn to look at science differently than the way they had it presented in class and the book. . . . There's a little bit of that, "Gosh, I thought everything we know is in this book!" And so they suddenly realize that there's so much that we don't know and that what's in a textbook may be just a guess. (Advisor)

I've made some great realizations. . . . I think a lot of people think science is truth, this all-encompassing certainty. . . . And what I found out is that often what research does is just to explain how something could happen or probably happens, and not necessarily how it does happen. So I think that has helped me a lot in understanding science better. (Student)

Faculty provided even fewer observations (2%) than their students (9%) of significant progress in understanding how to identify, frame, and refine new research questions, and how to select or develop research methods. When answering questions on students' abilities to propose a research question or develop an experimental design, faculty often added that undergraduates were unlikely to possess the level of knowledge and technical skills necessary to do this; rather, they expected these to be developed during graduate school.

Gains in knowledge. Gains in conceptual understanding, deepening of disciplinary knowledge, and an increased understanding of how ideas between and within the sciences were connected, are also cited as gains from UR (13% of faculty observations in this category; 16% of students'). Faculty noticed gains in both students' comprehension of science and in their ability to make conceptual and theoretical connections within their research:

> My students presented their work last Tuesday. . . . I wasn't sure that they really understood the point of what we were doing in the experiments. One of my colleagues asked a question of the young woman . . . and she answered it brilliantly. . . . I was so pleased because, intellectually, she has put all these things together and she's synthesizing what she's doing in respect to some of the things that have been done.

Some students felt they had gained a broader knowledge of their discipline, while others expressed learning in greater depth:

> Well, intellectually I think that it's helped me to understand chemistry better. Not just the chemistry that I happen to be doing in the lab, but also chemistry as a whole, just because my research does relate to many different areas of chemistry. And learning how to look through the primary literature and to really synthesize and understand the information about the project has helped me to better understand other areas of chemistry and pick things up more quickly.

> Just from being out in the field and asking (my advisor), "What's that plant there?" I've gotten a lot more knowledge of the basics. I think you do end up learning techniques or, you know, everything you ever wanted to know about milkweeds!

Other student observations on gains in knowledge. Students mentioned some gains in knowledge that faculty did not, notably, consolidating and deepening their knowledge through presentation and teaching others.

In sum, the category "Thinking and working like a scientist" represents the largest group of student gains identified by faculty and the second largest set of observations on gains offered by students. Each group reported similar intellectual gains from UR. Both emphasized hands-on engagement in authentic research as providing an enhanced intellectual and practical understanding of the processes of science research and the opportunity to directly exercise learning in a context that is unavailable in traditional coursework or class labs. Many students experienced increases in their ability to successfully apply critical thinking and problem-solving skills to the work at hand, including the capacity to analyze data in relation to scientific concepts and theories framing research. Fewer students developed a more complex epistemological understanding of the open-ended nature of scientific knowledge and that scientific "fact" may be subject to revision. Fewer students also gained a capacity to adequately develop a research question or design an experiment to test hypotheses. Results reported from the only two U.S. studies we know that carefully probed for and assessed students' higher order intellectual gains from UR experience (Kardash, 2000; Rauckhorst, 2001) are similar to ours. Thus findings suggest that active participation in UR offers the potential for students to move through a sequence of intellectual gains—from application to design to abstraction—though this process is neither easy nor guaranteed. Both faculty and students noted gains in students' knowledge and its transfer between research and course work.

"Becoming a Scientist"

The category "Becoming a scientist" ranks second (20%) in number of faculty observations on student gains from UR and fourth (12%) for students (see Table 7.1). It includes observations on the following student gains:

> Demonstrating attitudes and behaviors needed to become a scientist
> Understanding the nature of research work
> Understanding how scientists practice their profession
> Beginning to see themselves as scientists

These subsets of gains in "Becoming a scientist" are detailed in Table 7.3.

The high number of faculty observations documenting students' development as young research professionals is an especially interesting finding of this study, not least because this topic is not, as yet, well represented in the literature. It is also interesting because students who described these gains did not couch them in terms of "becoming scientists," but largely as issues of personal-professional (or other forms of) growth. When comparing faculty and student observations, we began to see that the perspectives of the participating faculty were important in understanding the wider significance of particular gains reported by students.

Demonstrated gains in attitudes and behaviors needed to be a scientist.
Faculty advisors' role as professional researchers influences their view of what they see students gain from UR: They look for and are aware of the development of traits that they see as necessary for the practice of science research. That stu-

Table 7.3. Comparison of faculty and student observations on gains in "becoming a scientist" (share of observations).

Type of Observation	% Faculty Observations (n = 450)	% Student Observations (n = 150)
Demonstrated gains in attitudes and behaviors needed to become a scientist: Student "takes ownership" of project—"intellectual engagement," creative and independent approach to decision making; demonstrates increased patience, perseverance; greater tolerance for setbacks, frustrations; shows commitment and initiative/goes beyond what is expected; shows willingness to take risks; becomes an "active learner"/takes responsibility for own learning	52	25
Understanding the nature of research work: Understanding that research is messy, riddled with problems/setbacks; can be tedious, boring, and slow; requires development of particular temperamental attributes	24	13
Understanding how scientists practice their profession: Awareness of attitudes, behaviors and norms required of professional practice; insight into the profession through attending and presenting at conferences; understanding collaboration with other peers/scientists as professional practice; increased understanding that thinking "creatively" and "taking risks" are necessary to science research; recognizing the importance of peer review and professional standards of behavior	14	5
Beginning to see oneself as a scientist: Beginning to adopt a professional identity as a scientist; readiness to undertake the work of a scientist (linked to growth of confidence)	10	57

dents report these gains but do not recognize them as indicators of professional growth is also the result of their relative viewpoint: They are, as yet, on the outside looking in. At this stage in their lives, students simply do not know what characteristics might be needed to become good scientists, and they are not conscious of developing such traits in themselves. However, as scientists, faculty *do* know, and, it is apparent from their comments that they notice if and when students start to take on particular attitudes and attributes that they deem necessary for professional practice. In this category of benefits, half (52%) of faculty observations described changes they observed in students' conduct, manner, and attitudes, noting how students began to exhibit behaviors and attitudes that underpin work as a researcher:

> What I look for, and to me, the mark of success in this kind of endeavor is ownership. . . . It's fun to see. . . . There's some transformation that occurs, where it suddenly becomes *their* project. And you *see* that.

> They approach me and say, "I know you always say I should at least run it by you . . . but I did this on my own and look what I got!" And there have been a few that have sort of just done it—around the sides without letting you know because they wanted to surprise you. That's a real transition point. . . . And, when you see that happen, you think, "Okay, we're all set here."

Faculty noticed students becoming less fearful of "being wrong" and more willing to take risks. They witnessed growth in students' intellectual creativity:

> One of the things that pleases me in a student is one who isn't afraid to get in there and just get their hands dirty, and just try something. That's what [he] did. He wasn't worried about wasting some reagents, some enzyme or something . . . to get it to work. Whereas, I've had other students who, if it doesn't work, the first thing they do is come to me. . . . The successful students are the ones that will just get in there and they'll try things on their own and get 'em to work.

Faculty described these shifts in attitudes and behaviors as "transformations" that indicated to them that their students were becoming young professionals.

Students also noted changes in their behavior and attitudes, but offered fewer reports of these gains and, unlike faculty, did not frame these gains as habits of the profession. A quarter (25%) of student comments in this category discussed learning to work and think independently and becoming active agents in figuring something out independently rather than relying on faculty. Students also talked about taking greater care with work to provide accurate results and feeling responsible for their project's progress. The following quotations illustrate how committed to and absorbed in their research these students had become:

> Just being able to sit down and concentrate on one thing and figure it out and understand. . . . We work with protein-DNA interactions. And so just for me to look at that and really, really understand it rather than just getting the big overview. And then, actually thinking about the problem critically and creatively and being, "Okay. Now what can I change to have

this effect and to have this outcome?" That's a whole new experience for me.

I'm being relied on to a certain extent. So if I'm not at least doing the 40 hours, not that I couldn't necessarily slip around it, but I feel that I should at least be in here working for 40 hours.

I was in the lab 8 hours a day and really working on large-scale projects and really having to start dealing with the issues of tedium and failure and, "This isn't just for me to write up in my lab book and turn in and get a grade. This is something that could eventually be published, that other people could base work on." It's more important for me to make sure that I'm doing it right, and that I record everything.

Understanding the nature of research work. By engaging in authentic research projects, faculty know that students will come to better understand the character of research work: that it is messy and slow, that it is often boring and tedious, that it may be necessary to repeat a procedure multiple times before it works properly, and that "failure" is often par for the course. These types of observations comprised nearly one quarter (24%) of faculty observations in this category:

They learn in the lab that science is an awful lot of frustration. They learn that it's not going to work a lot of the times. So this is one of their lessons that they come out with. (Laughs) So they get accustomed to the idea that things don't work and they have to figure it out.

As a corollary to understanding that such occurrences are a normal part of research work, faculty also saw in students a growing consciousness that to succeed as a scientist requires particular temperamental attributes, whether natural or acquired:

I think the most important thing they get out of it is just an understanding of what research is really like. . . . The first point this summer, when . . . they really realized how much work it was going to be, and how boring data collection can be. . . . And some of them realize they really like it, and some of them realize that this will drive them crazy.

A smaller number of student observations in this category (13%) also referenced gains in better understanding the character of research work and realizing that it requires a particular disposition:

You can't get too emotionally distraught over something . . . I have a tendency, especially when it's my own dumb mistake that's caused me to

lose several hours of work. . . . You have to just step back and deal with
the facts as they are and say, "Okay. I've messed up. I need to correct this.
It'll take a few hours, but then we'll move on."

Coming to an honest understanding of what real research entails—not only in terms
of its nature, but also recognizing that one must enjoy, or at the very least, be able
to tolerate its frustrations—is a benefit hard won from experience.

Understanding how scientists practice their profession. Fourteen percent of
faculty observations in the "Becoming a scientist" category identify students'
growth in understanding how scientists practice their profession. Faculty advisors were aware that UR provided students with an opportunity to witness firsthand how scientists operate as professionals. Students see that faculty must write
papers, pass peer review and publish, attend conferences, present papers, and learn
the professional practice of collaboration. Only 5% of student observations in this
category related to growth in understanding standards of professional practice.
These comments were framed almost entirely in personal terms, as leading to
increased confidence and their "feeling like scientists." Thus while students may
indeed be seeing "how" scientists practice their profession, they largely internal-
ize these gains, focusing on the immediate effects on their own self-development
rather than defining them (as do faculty) as habits of the profession.

Beginning to see themselves as scientists. In the final subset of observations
comprising the "Becoming a scientist" category, 10% of faculty comments linked
gains in confidence to students' beginning identification with science as a young
professional:

> The number one thing I see, and the thing they perhaps talk about the
> most, is self-confidence. You know, "Last week I couldn't spell engineer,
> and now I *is* one!" . . . To be able to get into the laboratory, posing some
> questions, using sophisticated techniques to try and address or answer
> those questions. Being able to interpret what the results are of their work.
> That they did it. . . . That self-confidence thing helps so much. They feel
> *so* good about it.

In contrast, the majority of student observations comprising the "Becoming a
scientist" category (57%) referenced increases in confidence. In conducting the
comparative analysis, faculty's observations made explicit some aspects of students' development of which students were largely unaware. For students, "feeling like a scientist" was framed entirely in the context of growth in confidence; it
was not projected as conscious development of "Becoming a scientist." Because
the two types of sentiments are highly related, they were counted as gains in both

the "Becoming a scientist" and the "Personal-professional gains" categories.[3] As gains in confidence are discussed by students primarily in terms of their personal development, we will elaborate on the growth of professional identity in our discussion of the "Personal-professional gains" category. However, one area in which students gained insight into how the science profession operates was in presenting at disciplinary conferences. Those students who had been to a conference typically emphasized how this had broadened their understanding of professional practice. These students saw firsthand how scientists practice professionally in the world. Some imagined what a career in science would be like, and some expressed an early sense of belonging to the profession:

> It gives you an idea, especially when I went to the [conference], it gives you an idea of where you might be working and if you would be interested in doing something like that, if you would like it, and types of problems that they have to deal with. It gives you an idea of where you are going to be at a certain point.

Faculty also saw the added value for students of getting to see how scientists worked beyond the walls of academe. They were aware that attending conferences helped students to see what a future in science might look like, encouraged a view of themselves as part of the scientific community, and held the potential to draw students into a science profession:

> When they get to the American Chemical Society meeting, they begin to realize that it's a whole lot bigger . . . and they've got connections to people who are out there . . . specific connections that show them the path of how they *can* get there.

In only a small proportion of student observations on increased confidence was it clear that students had come to understand the significance of developing a more practical understanding of the demands of professional science. Engaging in research, and finding that they could meet its challenges, evoked in some students a sense of becoming a scientist:

> The summer's research was sort of the first step in becoming a true biologist. The nature of the research is such that there are long periods of waiting before we can obtain data. And so some days were particularly trying, but as a whole, I look back on it fondly. I feel like I'm really learning what it's like to be a scientist.

Interestingly, learning that research is typically fraught with problems, that it requires patience and perseverance, that it is slow and often boring, and that a high incidence of "failure" is to be expected, was also seen by both faculty and students as applicable to life, in general:

> Life in the lab is tough. . . . I've spent years on some projects and not gotten a really great result out of it. And so students will spend a whole semester working on something and have to deal with "It didn't work this time. Didn't work this time. Didn't work this time." And it's not because it's a bad project. It's because they're in that troubleshooting phase that you must go through. You can't just buy a kit to do this experiment. You have to just troubleshoot yourself. And you *have* to go through that in order to get beyond it. And I would say that maturity of "Things don't always go the way I think they're going to go," is actually a very good life lesson to learn. (Advisor)

> I think the perseverance that it takes, the patience to be able to just keep working and not giving up on things, that is something that I think will be useful in other areas—learning to not expect things to happen right away, and suddenly, magically you have all your results. (Student)

In summary, in the "Becoming a scientist" category, faculty observations concern students' development as young scientists. Their observations describe the development of attitudes and behaviors that characterize aptitude for the profession and the adoption of the professional norms seen as necessary to science research work. Students' discussion of these types of gains referenced changes in their attitudes and behaviors in relation to research work; they did not frame their discussion of these gains in terms of professional development. Rather, as we will discuss next, students internalized these gains in terms of their own self-development.

Personal-Professional Gains

We called this category "Personal-professional gains" because students linked personal gains to their perceived professional value. While this category ranks fourth in faculty observations, it ranks first among student-identified gains (see Table 7.1). As Table 7.4 indicates, faculty and student observations that comprise this category refer largely to gains in confidence in doing research work. The benefits of establishing collegial relationships with faculty and peers were also discussed by both groups. However, it is evident from faculty advisors' comments that they are more aware than their students of the longer-term importance of both mentoring and developing working collegial relationships.

Increased confidence. Faculty acknowledged that students' increased confidence is a significant benefit of UR. Like students, faculty did not refer to confidence in

Table 7.4. Comparison of faculty and student observations on "professional gains" from UR (share of observations).

Type of Observation	% Faculty Observations (n = 420)	% Student Observations (n = 310)
Confidence		
Increases in confidence to do research/contribute to science	32	47
Increases in confidence in "feeling like a scientist" (students); "students beginning to see themselves as scientists" (faculty); attending and presenting at conferences; being taken seriously	11	27
Subtotal	43	74
Collegiality		
Establishing a collegial relationship with faculty; recognition of faculty advisors' positive influence on students	24	16
Peer/professional collegiality (i.e., with other UR students)	13	9
Subtotal	37	25
Total comparable observations	80	100
Noncomparable faculty observations on students' "personal-professional gains" from UR		
Seeing who/what a "real scientist" is/does; seeing faculty as "real people" at work	6	
Gains in maturity/self-discovery	6	
Belonging to a "community of learners"	4	
Gains in confidence due to: mentoring by more senior UR students of more junior UR students; mentoring by others (postdocs, other scientists, lab assistants, etc.)	4	
Total noncomparable faculty observations	20	

Note: Percentages do not sum to 100 due to rounding.

a general sense, but specifically linked students' increased confidence to their enhanced ability to engage in scientific research. However, the importance that faculty assign to this related set of gains is much less than that cited by their students (i.e., 43% of faculty-identified gains compared with 74% of student-identified gains in this category). Students broadly divided their observations on confidence between increased confidence to do research and contribute to science (47%) and accounts of how these confidence gains induced in some a feeling of being a "real" scientist (27%).

Students described growth in their confidence to do research as a change in themselves that, looking back, they could now see: They contrasted feeling daunted at the outset with their current feelings of competence, and they recognized a shift toward thinking and working independently. They also discussed gains in their technical know-how and feeling confident to tackle whatever new learning might be required in the future:

> At the beginning, I asked a lot of questions to get a good basis and a good idea when I didn't really know what I was doing. But by the end of the summer, I didn't speak to my advisor much, because I would just do it.

> I now feel confident that I can walk into any room with any instrument and figure out how to make that instrument work. And that's a very nice confidence to have because it makes me feel a lot more optimistic when I look at somebody's Web page and . . . I see this laundry list of 10, 15 different methods of analysis they're using, and I can look down that list and say, "I know how to do half of these, and another half of them I can figure out pretty easily, based on things I've done."

The most powerful source of their growing confidence as researchers was the realization that their work could make a useful contribution to the field:

> Contributing to the field is important . . . I really like the idea that I am doing science research and I feel like it's something that's new and exciting and it's been looked at sort of, but not really, the research that I'm doing. I get a lot of satisfaction out of the fact that I'm doing something new.

Faculty advisors affirmed the strong affective gains students take away from their research experience. Thirty-two percent of faculty observations in this category noted increased confidence in students' willingness to tackle new technical challenges and in their greater willingness to think creatively about alternative ways to approach a research question:

> You can see it a mile away. When they approach a new piece of equipment, it's more, "Well, where's the manual?" (Laughs) "Don't waste my time teaching me this. Just tell me how to turn it on and I'll figure it out." Self-confidence, maturity.

> I saw him able to approach problems with a little bit more creativity. With a little bit less, "It has to be done precisely one way." I really think he'd gained confidence.

Faculty advisors also concurred with students that a major source of increased confidence was the realization that they were able to make a meaningful contribution to science:

> I think when they see what they're doing connects with other people's work . . . that kind of validates a lot of what they do, so I think they like that. This summer we had a lot of requests for the clone that we've isolated . . . and I could see this one student was getting really excited.

Growth in students' confidence to do science and, thereby, to their beginning to *feel like* scientists are related to, but different from, the acquisition of the professional attributes needed to *become* a scientist that we discussed in the previous section. Both are essential elements in the processes whereby UR experiences contribute to the production of future scientists. However, faculty portray "the confidence to do science" as a necessary (if not sufficient) requirement for future scientists, while students present this growth of confidence as a valued personal benefit that may or may not lead them into a research career. We also distinguish between gains in students' confidence to contribute to science and their first steps in becoming a scientist, both of which arise out of the experience of attending and presenting at conferences. Both students and faculty described these gains, although faculty interpreted their significance in terms of bringing new talent into their profession, while students saw these benefits in terms of personal growth with transferable professional value. *Both* increased student confidence as well as bonding to professional identity and practice (11% of faculty observations and 27% of student observations) were prompted by the experience of presenting and discussing the results of their research work at formal end-of-program activities or at UR symposia. However, students especially observed these effects when they presented at disciplinary conferences:

> When you finish your research for the summer and you present your research, you put it in poster form. . . . I mean, there's a certain amount of pride that goes with that, and, you know, you feel like a scientist.

> When I was at the conferences, I felt truly that I was a scientist. I was
> amidst scientists. I was just, you know, completely surrounded by them,
> and they were . . . I was talking to them about my research and they
> were talking to me. And they, I could see them talking to me . . . not as
> if I was lower to them, but as equal to them. And that made me feel
> really good.

Faculty understood very well that publicly presenting research contributed in a
number of ways to students' increased confidence in themselves as emerging scientists and conscious of the role that presenting plays in students' professional
socialization:

> Watch them at their poster session, or watch them at a meeting, explaining
> what they've done to other chemists. . . . When you go to a [disciplinary]
> meeting, that's the key thing to do. And to watch all these chemists from
> Dow coming around to talk to students, . . . it's this big epiphany when
> they realize that what they're doing really is important and that somebody
> somewhere else actually cares about it, and they get into *real* scientific
> conversations: "Oh, well, did you try this?" "No, but I tried that!" When
> something like that happens, and the student gets truly excited about it,
> that's the moment there.

Faculty put considerable effort into arranging student presentation experiences
because they recognized the potential of these experiences to move promising
young scientists from a basic appreciation of increased confidence to do science
to a stronger identification with the profession of science.

Establishing a collegial relationship with faculty. The opportunity to build a
close, collegial relationship with faculty is a benefit of UR that is discussed by
both faculty and students. Descriptions of the importance to students of establishing collegial relationships were 24% of faculty and 16% of student observations
within the category of "Personal-professional gains." From the interview data, it
is clear that faculty advisors are very conscious of their mentoring role and are
more aware than are their students of the specific benefits of developing collegial
relationships. Students largely focus on the shift from a hierarchical and respect-
fully distanced relationship to one based on partnership; for them, such a shift is
quite powerful:

> I've gotten to know all the faculty. . . . I actually see them more as peers.
> As a researcher, they are your peers; you're working with them. . . . It
> gives a totally different aspect than being a student . . . and you don't have
> to be intimidated by them anymore.

Faculty also described the character of their interactions with their undergraduate researchers as one in which students became collaborators:

> Part of what I think works in this enterprise, is it's not this student-teacher relationship. It's a more collegial relationship. We're on fairly equal footing here. It's true I have a lot more experience, and I can give them the benefit of my general experience in thinking about mathematical problems, but I don't have any more specific insight into this problem. And it's wonderful when a student comes up with something and I say, "Well, that's really neat! I never thought of that." And they just beam, you know, "I got something!"

Students' observations on building collegial relationships with faculty provide insight into the mentoring role of faculty advisors. Faculty modeled how science is done, and, in doing so, gave their young colleagues the confidence that they too could handle the complexities of research:

> They're just a great resource. They're an expert in what you're doing, for one thing. So they have great ideas. And when you really hit that wall and you don't know what to do, and you've tried things, then you can go back to them and they will have some suggestions. . . . I think that's really important . . . the encouragement that you get from them. . . . I think that that can reflect to you, "Hey, you know I can do this! Look, she thinks I did a good job!" . . . I think when *you* start asking questions and when *you* are able to say, "What do you think about trying it this way?" and they go, "Oh, I hadn't thought about that," that's really nice.

That faculty are cognizant of the multiple ways in which they mentor their undergraduate researchers is evident in their observations on the value to students of establishing collegial relationships. Faculty reflected upon their experience of many long-lasting associations and ongoing friendships developed with former research students:

> There's a lawyer in Cedar Rapids that I've kept in touch with over the years. He was '76 class, something like that. And about every other year we get together someplace. We have a lot of mutual friends and we know what each other's doing. There's another guy, a faculty member, a mathematician . . . we see him all the time. He used to baby-sit for us. Their daughter was up a couple of weeks ago.

Gains in establishing professional collegiality with peers. Faculty and students also reported gains in collegiality among student peers (13% and 9%, respectively). Students described how the experience of working alongside other students provided good mutual support when things did not go smoothly, extra insight into problems with their research projects, and knowledgeable sources to turn to for ideas or critique when the research advisor was unavailable:

> We would also have meetings for lunch once a week where everybody from the two labs would get together and we'd discuss what we're working on. . . . Even though I'm not specifically working on that project, what their work is influences my project and vice versa. So we would . . . discuss what had been going on—new results, something good or bad that had happened. . . . Plus, that provides time for insight . . . maybe they're thinking about this problem a different way than you.

Faculty particularly noted the educational benefits of having students work together and the value of the camaraderie and confidence this can generate:

> I think . . . they learn a lot just from being around other students that do research. . . . They talk a lot. . . . The community aspect of it is very important in terms of support, like, "The other student has the same problem, so I'm probably doing okay. . . . I can do this!"

Other faculty observations. One-fifth of faculty observations in the "Personal-professional gains" category were not directly comparable to comments offered by students: the benefit of seeing faculty advisors as "real people"; gains in students' maturity and self-discovery; belonging to a community of learners; and gains from students' mentoring others.

Overall, the gains comprising this category speak to students' growing internal sense of self as young scientists and reflect the significance of building professional relationships with faculty and peers. Faculty and students emphasized UR as an opportunity to discover the confidence to work independently and creatively as researchers. For some, students' gains in confidence fostered "feeling like a scientist." The development of collegial relationships with faculty and research peers was also defined by students as a type of personal-professional gain whose significance was strongly acknowledged by faculty. Faculty, however, saw the longer term importance of collegial relationships that grew out of UR experiences, describing long associations with former undergraduate researchers.

Clarification, Confirmation, and Refinement of Career/Graduate School Intentions

The career clarification category is comprised of observations on the role of UR in increasing students' interest in science and science research and in helping them to clarify, confirm, and refine future career plans, including graduate school. By number of observations offered, this category ranks fourth for faculty and fifth for students (see Table 7.1). Table 7.5 presents faculty and student observations in this category.

Increased interest. A much higher percentage of observations were offered by faculty (57%) than by students (12%) on students' increased interest and enthusiasm for research or the field of study. This likely reflects faculty advisors' history of seeing many students extending their summer UR experience into the academic year and/or for several more summers:

> I've had students that worked with me during the summer, and then they've stayed the next year. Once they've started in the summer they enjoy the research and they stay during the academic year.

Table 7.5. Comparison of faculty and student observations on how UR clarified, confirmed, and refined career/graduate school intentions (share of observations).

Type of Observation	% Faculty Observations (n = 352)	% Student Observations (n = 131)
Increased student's interest/enthusiasm for field of study	57	12
Clarified/confirmed, student's interest in field of study; aided student in deciding which area of study to pursue; provided concrete recognition of fit between own interests and particular fields of study	20	36
Clarified that a research career was not what student wanted	11	5
Clarified/confirmed level of interest in graduate school/ increased likelihood of going to graduate school	9	39
Introduced student to new field of study	3	8
Total comparable observations	100	100
Noncomparable faculty observations on how UR clarified/ confirmed students' career/graduate school intentions		
Introduced idea of graduate school as a possibility/ going on to graduate school not previously thought of	<1	
Student has gone on to graduate school as a result of UR experience	<1	
Total noncomparable faculty observations	<1	

Students also discussed their increased interest, but spoke only from their experience of their recently completed summer research:

> I just gained a better love of the sciences and a better appreciation of them. And now that I've seen everything that's gone into [a research project], I have seen a little part of what goes into everything I've ever learned.

Confirmed "fit," "research is/is not for me." Also based on their long experience, faculty see UR as helping students to clarify their interest in an area of study and settling the question of whether "research is for me" (20% and 11%, respectively). Indeed, it is evident that many faculty value UR in part because it enables students to find out "what will make them happy" and whether going to graduate school would be a good choice for them:

> It's certainly nice to see them learn over the course of the summer, to see them doing more thinking for themselves, more autonomy, making good choices, making good decisions. It's nice to see them gain confidence in their role as research collaborators. It's nice to see them get to a point where they clarify what they do and don't want to do, because that really *does* often happen. . . . It's nice to see them clarify, "Yeah, that was interesting, but it's not my cup of tea," or "Oh, I loved it and this is what I want to do!"

Again, we note the significance (in this case for career decisions) of the tests of temperament posed by the essential character of real research work:

> I would actually say the majority of students that I've had over the years in the summer research program came in convinced that they wanted to get a PhD (laughs) and *that* changed their minds. I actually have had quite a few say that they're happy they had this experience because they never really realized what it was about, and that you have to be able to deal with frustrations and you have be patient and progress is very slow and all these things. You don't really understand that when you take a course at school.

Similarly, students emphasized how UR experience helped them to see how well an area of study or research fit with their prior notions of what work in that field was really like and whether they would be well suited to doing it (36%):

> I feel like I can more successfully say what I would like to specialize in. Whereas before I would just say, "Pure, general engineering. I have no idea what." I think bioengineering is the field that I want to go into.

For students, the experience of "seeing myself doing this" is revealed as a critical element in the career clarification process:

> Just the experience of realizing, "Okay this is what my life is going to be like if I decide to do this," and realizing, "Yeah, that's what I want to do. That's what I enjoy doing. That's what I love doing."

Sometimes, research experience caused some refocusing of earlier career aspirations:

> I've always had my eyes on medicine . . . but I think with my chemistry background, and especially with the recent experience, I think I'm much more leaning toward more of an experimental side of medicine. . . . I could see myself doing pharmaceutical research or something like that.

As faculty also noted, the UR experience clarified for some students that research was not well suited to their interests and/or temperament. In this sample of 76 students, seven found that "research is not for me":

> I really do enjoy doing research, but I can't see myself doing it for my entire life. I can't see myself in a lab, day in and day out.

For this group, as much as for those who embrace the research life, faculty emphasized the importance of students' being enabled to "see themselves" doing this work and using tests of temperamental fit in reaching career decisions.

Confirmed/increased interest in graduate school. Aside from the issue of settling whether research is a temperamental fit for students, both faculty and students appreciated the practical utility of UR experiences in confirming or increasing students' interest in graduate school. Statements on the value of UR in helping students determine their level of interest in, and commitment to, graduate education account for 9% of faculty comments in this category:

> We talked about graduate school a fair amount. He was sort of asking about "How do you decide where to go? How do you know if that's what you want to do?" I think he's fairly undecided about what he wants to do with his life, but I think he's pretty strongly considering graduate school . . . especially because he's finding out that he's enjoying the research probably more than he thought he would, that he's feeling a little more sure that he'll probably go to graduate school.

The much larger number of students' observations (39%) on gains in this category reflect students' immediate and dominant preoccupation with what they will do beyond graduation. Most of their observations either expressed an increased interest in attending graduate school or confirmed a preexisting interest in graduate school. Smaller percentages of faculty and students also mentioned the benefit of being introduced to a new field of study through UR (3% and 8%, respectively). Students' observations also show that UR experience provided greater confidence to choose the next steps in their lives:

> I've always been thinking and wanting to go to grad school, ever since I can remember, wanting to get a doctorate, but I actually truly decided, it was this summer when I said, "Yes, I'm going to go to grad school. It's what I want to do."

Other faculty observations. Only a very small number of faculty observations were not comparable to those offered by students (< 1%). Two faculty advisors reported they had worked with particular students for whom UR had been the mediating factor in their choice of graduate school. And while none of the students interviewed for this study were unfamiliar with the prospect of graduate school, these faculty cited two students who had never considered graduate education until their UR experience introduced this as a possibility. In both cases, the students came from underrepresented groups—one as a student of color, the other as a first-generation college student.

In summary, for this sample of students at liberal arts colleges, we did not find that UR experience had prompted their decisions to go to graduate school. Rather, most students had planned for and anticipated a graduate school education prior to college entry. Thus for this student group we found that the role of UR is to increase students' interest in and their probability of going on to graduate school, to confirm whether previous intentions to undertake graduate study were apposite, and to clarify or refine which fields of interest to pursue.

Enhanced Career/Graduate School Preparation

"Career and graduate school preparation" benefits rank fifth in number of faculty's and sixth in number of students' comments (see Table 7.1). That this set of observations has a relatively low ranking in the list of reported gains indicates that neither faculty nor students valued UR for predominantly instrumental reasons. Rather, both groups saw the pragmatic benefits of research experiences in preparing students for work or graduate education as ancillary rather than primary gains. As Table 7.6 shows, half of the benefits in this category mentioned by faculty and 20% offered by students described formal contributions to science by undergraduate researchers. They included students who had presented at conferences, were listed as lead or coauthors on articles, or who had made other contri-

Table 7.6. Comparison of faculty and student observations on how UR enhanced career/graduate school preparation (share of observations).

Type of Observation	% Faculty Observations (n = 228)	% Student Observations (n = 120)
Presenting/publishing		
Student *plans* to present at a conference		8
Student *plans* to attend a conference		8
Student has presented at a conference	23	0
Student *plans* to coauthor an article to be published		4
Student has coauthored/published an article based on UR work	23	0
Student has coauthored papers presented at conferences or abstracts submitted to conferences or student contribution is cited	4	0
Subtotal	50	20
Other		
Provides "real-world work experience" (students); good graduate school/job preparation (faculty)	12	32
Enhances résumé: good for graduate/medical school prospects	8	16
Offers opportunity to network with faculty, peers, other scientists	4	28
Subtotal	24	76
Total comparable observations	74	96
Noncomparable student observations on gains in their enhanced career/graduate school preparation		
Good for current education: good preparation for senior thesis, coursework		4
Working collaboratively enhances career/graduate school preparation		<1
Enhances career preparation, in general		<1
Total noncomparable student observations		5
Noncomparable faculty observations on students' gains in enhanced career/graduate school preparation		
Faculty have provided career advice/information; guided student's career plans/decisions	13	
Faculty have written letters of recommendation; facilitated student placement (in other UR opportunities, internships, jobs)	7	
Students have won academic awards/received grant awards (linked to UR participation)	6	
Total noncomparable faculty observations	26	

Note: Percentages do not sum to 100 due to rounding.

butions to their UR projects. Another 24% of faculty observations, but almost all (76%) of student comments in this category, described other benefits: how UR provided a good preparation for many types of work (from the faculty perspective) and "real-world work experience" (from the students' perspective); its role in enhancing student résumés and graduate or professional school applications; and its value in increasing students' possibilities of making important contacts with other faculty and scientists. A final group of faculty and student comments (26% and 5%, respectively) were not directly comparable.

Gains through presenting, conference attendance, and publication. Nearly half of faculty observations on students' gains in enhanced career and graduate school preparation specifically referenced numbers of students who had presented at conferences (23%) or served as lead or coauthors on published articles (23%). In the student interview data, we found that while many students had presented at UR symposia, only seven said that they had attended a professional meeting with their research advisor and only five students reported having been listed as a co-author on a published article.[4] However, some students explained that they planned to give a presentation at or to attend a professional conference as an outgrowth of their research work. Several students expected faculty to present or publish findings on their research at some point in the future:[5] discussion of plans to disseminate their research results were framed by the assumption that being publically credited for their role in the research would bring future benefits. The larger percentages of faculty estimates of career preparation gains clearly reflect the numbers of students they have brought to conferences and with whom they have published over the years. From their longer term perspective as professional scientists and educators, they also appear to view copresentation and shared publications with students as making valuable contributions to their own careers as well as having professional value for their students.

UR provides "real-world work experience"/good preparation. Twelve percent of faculty observations in this category described how UR had increased students' readiness for graduate work and a career in science:

> I know our graduates typically make the transition to graduate school very easily, because we are really taking them from a typical undergraduate experience into a typical graduate experience by their senior year. . . . So I know they enter graduate school—of course they're terrified—but they quickly realize that they're better prepared than most people there. . . . So certainly, I think we are giving them a tremendous advantage.

The highest percentage of student observations in this category (32%) discuss UR as providing "real-world work experience." Students saw this as being of transferable value as they compared UR to what they imagined it would be like to work professionally:

> You're given a lot of freedom and responsibility to do things, so I'm really getting out of it how to go about a professional type job or business, these kinds of things.

For those students who were more strongly considering graduate school, UR was seen as a preliminary glimpse of what graduate work would demand of them:

> I think the whole experience is great preparation because it's far more similar to what graduate school is actually like, I've been told.

Enhances résumé. Faculty and students were, of course, aware that listing research experience on a résumé or graduate school application would be of practical benefit to students. A small number of faculty observations in this category (8%), and a larger number of student observations (16%), discussed the competitiveness of graduate schools and recognized that UR experience would give a solid boost to résumés and graduate school applications:

> If you are interested in pursuing an advanced degree and you want to do it, of course, at a good institution, having research experience under your belt will be very, very helpful. Our students go to the best places, and I think, in large part, it's because, not only do they have As in the same math classes that students in other places do, but many of them have actual research experience. These graduate schools say, "This is not someone we have to gamble on." (Advisor)

> I'm interested in going to graduate school and I think it'll help my chances a lot in getting into graduate school to have done research as an undergraduate. (Student)

However, as we reported in our first article (Seymour et al., 2004), in a separate analysis of students' motivations for undertaking UR we found that 71% of students' statements cited intrinsic interest or a desire to learn what research work entails; only 17% mentioned doing UR as a way to enhance their résumé. Few students described their research experiences largely as a means to improve their career prospects, and no student described its benefits solely this way.

Offers opportunity to network with faculty, peers, other scientists. A few faculty reported that UR offered their students opportunities to network with other scientists (4%). Being able to meet and talk with other scientists helped students to envision what it would be like to be a working scientist. Again, faculty comments show understanding of the tacit role such experiences play in teaching students about work as professional scientists:

> The last two summers I've taken students with me to Duke University, and students like the idea that they might travel someplace. . . . There's multiple other things going on there. Being that this is an undergraduate institution, students don't naturally interact with graduate students here. I take them to Duke, they get to meet some grad students who hang out with them. And they get an idea of what they're getting themselves into.

Twenty-eight percent of student observations in this category also described UR as providing valuable professional connections. In their portrayal, this had both instrumental and purely intrinsic dimensions. In looking to the future, students valued meeting other scientists; they also appreciated the new possibilities that might be opened to them:

> I don't know if this will play out or not, or really how it works, but I have the added bonus of being connected with two or three other people in Seattle through this project. . . . So it sort of broadens my contacts. . . . And I hadn't thought of that at all when I started, but that may be something that later on turns out to be useful, something may turn up there.

Other student observations. Other gains that students (but not faculty) predicted would be helpful in the future were being better prepared to undertake a senior thesis or senior course work and learning to work collaboratively as a useful professional skill.

Other faculty observations. Additional student gains in this category cited by faculty included students' receiving career advice and information, letters of recommendation and help in procuring placement in other UR or internship positions, and scholarship awards based upon the high quality of their UR work.

All students' observations in this category reflect their preoccupation with imminent decisions about life and work beyond college. It is apparent that in the course of their UR experience students were enabled to more clearly understand what work as a scientist entailed and valued the ways in which it had helped them to feel better prepared to meet future challenges. Faculty advisors clearly noticed gains in students' readiness to undertake graduate work or careers in science and were aware that students' UR experience would be looked upon positively by prospective graduate schools and future employers. Some faculty also emphasized the additional opportunities UR provided for some students to travel to conferences, other institutions, and laboratories and saw these experiences as offering students insight into what graduate school or a career in science entailed. The majority of faculty observations in this category, however, focus on institutional measures of student achievement in UR, such as student coauthored publications, conference presentations, and so on. These extrinsic measures of student success may indeed enhance students' preparation, but faculty emphasis on the "products" of UR suggests a preoccupation with "proving" the value of their work to their institution, while their primary personal criteria for estimating its real value are clearly educational and professional.

Gains in Skills

The category of gains focused on increases in students' skills ranks sixth in number of faculty observations and third for student observations. The higher percentage of student observations likely reflects the steep learning curve they encounter at the beginning of UR projects when learning new lab techniques and instrumentation and, later, the challenge of learning to present and defend their research in a professional manner. Faculty also note students' gains in various skills, but, with the exception of presentation and communication skills, technical skills are reported less often. As Table 7.7 indicates, nearly half the gains in particular skills discussed by faculty and students concern communication skills (45% and 43%, respectively). Thirty-two percent of faculty observations in this category and 22% of student comments talk about gains in laboratory skills and techniques necessary for research work. Gains in work organization and time management skills, computer skills, the ability to effectively read science literature, and the ability to work collaboratively were also mentioned by both groups, but to lesser degrees.

Gains in communication skills. Faculty and students report nearly equal gains in learning to present and defend an oral argument (37% and 36%), while improvement in scientific and professional writing skills are cited at much lower levels (8% and 7%). All of the UR programs in this sample emphasized the importance of teaching students how to present scientific results. Indeed, teaching students presentation skills was one of the more overt, formal objectives of these programs. Faculty agreed that teaching students to explain, discuss, and critique their work is a significant aspect of learning professional practice. However, little or no formal writing was required for most end-of-summer presentations; most commonly, students provided a summary of the work that had been accomplished, along with their lab notebooks. As we have reported elsewhere (Seymour et al., 2004), few students were involved in assisting their research advisors in writing scholarly articles. Indeed, faculty discussed publishing coauthored papers as a benefit that "comes later" or beyond graduation. Since research often takes years, and faculty have difficulty finding the time to write up their results for publication, students may be well beyond graduation before faculty are ready to publish. Additionally,

Table 7.7. Comparison of faculty and student observations on gains in skills (share of observations).

Type of Observation	% Faculty Observations (n = 174)	% Student Observations (n = 214)
Communication skills		
Improvement of presentation skills/ability to defend oral argument	37	36
Improvement of writing skills	8	7
Subtotal	45	43
Other		
Lab/field skills: instrumentation, measurement, technical skills	32	22
Computer skills	8	9
Work organization skills: time management, note taking	5	11
Reading comprehension skills	4	8
Collaborative working skills	3	5
Subtotal	52	55
Total comparative observations	97	98
Noncomparable student observations on gains in their skills		
Information retrieval (library/Internet research skills)		2
Noncomparable faculty observations on students' gains in skills		
Communication skills: communicating "science," generally (not related to presenting/oral argument, writing, teaching others)	3	

Note: Percentages do not sum to 100 due to rounding.

helping students to learn professional writing skills requires more time and effort than is possible during the available 10 weeks.

Gains in other skills. Gains in laboratory techniques and learning instrumentation were noted among the highest skill gains by both faculty and students. Gains in computer skills are reported in lower numbers by faculty and students: Both groups commonly describe having to learn software programs used for modeling, analyses, or presentations, or learning programming languages. Smaller numbers of observations offered by faculty and students described increases in students' ability to manage their time effectively, comprehend and critique literature, and work collaboratively. A few students added as a gain learning how to do library, Internet, and database searches to find information.

CONCLUSIONS

The comparative analysis of data from the faculty advisor interviews with that from the first student researcher interviews produced strong concurrence on the extent and nature of UR benefits. First, there was a high level of agreement between students and faculty that the UR experience was highly beneficial: 90% of faculty and 92% of students' evaluative observations contained accounts of specific gains from UR participation.

Second, faculty observations on student gains from UR also correspond strongly with those described by students. No major types of gains were identified by faculty that we did not also find among students in our earlier published analysis (Seymour et al., 2004). This finding encourages us to think that the range and type of student gains that we have identified in the context of liberal arts college summer UR programs are qualitatively valid.

We also found a high degree of congruence between faculty and student benefits, both in broad statements and in the detail offered. The categories that we labeled "Thinking like a scientist," "Becoming a scientist," and "Personal-professional gains" are notably interdependent and reciprocal. Taken together, these three categories account for 62% of all gains observations offered by faculty and by students. Thus almost two thirds of the gains statements reported by faculty and students describe growth in understanding both salient areas of science and how to apply knowledge to the professional practice of science; concomitant development of students' confidence and competence in doing research; personal growth in the attitudes, behaviors, and temperament required in a researcher; and the beginnings of identification with and bonding to science as an enterprise. Faculty accounts of student gains emphasize even more clearly than did student reports the critical role played by UR experiences in helping students find themselves as young scientists. Both faculty and student observations affirm UR as an intellectual-experiential process: It provides students a hands-on learning experience of what it is to do science, and to some degree, to develop a more complex understanding of the nature of science. Our findings support recommendations by the Boyer Commission Report (2001) and funding agencies and organizations promoting college science education (National Science Foundation, 2000, 2003; National Research Council, 1999, 2000, 2003a, 2003b) that UR in this type of program is (as many faculty claim, but few studies have documented) an ideal way to learn science. These UR programs provided a learning context that affords the opportunity for personal growth and self-understanding that Baxter-Magolda (1991) describes as "self-authorship."[6] As we concluded in our first article (Seymour et al., 2004), to focus on institutional and extrinsic measures of success for UR, rather than on students' personal, intellectual, and professional growth, is missing the point.

Although there were no categories of gains identified by faculty that were not also identified by students, faculty and students explained the significance of particular gains differently; that is, drawing on different time frames and from perspectives shaped by their experiences, priorities, career focus, and life stages. The divergence of ways in which faculty and students valued UR was particularly sharp in the category of observations that we labeled "Becoming a scientist." Each subset of observations in this category is distinctively framed. The interview data that inform this account were gathered as students were finishing their 10-week intensive UR experience and about to enter their senior year. Students' dominant focus on the decisions and life transitions lying just ahead of them is evident in the ways in which they evaluated the UR experience. The prominence among students of the "Personal-professional" category of benefits reflects their focus on their own processes of growth and their uncertainties about the future. Their emphasis on the transferable nature of many benefits also reflects that they are in a life stage when career options are open.

Faculty advisors report the progress and growth of their current crop of summer researchers, but their evaluation statements also reflect their own professional goals and cumulative experiences as advisors to many students over time. Because they remain in touch with many former research students and often continue to play a role in their career development, they understand the longer-term significance of particular growth signs from early encounters with authentic research. They assess the collective effects of UR over time for all of their student researchers, not just for individual, outstanding ones. Embedded in faculty observations are evidence both of their intrinsic pleasure in seeing the growth of their young researchers and of their perspectives as educators, scholars, professional scientists, and mentors. As teachers, they foster students' intellectual growth and maturity as young colleagues. As scholars, they count as coups achievements such as conference presentations, coauthorship on published work, and the career success of particular students because these have significance for their own professional reputation and progress. As scientists and mentors, they share a professional responsibility to recruit and support potential scientists and, accordingly, look for and encourage in their student researchers indicators of an aptitude for research work and the kinds of thinking it demands.

The findings of our study thus far strongly underwrite the faith that faculty, institutions, and UR program funders have placed in the value of UR experiences for science students. However, our findings place more emphasis on intrinsic, educational, and professional benefits and less on extrinsic and institutional gains than may be found in some institutional claims for their UR programs. Our hope is that these findings will enable some common agreement as to what constitutes "success" in UR and lead to better documentation of the success of any particular UR program.

ACKNOWLEDGMENTS

This research was sponsored in part by NSF-ROLE grant (#NSF PR REC-0087611): "Pilot Study to Establish the Nature and Impact of Effective Undergraduate Research Experiences on Learning, Attitudes and Career Choice"; and Howard Hughes Medical Institute Special Projects Grant, "Establishing the Processes and Mediating Factors that Contribute to Significant Outcomes in Undergraduate Research Experiences for Both Students and Faculty: A Second Stage Study."

NOTES

1. An extensive review and discussion of the literature on UR is presented in Seymour et al., 2004.

2. The protocol is available by e-mail request to the authors via abhunter@colorado.edu

3. The placement of 85 comments both in the "Becoming a scientist" and the "Personal-professional gains" categories increases the percentage of students' observations on their UR gains to 92% of all student observations. In Seymour et al. (2004), this was originally reported as 91%. For a detailed description of how student gains were recategorized in the comparative analysis, see Hunter, Laursen, & Seymour (2006), the paper on which this chapter is based.

4. Because student mentions of these accomplishments were framed in terms of gains in confidence and feeling like a scientist, not in terms of how these helped to prepare them for the future, these observations were counted in the "Personal-professional gains" category and thus are not listed in Table 7.6.

5. In our third-round interviews with students we are checking to see if this is the case.

6. In Hunter, Laursen, and Seymour (2007), we discuss the apprentice-style model of UR as a community of practice and processes of students' professional socialization based on these comparative findings.

REFERENCES

Adhikari, N., & Nolan, D. (2002). "But what good came of it at last?": How to assess the value of undergraduate research. *Notices of the AMS, 49*(10), 1252–1257.

Barlow, A., & Villarejo, M. (2004). Making a difference for minorities: Evaluation of an educational enrichment program. *Journal of Research in Science Teaching, 41*(9), 861–881.

Bauer, K. W., & Bennett, J. S. (2003). Alumni perceptions used to assess undergraduate research experience. *Journal of Higher Education, 74*(2), 210–230.

Baxter-Magolda, M. (1991). *Making their own way: Narratives for transforming higher education to promote self-development.* Sterling, VA: Stylus.

Berger, P. L., & Luckman, T. (1967). *The social construction of reality.* London: Penguin Press.

Blumer, H. (1969). *Symbolic interactionism: Perspectives and methods.* Englewood Cliffs, NJ: Prentice Hall.

Boyer Commission on Educating Undergraduates in the Research University. (2001). *Reinventing undergraduate education: Three years after the Boyer Report.* Retrieved January 4, 2008, from http://www.sunysb.edu/pres/pdfs/0210066-Boyer%20Report%20Final.pdf

Garfinkel, H. (1967). *Studies in ethnomethodology.* Englewood Cliffs, NJ: Prentice Hall.

Hathaway, R., Nagda, B., & Gregerman, S. (2002). The relationship of undergraduate research participation to graduate and professional educational pursuit: An empirical study. *Journal of College Student Development, 43*(5), 614–631.

Hunter, A.-B., Laursen, S. L., & Seymour, E. (2006, February 10–11). Benefits of participating in undergraduate research in science: A comparative analysis of student and faculty perceptions. Paper presented at To Think and Act Like a Scientist conference at Texas Tech University, Lubbock, TX.

Hunter, A.-B., Laursen, S. L., & Seymour, E. (2007). Becoming a scientist: The role of undergraduate research in students' cognitive, personal, and professional development. *Science Education, 91*(1), 36–74.

Kardash, C. M. (2000). Evaluation of an undergraduate research experience: Perceptions of undergraduate interns and their faculty mentors. *Journal of Educational Psychology, 92*(1), 191–201.

Lopatto, D. (2004). Survey of undergraduate research experiences (SURE): First findings. *Cell Biology Education, 3*, 270–277.

Mead, G. M. (1934). *Mind, self, and society.* Chicago: University Press of Chicago.

Nagda, B. A., Gregerman, S. R., Jonides, J., von Hippel, W., & Lerner, J. S. (1998). Undergraduate student-faculty research partnerships affect student retention. *Review of Higher Education, 22*(1), 55–72.

National Research Council. Committee on Undergraduate Science Education. (1999). *Transforming undergraduate education in science, mathematics, engineering and technology.* Washington, DC: National Academy Press.

National Research Council. Committee on Developments in the Science of Learning and Committee on Learning Research and Educational Practice. (2000). *How people learn: Brain, mind, experience, and school* (expanded ed.). Washington, DC: National Academy Press.

National Research Council. Committee on Undergraduate Biology Education to Prepare Research Scientists for the 21st Century. (2003a). *BIO 2010: Transforming undergraduate education for future research biologists,* Washington, DC: National Academies Press.

National Research Council. Committee on Recognizing, Evaluating, Rewarding, and Developing Excellence in Teaching of Undergraduate Science, Mathematics, Engineering, and Technology. (2003b). *Evaluating and improving undergraduate teach-*

ing in science, technology, engineering, and mathematics. Washington, DC: National Academies Press.

National Science Foundation. (2000). *NSF GPRA Strategic Plan, FY 2002–2006* (NSF Publication 0104). Washington, DC: Author. Retrieved October 25, 2007, from http://www.nsf.gov/pubs/2001/nsf0104/start.htm

National Science Foundation. (2003, March 30–April 1). *Exploring the concept of undergraduate research centers: A report on the NSF workshop*. Arlington, VA: Author.

Rauckhorst, W. H. (2001, July). *Measuring the impact of the undergraduate research experience on student intellectual development*. Paper presented at Project Kaleidoscope Summer Institute, Snowbird, UT.

Russell, S. H. (2005, November). *Evaluation of NSF support for undergraduate research opportunities: Survey of STEM graduates*. Contributors C. Ailes, M. Hancock, J. McCullough, J. D. Roessner, and C. Storey. (Draft Final Report to the NSF.) Menlo Park, CA: SRI International. Retrieved February 19, 2006, from http://www.sri.com/policy/csted/reports/university/index.html#urostem.

Schutz, A., & Luckman, T. (1974). *The structures of the life world*. London: Heinemann.

Seidel, J. V. (1998). The Ethnograph: A program for the computer-assisted analysis of text-based data (Version 5.0) [Computer software]. Thousand Oaks, CA: Qualis Research; distributed by SCOLARI Sage Publications Software.

Seymour, E., Hunter, A.-B., Laursen, S. L., & DeAntoni, T. (2004). Establishing the benefits of research experiences for undergraduates in the sciences: First findings from a three-year study. *Science Education, 88*(4), 493–534.

Ward, C., Bennett, J., & Bauer, K. (2002). *Content analysis of undergraduate research student evaluations*. Retrieved March 10, 2005, from http://www.udel.edu/RAIRE/content.pdf

Zydney, A. L., Bennett, J. S., Shahid, A., & Bauer, K. W. (2002). Impact of undergraduate research experience in engineering. *Journal of Engineering Education, 91*(2), 151–157.

Critical Factors in the Undergraduate Research Experience

Roman Taraban, Eric Prensky, and Craig W. Bowen

OVER THE LAST 40 years, a commitment to science and the methods of scientific discovery has permeated all levels of instruction, from the elementary to postsecondary grade levels. The National Research Council (NRC, 2003), National Science Foundation (NSF, 1996, 2003), and Research Corporation (Doyle, 2000) recommend that *all* undergraduate students be encouraged to pursue research projects, and that they get involved in research as early as practicable in their school programs. This has been achieved, in part, through research-based teaching (Gavin, 2000), and by getting students to work on research projects in lab and field settings under the guidance of faculty mentors (Vesilind, 2001) beginning as early as their freshman and sophomore years (Boyer Commission on Educating Undergraduates in the Research University, 1998; Chaplin, Manske, & Cruise, 1998; Hutchison & Atwood, 2002; Spilich, 1997). A "sustaining relationship" (NRC, 2003, p. 17) with a faculty mentor is effective in integrating undergraduate students into the culture of science. Engaging in research activities is regarded as the "key determinant" (NSF, 2003) in drawing students to science careers. From a pedagogical view, mentoring students in the laboratory has been described as "the purest form of teaching" (NRC, 2003, p. 87). This chapter focuses on the development of science-oriented thinking and scientific-inquiry skills at the undergraduate level. The range of activities that draw undergraduate students into the contemporary culture of science and integrate them more fully into the practice of inquiry and research will be termed the undergraduate research experience (URE).

All UREs are not the same. The general degree requirements at the college level often require students to take two or more courses in science that include a lab experience. In this context, students are exposed to the scientific method and carry out predictable experiments, in a manner consistent with elementary and secondary science curricula (O'Neill & Polman, 2004). We will refer to this as the *exposure* condition. In another variant, students may get involved in individual research projects. Nikolova Eddins and Williams (1997) describe this situation as a *traditional* undergraduate research experience involving a one-on-one relationship between a motivated student and faculty member. Early in the experience, the student assists in rudimentary tasks, over time is given greater responsibility, and eventually may develop an individual project. Under this model, the student may gain valuable experience that looks good on a résumé, but the experience lacks "sustained learning and research opportunities" (p. 81). Often, no final product emerges from the effort, either for the student or faculty member. An *ideal* URE differs from the traditional kind in several ways (Howard Hughes Medical Institute, 1997; NRC, 2003; Nikolova Eddins & Williams, 1997). Students work collaboratively in faculty-student research groups. They develop domain knowledge, appropriate research methods, and research questions, partly through course work and partly through their interactions in a research group. Students are engaged in research over an extended period of time, and experience multiple and diverse learning and research opportunities that include many hands-on activities. The ideal URE changes the academic culture in which students learn. As Nikolova Eddins and Williams describe, "it is designed to be a regular and integral part of the students' lives and is organically connected with the undergraduate curriculum" (p. 84). The ideal experience is intense, sustained, coherent, and collaborative.

This chapter considers the nature and characteristics of research opportunities that students experience across a continuum of kinds of experiences, from exposure experiences that are offered through regular college curricula to ideal experiences gained through research apprenticeships. The overall goal of this research was to measure gains undergraduates made in learning the norms and practices of scientific research and discourse. We began by identifying critical elements of a successful undergraduate research experience, using interview data from undergraduates participating in ideal research experiences. These data formed a framework for construction of a questionnaire for assessing student gains in learning science. We then used the questionnaire to examine changes in science knowledge and skill across time. We also examined correlations between growth of knowledge and skills with specific academic factors and experiences. We hypothesized that traditional venues like the classroom build knowledge required for active participation in knowledge-producing practices in specific domains, and that students excel when placed in "rich social, cultural, and material environments" (Nersessian, 2005, p. 18) that enable them to learn and contribute to the norms and practices of a research community.

DEVELOPING THE UNDERGRADUATE RESEARCH QUESTIONNAIRE

In order to develop items appropriate for a questionnaire that could be used with a broad college population, we drew on the experiences of science majors who were involved in laboratory research, specifically students in the Texas Tech University Howard Hughes Medical Institute (TTU/HHMI) Undergraduate Science Education Program. The TTU/HHMI program exemplifies one variant of an ideal URE. Research scholars commit to projects through mutual agreement with faculty mentors. They spend 10–20 hours each week in a lab during regular semesters and 40 hours each week during the summer. Their commitments to research projects extend over periods of 1 to 3 years. Throughout the URE, there is a great deal of collaboration with mentors and peers. Research scholars are encouraged to present their research findings at university-sponsored research conferences, and they are provided with support to travel to professional conferences to make presentations and interact with professional colleagues. The program includes academic enrichment activities, such as hosting scientists from off campus to interact with the research scholars. It provides scholars with numerous opportunities for community service, including science education outreach activities. Overall, the program is oriented toward building knowledge, skills, and confidence among the scholars, but also increasing camaraderie among them and preparing them for graduate school in academic research areas. (Additional information about the program can be obtained via the internet at http://www.ciser.ttu.edu/hhmit).

We reasoned that data from interviews of TTU/HHMI scholars about their research experiences could be used to develop a questionnaire because their experiences incorporated all the known elements of an ideal research experience and thus their comments about research would provide an inclusive set of statements about the undergraduate research experience. We further reasoned that these students had sufficient exposure to science and research to allow them to verbalize their experiences with a reasonable measure of clarity and confidence, thereby providing additional support for using their verbal data as the basis for the questionnaire. However, because the questionnaire was meant to be used with a broad range of students, we ultimately sought to select items that would make sense to undergraduates at all levels of UREs at different institutions.

The questionnaire was developed through several iterations. As part of formative evaluations of the program that were completed prior to the present study, Bowen (1999, 2003) interviewed TTU/HHMI research scholars. Scholars' responses to focused interview questions were developed into a preliminary questionnaire consisting of 178 statements that described all the distinct aspects of academic life mentioned by these scholars. In the first iteration of development, the questionnaire was administered to 348 undergraduate volunteers. According to normal practice, the sample size was small given the number of variables. However, because we had set a high criterion for factor loadings on problem variables, and because we were expecting a modest number of factors (between

5 and 10), the sample size was justified (for additional details on sample size, see MacCallum, Widaman, Zhang, & Hong, 1999; Tabachnick & Fidell, 2001).

The participants were recruited through the Psychology Department subject pool, which draws on undergraduates from nearly every discipline and every level at the university, and participated for course extra credit. Self-reported demographic data indicated that 211 (60.9%) participants were female and 137 (39.4%) were male, and 70 distinct college majors were represented, with three majors accounting for about half of the total (Psychology 28.1%, Biology 10.6%, and Cell and Molecular Biology 9.0%). Regarding class level, 198 (56.9%) were freshman, 84 (24.0%) were sophomores, and the remainder were juniors and above.

In this round of data collection, and all that follow, the questions were presented via computer in random order, and responses were made using a 5-point Likert-type scale (*I agree with the statement* 1: not at all, 2: barely, 3: on average, 4: very much, 5: extremely) and were automatically stored on a computer server for later analysis. The instructions presented on the computer indicated that the purpose of the survey was to collect information on student experiences with college life, research, and academics in general. At the conclusion of the questionnaire, participants completed several demographic items.

The data were independently analyzed by the three authors, according to the following steps and criteria. Exploratory factor analysis, using a principal component method, was used to reduce the number of questionnaire items. The principal component analysis applied Varimax rotation with Kaiser normalization, which is an orthogonal rotation method that simplifies the interpretation of the factors and is commonly used for data like these (Tabachnick & Fidell, 2001). Decisions about items to retain were the result of mutual agreement among the three authors. Several criteria were used: Items had to have a high loading on one factor and low loadings on the other factors; the factors had to be interpretable; and the items were selected to cover different aspects of a construct (e.g., feedback on writing, feedback on oral presentations) in order to maintain the general utility of the instrument. The number of factors to retain was based on the Kaiser criterion (eigenvalues > 1) and an examination of the scree plot. These criteria reduced the number of questionnaire items to 38.

In a second iteration, participants were recruited and compensated in the same manner as the previous group. Self-reported demographic data for the 323 participants indicated that 161 (49.8%) were female, 162 (50.2%) were male, 212 (65.6%) were freshman, 73 (22.6%) were sophomores, and the remainder were juniors and above. Data were collected as in the first iteration. By applying the same criteria for the assignment of items to factors, six additional items were eliminated, resulting in a final instrument with 32 items representing five factors. The analysis of the 5-factor structure with 32 items yielded factors with eigenvalues equal to 8.93, 3.22, 2.10, 1.82, and 1.51, an inflection point in the scree plot between the fifth and sixth factors (sixth factor eigenvalue = 1.05), and accounted for 54.89% of the variance. The scales, item loadings, and communalities are displayed in Table 8.1. An analysis

Table 8.1. The 32 items included in the final version of the URQ, organized by scales.

	F1	F2	F3	F4	F5	CM
Research Mindset						
Due to my experience conducting research, I want to pursue a career in science.	**.785**	.014	.150	.000	.107	.650
My motivation to pursue a science career has increased.	**.789**	.172	.345	.148	.261	.655
It is important to be excited about science.	**.763**	-.003	.209	.152	.076	.589
I am more interested in research due to my research experience.	**.798**	.179	.408	.290	.253	.501
The academic environment I am in encourages me to consider a research career.	**.733**	.145	.170	.147	.026	.490
My research experience has helped me think more scientifically.	**.750**	-.019	.357	.267	.192	.528
Doing research is an important part of my undergraduate experience.	**.603**	.241	.252	.045	.117	.418
My self-confidence has increased due to my involvement in research.	**.685**	.380	.429	.221	.304	.366
Faculty Support						
A faculty member has encouraged me to excel in my course work.	.164	**.782**	.011	.080	.070	.650
I received academic support from a faculty mentor.	.291	**.796**	.149	.260	.280	.627
A faculty member encouraged me in my academic goals.	.074	**.750**	.128	.034	.204	.673
A faculty member has been a good role model for me.	.245	**.780**	.242	.227	.388	.571
It has been easy to discuss ideas about career options with a faculty member.	.149	**.742**	-.039	.217	.228	.480
It is easy to discuss ideas in my area of study with a faculty member.	.304	**.803**	.121	.395	.432	.451
A faculty member has given me useful feedback about my writing.	.166	**.718**	.016	.121	.115	.441

176

	F1	F2	F3	F4	F5	CM
Research Methods						
I can design experiments.	.286	.076	**.747**	−.009	.072	.651
	.469	.208	**.796**	.140	.210	
I troubleshoot experiments.	.247	.140	**.735**	.124	.022	.637
	.451	.275	**.792**	.267	.189	
I understand how to report experimental results.	.133	.170	**.720**	.097	.106	.586
	.354	.295	**.757**	.238	.248	
Generating hypotheses is something I can do.	.155	.009	**.685**	.055	.069	.501
	.331	.128	**.704**	.163	.172	
Data analysis is something I can do.	.269	.080	**.685**	.073	.045	.555
	.447	.212	**.740**	.207	.189	
Carrying out experiments is something I can do.	.169	.016	**.644**	.187	.087	.486
	.357	.159	**.684**	.290	.209	
Academic Mindset						
Being efficient in my academic work is something I have learned.	.166	.103	.021	**.719**	.230	.608
	.316	.295	.167	**.763**	.379	
Balancing my class schedule with other obligations is something I have learned.	.007	.199	.077	**.715**	.043	.559
	.165	.331	.176	**.736**	.200	
I have better time-management skills.	.099	.042	.161	**.714**	.087	.555
	.255	.213	.265	**.734**	.231	
I have become more independent academically.	.049	.119	.118	**.695**	.125	.529
	.213	.279	.221	**.723**	.268	
I have developed a routine for completing my schoolwork.	.178	.241	.074	**.685**	.129	.581
	.339	.409	.223	**.752**	.316	
I have become more academically responsible.	.291	.291	.072	**.654**	.023	.603
	.430	.448	.242	**.734**	.242	
Peer Support						
Other students have encouraged me to excel in my course work.	.055	.099	.105	.203	**.716**	.578
	.235	.283	.206	.326	**.747**	
Other students have helped me clarify my professional goals.	.178	.208	.090	−.019	**.713**	.592
	.329	.364	.210	.150	**.756**	
Other students have been good role models for me.	.204	.096	.016	.203	**.670**	.541
	.345	.285	.153	.332	**.721**	
I have received academic support from students in my major.	.080	.159	.120	.129	**.657**	.494
	.250	.321	.220	.265	**.699**	
Fellow students gave me useful feedback about my oral presentations.	.184	.263	.036	.066	**.555**	.417
	.317	.397	.161	.217	**.627**	

Notes: First row of each item shows factor pattern and communalities based on principal component analysis using Varimax rotation with Kaiser normalization; second row shows factor structure based on principal component analysis using Promax rotation with Kaiser normalization. F1–F5 = Factor 1–Factor 5 correlations between factors and variables, respectively. CM = communalities. The highest correlation coefficients are shown in boldface.

using Promax (oblique) rotation was also conducted. Item loadings for this analysis, which allows for correlations between factors, are also included in Table 8.1. The factor correlations from the oblique rotation, shown in Table 8.2, indicate moderate correlations between factors, suggesting that these elements of students' academic experience are related. Cronbach's alpha coefficients were computed for each scale (defined in the next section)—for Research Mindset (α = .86), for Faculty Support (α = .86), for Academic Mindset (α = .84), for Research Methods (α = .84), and for Peer Support (α = .76)—and confirmed that the scales had high internal consistency.

FACTORS IN THE UNDERGRADUATE RESEARCH EXPERIENCE

The factor analyses provided five scales for measuring undergraduate research experiences. These scales form the basis for the Undergraduate Research Questionnaire (URQ). The most general scale is *Academic Mindset*, which reflects students' skills in organizing their academic lives in effective and efficient ways, and dispositions toward academic responsibility and independence. Two scales are directly related to research. The first, *Research Mindset*, reflects students' excitement about science, confidence in their ability to think like scientists, self-confidence in conducting research and a commitment to research, and enthusiasm for science careers. The second, *Research Methods*, expresses students' confidence in their ability to design experiments, generate hypotheses, carry out experiments, analyze data, and report experimental results. The final two scales capture the social nature of learning and doing science. The *Faculty Support* scale highlights the role of teachers and mentors in providing role models for students, for encouraging them in their course work and academic goals, for providing feedback, and

Table 8.2. Correlations between factors based on principal component analysis with Promax rotation.

	1	2	3	4	5
1 Research Mindset	1.00	.36	.50	.35	.40
2 Faculty Support		1.00	.28	.41	.45
3 Research Methods			1.00	.28	.26
4 Academic Mindset				1.00	.34
5 Peer Support					1.00

being available to discuss students' major areas of study and career options. The *Peer Support* scale emphasizes a role for peers that mirrors the supportive roles of teachers and mentors.

CASE STUDY: ASSESSING DIFFERENCES IN UNDERGRADUATE RESEARCH EXPERIENCES

The goals of this case study were twofold. One was related to academic development: We asked if there was an increase in the strength of the five URQ factors over the course of students' undergraduate years. The second goal was to identify the academic activities and contexts that were correlated with growth in URQ factors. Because skill develops through meaningful practice, collaboration, and engagement with problems in the domain (Ericsson, 2002; VanLehn, 1996), we predicted that academic level and the intensity of students' research exposure would be associated with the depth and quality of their research experience, as indicted by the URQ scales.

Materials, Participants and Procedure

The materials were the 32-item URQ, demographic questions, and questions requesting estimates of academic behaviors and outcomes (cf. Tables 8.3 and 8.4). The 32 items were presented in random order, followed by the demographic items. Participants also provided estimates of behaviors (e.g., conducting research, meeting with faculty mentor and other students, and interest in applying to graduate schools), for the semester in which the questionnaire was completed; these items were presented to each student in a different random order.

Participants were recruited through upper-level life sciences and psychology courses, and through the TTU/HHMI program. Additional participants were recruited through general psychology, as in the previous studies. Across all cases, the recruitment procedure was uniform, participation was voluntary, and participants were compensated through extra course or lab credit. Demographic data indicated that 125 (67%) were female and 61 (33%) were male; 26 (14%) were freshman, 29 (16%) were sophomores, and the remainder were juniors and above. Seventy-five percent of the participants were classified as majoring in a discipline that involved experimental research (e.g., microbiology, chemistry, psychology). The remaining participants represented majors like business, political science, and Spanish. The 186 participants received the questionnaire by e-mail and submitted their responses by replying to the e-mail. Overall earned credit hours, credit hours for courses with a lab component, and SAT Verbal, Math, and Composite scores were obtained from students' transcripts.

A Confirmatory Analysis of the URQ

Prior to addressing the primary questions in this study, a confirmatory analysis was conducted using structural equation modeling through the EQS program (Byrne, 1994). This test was important before proceeding with the remaining analyses because of the shift in the sample from a largely freshman-sophomore cohort in the exploratory studies to a junior-senior cohort in the present study. Russell (see Chapter 4) has shown that the larger proportion of undergraduate researchers are juniors and seniors, therefore, we wanted to test whether the URQ, which was developed predominantly with freshman-sophomore cohorts would apply to a sample that better approximated the population of undergraduates who participated in research. A confirmation of the URQ item assignments would indicate that the model is robust across samples of students.

Structural equation modeling requires that the patterns of variable and factor relations be specified a priori in the form of hypotheses, which are then tested statistically, either confirming or disconfirming the hypothesized variable and factor relations. Variables in this analysis were the URQ statements. Variables were linked to factors, as indicated in Table 8.1, with each item assigned to a single factor, except for the item, "My research experience has helped me think more scientifically," which was linked to the factors Research Mindset and Research Methods, due to a loading > 0.30 to the latter factor in the orthogonal rotation. Because the factors were partially correlated (see Table 8.2), the factors were allowed to covary in the EQS model. The two critical outcomes in the first pass were a comparative fit index (CFI) = .901 and root mean-square error of approximation (RMSEA) = .059 (confidence interval: 0.051, 0.066), both which indicated an acceptable fit to the hypothesized model (Byrne, 1998). The CFI improved to 0.908, and the RMSEA to 0.056 (confidence interval: 0.049, 0.064) after implementing one suggestion generated by the EQS program for allowing an additional URQ statement to covary with another factor ("Fellow students gave me useful feedback about my oral presentations" with the Faculty Support factor).

The Impact of Academic Level and Scholastic Ability on URQ Factors

Skill acquisition theory predicts that skill develops over time through experience and practice. To test this possibility, completed college credits and credit hours in courses with labs were correlated with URQ factor scores. Because skill acquisition can be affected in small part by talent or ability (Ericsson & Lehmann, 1996), the associations between SAT-Verbal, SAT-Math, and SAT-Composite scores with the URQ factors were also considered. Factor scores were calculated for each student by summing the ratings for the questions for each factor and dividing by the number of questions for that factor. We chose to use Spearman (ρ) nonparametric correlation tests (Conover, 1999) in our analysis because Kolmogorov-Smirnov tests for normality (SPSS, 2004) indicated that for many of the variables the normality assumption required for parametric correlations was violated. Because the Spearman test overcomes these violations through a rank-order method, we decided to consistently apply nonparametric tests for our analyses.

Before conducting the analyses, it was important to review the URQ questions in order to ascertain the implications of significant correlations, should they be found. All the URQ statements are worded in an active form—*I want to . . . , has helped me . . . , I can . . .* Many of the statements are worded in an active form that includes change—*my motivation has increased . . . , I am more interested. . . .* If participants' agreement ratings for the statements capture fixed traits, abilities, or dispositions, factor scores would not correlate with academic level. On the other hand, positive correlations with earned credits would suggest that as a student progresses through the curriculum, he or she perceives gains in particular abilities or dispositions. As shown in Table 8.3, there were significant positive associations between completed college credits and Research Mindset, Research Methods, and Peer Support. The correlation with Research Mindset reflects the association between students' overall earned college credits and their excitement about science, confidence in their ability to think like scientists, self-confidence in conducting research and a commitment to research, and enthusiasm for science careers. The correlation with Research Methods reflects the association of earned credits with students' confidence in their ability to design experiments, generate hypotheses, carry out experiments, analyze data, and report experimental results. The correlation with Peer Support indicates an association between earned credits and academic supports provided through interactions and collaborations with peers. A further examination of Table 8.3 shows that the correlations with URQ factors are even stronger when one considers credit hours for courses with labs. This suggests that the number of courses

Table 8.3. Spearman correlations (ρ) between student descriptors and URQ factors.

	M	SD	Research Mindset	Faculty Support	Research Methods	Academic Mindset	Peer Support
Completed college credits	79.13	41.65	.22**	.09	.25**	.08	.18*
Credits for courses with labs	7.12	9.60	.38***	.06	.26**	.06	.20**
SAT-Verbal	532.03	84.71	.16*	.09	.14	−.04	−.15
SAT-Math	543.60	91.03	.14	.10	.14	.01	−.05
SAT-Composite	1076.57	159.32	.16*	.09	.14	−.02	−.13

Notes: $N = 172$ for SAT correlations; $N = 181$ for credits correlations.
* $p < .05$, two-tailed. ** $p < .01$, two-tailed. *** $p < .001$, two-tailed.

with labs that a student has completed may be a better indicator of research-related factors than overall college credits. SAT scores were weakly correlated with a single factor—Research Mindset—which suggests that ability measures taken in high school may lose their predictive capacity as students progress through the undergraduate curriculum.

The Impact of Students' Current Situation on URQ Factors

The questionnaire also asked students to report on their current learning context. (See Table 8.4 for the questions.) Five of the six questions began with "This semester, I anticipate that I will . . ." and requested quantitative estimates of activities that were considered central to an ideal research experience (see Bauer & Bennett, Chapter 5; also Bauer & Bennett, 2003; Boyer Commission on Educating Undergraduates in the Research University, 1998; Chaplin et al., 1998; Gavin, 2000; Howard Hughes Medical Institute, 1997; Hutchison & Atwood, 2002; Kardash, 2000; Kremer & Bringle, 1990; NRC, 2000, 2003; Nikolova Eddins & Williams, 1997; Shellito, Shea, Weissmann, Mueller-Solger, & Davis, 2001; Vesilind, 2001). The use of the wording "anticipate that I will" was used to allow students to think broadly about the semester when making their estimates. The sixth question was about prospective graduate study, which is also considered part of a successful research experience.

Table 8.4 shows significant positive correlations between the URQ factors and time spent working in a laboratory, time spent doing research, number of meetings with faculty mentors, number of meetings with peers, and number of papers and posters being prepared for a conference. Very clearly, the number of hours working in a laboratory was the strongest associate of the URQ factors. This suggests that the strongest immediate factor contributing to students' research mindset, research skills, and perceived academic support from faculty and peers is associated with active participation in a research laboratory. The positive direction of the correlation indicates that the higher the lab hours the stronger the association with these URQ factors. The strong correlations overall support claims in the literature about the benefits of research experiences. They also provide support for the construct validity of the URQ.

The one factor that was not significantly correlated in these tests, or those involving credits and SAT scores, was academic mindset. Interestingly, this is not because students consider themselves weak on organizing their academic lives in effective and efficient ways, nor in their dispositions toward academic responsibility and independence. To the contrary, mean ratings for this factor ($M = 3.82$) were the highest of all. Whether this is due to good academic management skills upon entry to college or very early development of these skills in college is not clear. In any case, the correlation patterns indicate that academic management skills are not associated with the emergence of research ability and mindset over time.

Table 8.4. Spearman correlations (ρ) between questionnaire statements and URQ factors.

Statement	Research Mindset	Faculty Support	Research Methods	Academic Mindset	Peer Support
This semester, I anticipate that I will . . .					
conduct research in a laboratory __ hours per week.	.62***	.32***	.38***	.06	.23**
spend approximately __ hours per week conducting research.	.58***	.35***	.31***	.11	.19*
meet with my faculty mentor __ times per week to discuss ideas.	.50***	.50***	.31***	.12	.20**
meet with other students __ times per week to discuss ideas.	.24**	.22**	.14	.09	.36***
work on __ paper or poster presentations for a conference.	.25**	.27***	.16*	.12	.05
I am considering __ schools for graduate work or advanced training.	.33***	.30***	.23**	.03	.23**

Notes: $N = 186$.
* $p < .05$, two-tailed. ** $p < .01$, two-tailed. *** $p < .001$, two-tailed.

THE BENEFITS OF RESEARCH ACROSS A CONTINUUM OF EXPERIENCES

The Undergraduate Research Questionnaire (URQ) was developed from the formative analyses of Bowen (1999, 2003) who interviewed students engaged in intense research experiences in the sciences. The URQ measures college students' perceptions of their academic and research experiences. It is presently the only available instrument that affords a uniform basis for quantifying students' research knowledge and experiences across a broad range of learning contexts, from exposure experiences in traditional classroom instruction to intense research in ideal settings, like summer and year-round internships.

Exploratory and confirmatory factor analyses indicated five factors as discriminating constructs in the undergraduate experience. These are Research Mindset, Faculty Support, Research Methods, Academic Mindset, and Peer Support. Research Mindset accounted for the greatest proportion of variance in the exploratory factor analyses, and on that basis was the most significant factor. The remaining factors accounted for progressively less variance, as indicated in the order presented here. The URE identifies critical dimensions of the undergraduate experience that are consistent with other studies (see Hunter et al., Chapter 7, and Lopatto, Chapter 6; also Kardash, 2000; Lopatto, 2003, 2004; Seymour, Hunter, Laursen, & DeAntoni, 2004), and makes explicit the dimensions along which students excel in an ideal research setting (Nikolova Eddins & Williams, 1997).

Skill development theories and contemporary views of the role of research in learning predict that students should differ in their knowledge of the norms and practices of science according to the extent and quality of their research experiences. Academic level was significantly correlated with higher scores for Research Mindset, Research Methods, and Peer Support. Even stronger correlations were uncovered when using credit hours for courses that included labs and students' self-reports of the number of hours they were working in labs during the semester in which they completed the questionnaire. Overall, our predictions that students farther along in the curriculum and those involved in intense research experiences would show greater evidence of URQ constructs was upheld for four of the five constructs. These outcomes are consistent with theories of skill acquisition (Ericsson, 2002; Ericsson & Lehmann, 1996; VanLehn, 1996) and sociocultural constructivism (Lave, 1991; Lave & Wenger, 1991).

These data also indicate that students have developed adaptive academic skills that may be a necessary precursor to participating in research experiences, but not connected directly to research practices. Strikingly, the ratings for Academic Mindset were over one standard deviation greater than the neutral rating of 3, suggesting that students either enter college with highly refined strategies for school success or develop them early in their college careers.

The time factor associated with UREs has been ignored in past studies. Kardash (2000), for instance, combined yearlong interns with summer interns in her analyses. Based on students' low ratings at the end of the experience for skills like identifying research questions and testing hypotheses, she concluded "that although UREs are clearly successful in enhancing a number of basic scientific skills, the evidence is less compelling that UREs are particularly successful at promoting the higher order inquiry skills that underlie the foundation of critical, scientific thinking" (p. 196). The positive correlations found here between URQ factors and academic level, lab course credits, and time working in a lab, suggest that the extent and nature of UREs must be considered when drawing conclusions about the success of experiences.

The present studies caution against defining the pathways to success in science too narrowly, namely, in terms of internships, research experience, and lab skills (cf. Kardash, 2000). Faculty and peer encouragement, feedback, and discussion may begin to develop in didactic contexts like the classroom and may set the stage for more intense experiences later on.

For purposes of developing curriculum, it may be more helpful to think of traditional students as on a continuum with those students engaged in intense research, rather than as a different kind of student. It may also be feasible for post-secondary institutions to use existing resources to create the physical conditions and the research opportunities that allow students to engage more fully in the authentic practices of inquiry and research. Models of such revised curricula have been described in a number of places in the literature (see Trosset et al., Chapter 3; also

Gavin, 2000; Gentile, 2000; Lichter, 2000; Lopatto, 2003; Spilich, 1997; Stewart, 2003).

Even though traditional learning contexts can lead to growth of knowledge of research norms and practices, we should not lose sight of the gains that are made through intense, directed practice. Students on a trajectory for graduate study and professional preparation should be made more cognizant of the benefits of a deep commitment to inquiry and research, vis-à-vis skill acquisition theory: "Until ordinary individuals recognize that sustained effort is required to reach expert performance, they will continue to misattribute lesser achievement to lack of natural gifts, and thus fail to reach their own potential" (Ericsson, 2002, p. 51).

The present research is limited by a methodology that relied on correlations and that did not collect multiple measures from the same students at different points in their undergraduate careers. We are assuming individual development by showing cohort differences, which is not as strong as repeated measures on individuals, but still provides supporting evidence. A particular interest from here forward is to learn more about the developmental transitions that take place over the course of sustained research experiences, in terms of changes in epistemic beliefs (Baxter-Magolda, 2004; Perry, 1970; Ryder, Leach, & Driver, 1999; Schraw, Bendixen, & Dunkle, 2002; Wickman, 2004), as well as in terms of learning specific norms and skills in the research contexts in which students find themselves. Data like these will provide a necessary dimension of knowledge about UREs and will further our understanding of how undergraduate research experiences change students' knowledge, dispositions, and behaviors.

ACKNOWLEDGMENT

This research was supported in part by a Howard Hughes Medical Institute grant through the Undergraduate Science Education Program to Texas Tech University.

REFERENCES

Baxter-Magolda, M. B. (2004). Evolution of a constructivist conceptualization of epistemological reflection. *Educational Psychologist, 39*(1), 31–42.

Bauer, K. W., & Bennett, J. S. (2003). Alumni perceptions used to assess undergraduate research experience. *Journal of Higher Education, 74*(2), 210–230.

Bowen, C. W. (1999). *Evaluation of the undergraduate research program of the Texas Tech University Howard Hughes Medical Institute Project.* Cofton, MD: Botz Education Group.

Bowen, C. W. (2003). *Evaluation of the undergraduate research fellows program of the Texas Tech University Howard Hughes Medical Institute Project.* Baltimore, MD: Botz Education Group.

Boyer Commission on Educating Undergraduates in the Research University. (1998). *Reinventing undergraduate education: A blueprint for America's research universities.* New York: Author.

Byrne, B. M. (1994). *Structural equation modeling with EQS and EQS/Windows: basic concepts, applications, and programming.* Thousand Oaks, CA: Sage.

Byrne, B. M. (1998). *Structural equation modeling with Lisrel, Prelis, and Simlis.* Mahwah, NJ: Erlbaum.

Chaplin, S. B., Manske, J. M., & Cruise, J. L. (1998). Introducing freshmen to investigative research: A course for biology majors at Minnesota's University of St. Thomas. *Journal of College Science Teaching, 27*(5), 347–350.

Conover, W. J. (1999). *Practical nonparametric statistics* (3rd ed.). New York: John Wiley.

Doyle, M. P. (Ed.). (2000). *Academic excellence.* Tucson, AZ: Research Corporation.

Ericsson, K. A. (2002). Attaining excellence through deliberate practice: Insights from the study of expert performance. In M. Ferrari (Ed.), *The pursuit of excellence through education* (pp. 21–55). Mahwah, NJ: Erlbaum.

Ericsson, K. A., & Lehmann, A. (1996). Expert and exceptional performance: Evidence of maximal adaptation to task constraints. *Annual Review of Psychology, 47,* 273–305.

Gavin, R. (2000). The role of research at undergraduate institutions: Why is it necessary to defend it? In M. P. Doyle (Ed.), *Academic excellence* (pp. 9–17). Tucson, AZ: Research Corporation.

Gentile, J. M. (2000). Then and now: A brief view of Hope College today. In M. P. Doyle (Ed.), *Academic excellence* (pp. 79–85). Tucson, AZ: Research Corporation.

Howard Hughes Medical Institute. (1997). *Assessing science pathways.* Chevy Chase, MD: Author.

Hutchison, A. R., & Atwood, D. A. (2002). Research with first- and second-year undergraduates: A new model for undergraduate inquiry at research universities. *Journal of Chemical Education, 79*(1), 125–126.

Kardash, C. M. (2000). Evaluation of an undergraduate research experience: Perceptions of undergraduate interns and their faculty mentors. *Journal of Educational Psychology, 92,* 191–201.

Kremer, J. F., & Bringle, R. G. (1990). The effects of an intensive research experience on the careers of talented undergraduates. *Journal of Research and Development in Education, 24*(1), 1–5.

Lave, J. (1991). Situating learning in communities of practice. In L. B. Resnick & J. M. Levine (Eds.), *Perspectives on socially shared cognition* (pp. 63–82). Washington, DC: American Psychological Association.

Lave, J., & Wenger, E. (1991). *Situated learning: Legitimate peripheral participation.* Cambridge, MA: Cambridge University Press.

Lichter, R. L. (2000). Research is important, but . . . In M. P. Doyle (Ed.), *Academic excellence* (pp. 41–54). Tucson, AZ: Research Corporation.

Lopatto, D. (2003). The essential features of undergraduate research. *Council on Undergraduate Research Quarterly, 24,* 139–142.

Lopatto, D. (2004). Survey of Undergraduate Research Experiences (SURE): First findings. *Cell Biology Education, 3,* 270–277.

MacCallum, R. C., Widaman, K. F., Zhang, S., & Hong, S. (1999). Sample size in factor analysis. *Psychological Methods*, *4*(1), 84–99.

National Research Council (NRC). Committee on the Development of an Addendum to the National Science Education Standards on Scientific Inquiry. (2000). *Inquiry and the national science education standards: A guide for teaching and learning*. Washington, DC: National Academy Press.

National Research Council (NRC). Committee on Undergraduate Biology Education to Prepare Research Scientists for the 21st Century. (2003). *BIO 2010: Transforming undergraduate education for future research biologists*. Washington, DC: National Academies Press.

National Science Foundation (NSF). (1996). *Shaping the future: New expectations for undergraduate education in science, mathematics, engineering and technology*. Washington, DC: Author.

National Science Foundation (NSF). (2003, March 30–April 1). *Exploring the concept of undergraduate research centers: A report on the NSF workshop*. Arlington, VA: Author.

Nersessian, N. J. (2005). Interpreting scientific and engineering practices: Integrating the cognitive, social, and cultural dimensions. In M. E. Gorman, R. D. Tweney, D. C. Gooding, & A. P. Kincannon (Eds.), *Scientific and technological thinking* (pp. 17–55). Mahwah, NJ: Erlbaum.

Nikolova Eddins, S. G., & Williams, D. F. (1997). Research-based learning for undergraduates: A model for merger of research and undergraduate education. *Journal on Excellence in College Teaching*, *8*(3), 77–94.

O'Neill, D. K., & Polman, J. L. (2004). Why educate "little scientists?" Examining the potential of practice-based scientific literacy. *Journal of Research in Science Teaching*, *41*(3), 234–266.

Perry, W. G. (1970). *Forms of intellectual and ethical development in the college years: A scheme*. New York: Holt, Rinehart, & Winston.

Ryder, J., Leach, J., & Driver, R. (1999). Undergraduate science students' images of science. *Journal of Research in Science Teaching*, *36*, 201–219.

Schraw, G., Bendixen, L. D., & Dunkle, M. E. (2002). Development and validation of the Epistemic Belief Inventory (EBI). In B. K. Hofer & P. R. Pintrich (Eds.), *Personal epistemology: The psychology of beliefs about knowledge and knowing* (pp. 261–275). Mahwah, NJ: Erlbaum.

Seymour, E., Hunter, A., Laursen, S. L., & DeAntoni, T. (2004). Establishing the benefits of research experiences for undergraduates in the sciences: First findings from a three-year study. *Science Education*, *88*, 493–534.

Shellito, C., Shea, K., Weissmann, G., Mueller-Solger, A., & Davis, W. (2001). Successful mentoring of undergraduate researchers. *Journal of College Science Teaching*, *30*(7), 460–464.

Spilich, G. (1997). Does undergraduate research pay off? *Council on Undergraduate Research*, *18*, 57–59, 89–90.

SPSS, Inc. (2004). *SPSS for Windows* (Release 12.0). Chicago, IL: Author.

Stewart, S. A. (2003). Immersion theory. *University of Chicago Magazine*, *96*(2), 40–42.

Tabachnick, B. G., & Fidell, L. S. (2001). *Using multivariate statistics* (4th ed.). Needham Heights, MA: Allyn & Bacon.

VanLehn, K. (1996). Cognitive skill acquisition. *Annual Review of Psychology, 47,* 513–539.

Vesilind, P. A. (2001). Mentoring Engineering students: Turning pebbles into diamonds. *Journal of Engineering Education, 90*(3), 407–411.

Wickman, P. (2004). The practical epistemologies of the classroom: A study of laboratory work. *Science Education, 88,* 325–344.

PART IV

Women in Science

Undergraduate Research Experiences: Male and Female Interns' Perceptions of Gains, Disappointments, and Self-Efficacy

CarolAnne M. Kardash, Michael Wallace, and Linda Blockus

A GROWING DATABASE reveals considerable consensus regarding student-identified benefits of participation in undergraduate research experiences (UREs) (Bauer & Bennett, 2003; Hunter, Laursen, & Seymour, 2007; Lopatto, 2004; Seymour, Hunter, Laursen, & DeAntoni, 2004; Zydney, Bennett, Shahid, & Bauer, 2002). In previous studies, we have described gains in specific research skills acquired by students during their UREs (Kardash, 2000) as well as their perceptions of what they learned by their participation (Kardash, Wallace, & Blockus, 2008). To our knowledge, however, little attention has been devoted to the possibility that UREs may have unanticipated, negative side effects. Thus in this study we questioned research interns on what they perceived to be the most satisfying and the most disappointing aspects of their experiences. We asked about how the URE affected their career goals. Given the important role played by perceived self-efficacy in young people's career plans (Eccles (Parsons), 1984), we also collected data on interns' perceived self-efficacy at both the beginning and end of the URE.

Most important, given the continuing underrepresentation of females in the fields of science, mathematics, engineering, and technology, as well as the well-documented gender differences in perceptions of science classes at the undergraduate level (c.f., Kardash & Wallace, 2001; Seymour & Hewitt, 1997) and the notion that Western practices of scientific inquiry do not take into consideration women's ways of knowing and learning (Brickhouse, 2001; Davis, 2001; Rosser, 1990), we were particularly interested in whether male and female research interns perceived their experiences similarly. This question is important since Cronin and Roger (1999) have proposed that simply having access to the same opportunities and treatments may produce vastly different results for men and women.

A STUDY OF RESEARCH EXPERIENCES FOR UNDERGRADUATES

Description of the URE and Participants

Participants were undergraduate science research interns at the University of Missouri–Columbia whose UREs were supported by monies from the National . Science Foundation (NSF) and the Howard Hughes Medical Institute (HHMI). Students participated in theoretical, field, or laboratory research with faculty mentors during an 8-week summer session or during the academic year. Summer interns worked 40 hours per week in their mentors' laboratories. Their UREs culminated with poster presentations of their work on the university's campus. Academic year interns worked 12 hours per week in their mentors' laboratories for a 32-week period. Their UREs culminated with oral presentations of their projects at a statewide science conference.

Data for the present study were collected from summer 1996 through summer 1999. Table 9.1 displays interns' participation by gender and time of year. Of a total of 189 interns (113 women, 76 men), 146 (77.2%) were funded by HHMI, and 43 (22.8%) by NSF Research Experiences for Undergraduates (REU).

Materials

At the end of their internship, interns responded in writing to three open-ended questions: (1) How has the research internship influenced your future career goals,

Table 9.1. Interns' participation by gender and time of year.

Semester	Women	Men
Summer 1996	26	17
Academic year 1996–97	1	3
Summer 1997	31	13
Academic year 1997–98	4	9
Summer 1998	29	21
Summer 1999	22	13

if at all? (2) What, in your estimation, was the most personally beneficial and satisfying aspect of the internship? (3) What, in your estimation, was the most personally disappointing or frustrating aspect of the internship?[1]

Interns were also asked a total of 13 close-ended items, of which 6 were about self-efficacy and interest, 5 were about future career plans, and 2 were about the URE itself. Four close-ended items that dealt with interns' perceptions of their ability, motivation, interest, and desire to pursue a career in science (refer to Table 9.5 later in the chapter) were rated immediately prior to the internship and again at the end of the internship. Two additional efficacy items dealing with the extent to which the internship increased or decreased participants' self-confidence and interest in becoming a research scientist appeared on the exit survey only. All six items were rated on a 5-point scale ranging from 1 (*strongly disagree/ decreased*) to 5 (*strongly agree/increased*).

To the five close-ended items that dealt with the impact of the URE on interns' future career plans, interns responded by marking *yes* or *no*. (Refer to Table 9.6 later in the chapter.) In the final group of close-ended items on the survey, the first asked interns to characterize the overall internship experience using the following scale: 1 (*routine and less stimulating than expected*), 2 (*about as challenging and stimulating as expected*), and 3 (*exceptionally challenging and stimulating*). The last item asked, "To what extent were your original goals for the internship met?" Interns responded to this item using a scale ranging from 1 (*not at all*) to 5 (*a great deal*).

Procedures

One day prior to beginning their internship, the authors described the evaluation effort to the interns. Those who volunteered to participate completed informed consent. Participants were advised that they could skip any questions they preferred not to answer.[2] The confidential nature of the surveys was stressed. The open-ended questions and close-ended exit survey were distributed on the last day of the internship with a request to return it within 2 weeks.

Scoring of Open-Ended Questions

Interns' responses to each open-ended question were first examined for recurring responses and themes, with preliminary categories formed on that basis (Strauss & Corbin, 1998). The first two authors coded all participant responses by assigning individual responses to the preliminary categories. Disagreements were resolved by consensus, leading to successive refinements of the categories. The number of categories was further reduced by taking into account the frequency with which certain responses fell into a particular category and by a logical analysis of the similarity among the various categories (Berg, 1998).

RESULTS

Open-Ended Questions

***How has the research internship influenced your future career goals, if at
all?*** As displayed in Table 9.2, over one third of the interns indicated the URE
provided an opportunity to think more deeply about and to clarify their career goals.
Typical comments included: "This experience has influenced me to take some time
off before college and grad school to make sure that I am entering the right field.
I might work a year or so before going to grad school. I now want to enter the job
market." Another student wrote, "I was considering a career in veterinary medicine; my research has also steered me to consider biomedical research."

About 22% of the interns reported the internship increased their interest in
pursuing a career in research science: "Since I have enjoyed my internship, I know
that research is a path I want to take—I have discovered that getting my master's
is the path I want to take because I enjoy doing the bench science work."

For about 23% of the interns, however, the research experience decreased
their interest in pursuing a research career. "I realized that the field of science I
enter must have a good amount of people interaction for me to be happy. If there
was any influence, it is that I like research, but I would rather work with people.
I know that being a research scientist in academia is not for me." Approximately
13% of the interns reported that the internship had no effect on their career goals.
Although the experience did not alter career goals for this group of interns, some
students noted it did increase their appreciation for research: "It has not changed
my career goals, but it has increased my interest and appreciation for biomedical
research."

About 12% of the students reported that the exposure the internship provided
to the everyday life of a scientist affected their career goals. As one student commented, "It gave me a more realistic picture of what the career's like." For some,
this insight into a scientist's lifestyle seemed to raise doubts about a career in research. One female noted, "It's made me realize how hard it will be to have kids
and a job in academics." For others, exposure to the lifestyle of scientists seemed
to increase their interest in research: "Attending the Society for Neuroscience
meeting gave me an insider's view and answered my lingering questions concerning the lifestyle of a scientist—it definitely helped me make up my mind that I
want to go to grad school."

For about 9% of the interns, especially those with a longstanding interest in
pursuing a medical degree, the URE piqued their interest in a combined PhD/MD
degree. Typical comments included: "Prior to my internship, I had not planned
on pursuing a degree of MD/PhD, only an MD. Since my experience I have realized what an important and rewarding career research can be and I want to be part
of it."

Table 9.2. Interns' perceptions of how participation in the URE influenced their career goals (percent of respondents).

	Total (N = 128)	Men (n = 50)	Women (n = 78)
Career clarification	34.4	32.0	35.9
Decreased interest in pursuing a career in science research	22.7	8.0	32.1**
Increased interest in pursuing a career in science research	21.9	24.0	20.5
Had no effect on career aspirations	12.5	18.0	9.0
Provided exposure to the life of a research scientist	11.7	14.0	10.3
Increased interest in pursuing a combined PhD/MD degree	8.6	4.0	11.5
Enhanced self-efficacy	7.8	16.0	2.6**
Increased likelihood of intern's incorporating some aspect of research into career	7.0	8.0	6.4
Increased knowledge of content and laboratory skills	4.7	8.0	2.6
Decreased self-efficacy	2.3	0.0	3.8
Provided career-enhancing outcomes	1.6	2.0	0.0

$**p < .01$, two-tailed.

About 8% of the interns indicated that the URE influenced their career plans by its effect on their self-efficacy. "It has shown me that if I decide it's what I want to do, I am capable of and good at doing research." For 7% of the students, the URE increased the likelihood that they would incorporate research into whatever career they ultimately chose. "While I am still most interested in becoming a clinical doctor, I wish to find ways to work research into my career."

There were two significant gender differences. More male (16.0%) and fewer female (2.6%) interns than expected mentioned that the URE enhanced their sense of self-efficacy.[3] In addition, fewer men (8.0%) and more women (32.1%) than expected mentioned that participation in the URE had decreased the likelihood of their choosing a science career.[4]

What, in your estimation, was the most personally beneficial and satisfying aspect of the internship experience this past summer (academic year)? As shown in Table 9.3, approximately 30% of the interns viewed gains in research skills and insights into the research process as the primary benefit of the internship. Within this category, almost 20% of the interns mentioned an increased appreciation for research and insight into the lifestyle of research scientists. One student said, "Working with my mentor to see what a scientist's life is really about." Approximately 6% indicated that what they most valued was an increase in their ability to think like a research scientist ("learning how to approach questions related to science and setting out to answer those questions"). Another 3% wrote of gains in specific research skills such as designing experiments ("designing the experiments rather than following the ones written in labs for classes"), interpreting results ("to be able to look at data and know what it means because you collected the data in your own experiment"), and reformulating hypotheses and experimental protocols.

The next most frequently valued benefit, mentioned by 29% of the interns, was development of collaborative relationships with faculty mentors and laboratory personnel. Within this category, approximately 11% of the students specifically mentioned appreciation for their faculty mentor: "Working with Dr. X helped teach me what being professional is all about." Another 17% noted they enjoyed simply meeting and talking with others in their laboratory about science and other topics.

Table 9.3. Interns' perceptions of the most beneficial and satisfying aspects of the URE (percent of respondents).

	Total (N = 121)	Men (n = 46)	Women (n = 75)
Gains in research skills and insights into the research process	29.8	34.8	26.7
Collaborative relationships	28.9	19.6	34.7
Gains in knowledge and skills	26.4	23.9	28.0
Pride in accomplishments	24.0	28.3	21.3
Gains in perceived self-efficacy and independence	19.8	4.3	29.3***
Career clarification	11.6	13.0	10.7
Money or secure income	2.5	6.5	0.0
Career-enhancing outcomes	1.7	4.3	0.0
Increases in persistence, perseverance, and ability to accept setbacks	1.7	4.3	0.0

*** $p < .001$, two-tailed.

Twenty-six percent of the interns viewed gains in general knowledge and skills as the most beneficial aspect of their internship. Ten percent specifically commented on increases in their content knowledge: "I have a much deeper understanding of so many biological processes." Another 10% commented on increases in their laboratory skills, and approximately 5% noted gains in communication skills that emerged as a consequence of preparing for their poster sessions ("The poster tied everything together at the end.")

Twenty-four percent noted pride in their accomplishments as the most beneficial and satisfying aspect of the internship. Of these, 10% referred to presentation of their research at poster sessions and conferences. Another 10% noted the pride they felt when research results confirmed their hypotheses ("the fact that I finished and had good data to support my hypothesis"). Almost 7% commented on having made a meaningful contribution to the work of the laboratory. Typical phrases included: "beginning to understand how significant my research is to my mentor and those who follow his work."

Pride in accomplishments was closely linked to gains in perceived efficacy and independence, mentioned by about 20% of the interns. In this category, both increases in self-confidence and the ability to work independently were mentioned by approximately 10% of the interns. Remarks typical of those expressing increased self-confidence were: "the increased confidence from being trusted with my project"; and "finding that I could actually do the research—I thought it would be too difficult." Increases in the ability to work independently were typified by comments such as, "When I actually started working on my own focusing on a specific question."

Career clarification again emerged as an important aspect of the URE. About 12% mentioned it as the most beneficial outcome of the internship, with 7% of the interns mentioning specifically that the internship provided information to aid in their career decision-making. Typical remarks included: "I now know what to expect with a career in research and am looking forward to pursuing it."

Career-enhancing outcomes, money, and increases in perseverance and in the ability to accept temporary setbacks were benefits mentioned infrequently and by male interns only.

Chi-square analyses revealed that more female (29.3%) and fewer male (4.3%) interns than expected mentioned gains in perceived self-efficacy and independence as the most beneficial and satisfying aspect of the internship.[5] One marginally significant difference emerged as well. More female (34.7%) and fewer male (19.6%) interns than expected mentioned collaborative relationships as the most satisfying aspect of the internship.[6]

What, in your estimation, was the most personally disappointing or frustrating aspect of the internship experience? As displayed in Table 9.4, over 55% of the interns mentioned aspects of the research process as the most disappointing

Table 9.4. Interns' perceptions of the most disappointing and frustrating aspects of the URE (percent of respondents).

	Total (N = 114)	Men (n = 41)	Women (n = 73)
Aspects of the research process	55.3	56.1	54.8
Logistical problems	27.2	24.4	28.8
Problems with faculty mentor	15.8	12.2	17.8
Self-perceived inadequacies	14.0	12.2	15.1
Other aspects of the URE	8.8	7.3	9.6

and frustrating part of their internship experience. Within this category, 25% mentioned "disappointing results" from their research projects. Typical comments included: "a lot of unsuccessful experiments," "having experiments not work," and "lack of results due to random problems." Approximately 17% voiced frustrations with the "ups and downs" of the research process: "I found out that all the work I had done was with the wrong DNA and all my data was worthless." Approximately 12% of the interns voiced disappointment with the time needed to obtain results: "Things always took about three times longer than I expected them to." Other interns expressed dismay with the monotony and tedium associated with benchwork. One student mentioned "the constant reproduction of what was done in the past to retry one aspect."

The next most frequently voiced disappointment concerned logistical problems (27.2%). The largest subcategory in this area dealt with insufficient time to complete the research project. Other logistical issues included equipment failures or lack of necessary equipment. As one intern put it, "The equipment was broken. We couldn't buy a new spectrophotometer due to a lack of grant dollars."

For approximately 16% of the interns, the major disappointment involved problems with their faculty mentors: "The relationship with my professor. He made me feel like nothing, but this did not stop me from learning everything on my own and using my own opinions and ideas . . . having confidence in myself."

Fourteen percent of the interns viewed themselves as primarily responsible for any disappointing or frustrating aspects of their experiences. Some questioned their own self-efficacy: "I did not feel I had the intellectual skills to understand what I was doing and made many mistakes." Others expressed concern with their lack of content knowledge: "In some areas of my research my knowledge was somewhat lax and put me at a disadvantage." Yet others expressed concerns about their laboratory skills: "Being so dependent on everyone else in the lab, I wasn't able to do anything without help."

Finally, about 9% voiced frustration with efforts to incorporate social events into the experience, some of the seminars that featured guest speakers, and making their posters. Not surprisingly, a few interns expressed frustration with the number of surveys they were asked to complete for the evaluation effort!

Chi-square analyses yielded no significant gender differences.

Close-Ended Self-Efficacy and Interest Items

Means and standard deviations for interns' ratings on the four self-efficacy and interest items as a function of gender are displayed in Table 9.5.[7] Interns' mean ratings of their ability and their interest demonstrated statistically significant declines,[8] and mean ratings on the motivation and desire items marginally significant declines,[9] from the beginning to end of the URE.

Table 9.5. Interns' mean ratings of self-efficacy and interest items by gender.

| | Beginning of URE | | | | End of URE | | | |
| | Males (n = 50) | | Females (n = 83) | | Males (n = 50) | | Females (n = 83) | |
	M	SD	M	SD	M	SD	M	SD
I'm the kind of person who has the ability to have a successful career as a scientist.	4.50	0.61	4.25	0.71	4.34	0.80	3.99	0.99
I'm the kind of person who has the motivation and persistence required for a career in some field of science.	4.72	0.45	4.51	0.59	4.58	0.61	4.42	0.77
I have a strong interest in pursuing a career as a scientist.	4.20	1.01	4.18	0.92	3.82	1.21	3.82	1.07
My desire to become a scientist is strong enough to help me overcome most barriers that I might encounter in pursuit of this career goal.	4.02	0.94	3.95	0.97	3.94	1.00	3.73	1.04

Notes: At the end of the URE, each item was preceded by the phrase, "My experience this summer (academic year) as an undergraduate research intern has strengthened my belief that . . . ." Items were rated on a 5-point scale ranging from 1 (strongly disagree) to 5 (strongly agree).

At the end of the URE, interns use a 5-point scale ranging from 1 (*strongly decreased*) to 5 (*strongly increased*) to respond to the following two items: "To what extent did the internship either increase or decrease your self-confidence in terms of being a successful research scientist?" and "To what extent did the internship either increase or decrease your interest in becoming a research scientist?" Male interns ($n = 58$) rated their confidence levels $(M = 3.83, SD = 0.68)$ significantly higher than did female interns ($n = 90; M = 3.53, SD = 0.91$).[10] Male ($n = 56; M = 3.41$) and female ($n = 89; M = 3.31$) mean ratings for the interest item did not differ significantly.

Interns' Evaluation of Effects of the URE on Their Overall Career Plans

Table 9.6 presents interns' evaluation of the impact of the URE on their future career plans. The number of interns responding to these items ranged from 137 to 141. The URE played an important role in interns' career plans, especially in broadening their outlooks on careers. Eighty-two percent of the interns indicated the URE opened their eyes to new career possibilities, and almost 74% indicated it helped them identify an area of science they enjoyed. Approximately 44% indicated the URE helped them decide to pursue a career in research science, whereas almost 33% indicated it helped them decide against a research science career. Fifty-six percent indicated the URE helped them decide on a career in medicine.

Interestingly, only one gender difference emerged. More women (90.7%) and fewer men (68.5%) than expected indicated the URE opened their eyes to new career possibilities.[11]

Table 9.6. Interns' evaluations of the impact of the URE on their career plans (percent of respondents).

	% Responding Yes		
Question	Total	Men	Women
Has the internship . . .			
Helped you to decide to pursue a career in research?	43.5	46.4	41.5
Helped you to decide against a career in research?	32.8	28.1	36.3
Helped you to identify an area of science you enjoy?	73.6	73.2	73.8
Helped you to decide to pursue a career in medicine?	56.0	51.8	58.8
Opened your eyes to new career possibilities?	82.1	68.5	90.7***

*** $p < .001$, two-tailed.

Interns' Overall Ratings of the URE

One hundred forty-three interns rated their overall impression of the URE. Forty-seven percent rated it "exceptionally challenging and stimulating," another 47% rated it "about as challenging and stimulating as expected," and 6% rated it as "routine and less stimulating than expected." Significantly more male (63.2%) and fewer female (36.0%) interns than expected rated the URE as "exceptionally challenging and stimulating," whereas significantly more female (57.0%) and fewer male (31.6%) interns than expected rated the URE as "about as challenging and stimulating as expected."[12]

One hundred nineteen interns responded to, "To what extent were your original goals for the internship met?" using a 5-point scale ranging from 1 (*not at all*) to 5 (*a great deal*). Interns' mean rating was 4.24 ($SD = 1.03$). There were no significant differences in male ($M = 4.20$) and female ($M = 4.27$) interns' mean ratings.

DISCUSSION

Overall Findings

The gains and benefits that students identified from URE participation in this study bear striking resemblance to those identified by others (cf., Seymour et al., 2004). At the same time, our study extends and further informs the extant literature on UREs by providing insights into what interns viewed as the most disappointing and frustrating aspects of UREs. Interestingly, there was considerably more uniformity among students in their descriptions of the most disappointing and frustrating aspects of the UREs than in their descriptions of the most important and beneficial things learned. By far the most common responses to this question derived from interns' increased insight into the research process. Over 55% noted aspects such as: disappointing results; the time required to obtain results; dealing with setbacks and failures due to the "unpredictability" of research results; the monotony and tedium associated with bench work; the need to work long hours; and the physical isolation of the laboratory. For some, these insights may have led them to indicate that the URE had decreased their interest in pursuing a career as a research scientist. Other disappointing and frustrating aspects of the UREs, such as logistical problems with equipment, problems with faculty mentors, and perceptions of self-identified inadequacies in content knowledge and laboratory skills were mentioned far less frequently.

A very unexpected and surprising finding was the statistically significant decrease from the beginning to end of the URE in interns' ratings of their ability and interest in a career as a research scientist. On the one hand, interns' ratings of their ability levels and motivation were still fairly high at the end of the URE, with interns generally "agreeing" that they had the ability and motivation to succeed at a research career. On the other hand, their ratings at the end of the URE fell a bit short of agreement with the two statements that tapped their interest and their belief that their desire to become research scientists would be sufficient to overcome any obstacles they encountered in pursuit of that goal. In addition, when asked at the end of the URE about the extent to which the experience had increased their self-confidence and interest in terms of becoming research scientists, the mean ratings for both items again fell just shy of the point on the scale that indicated "increased." A probable explanation for these findings is that interns may have initially overestimated both their interest and ability at the beginning of the URE. Participation in the URE, by allowing students to engage meaningfully in the "real lives of scientists" over an extended period of time, likely provided an opportunity for interns to more carefully and realistically assess their own abilities and career interests.

When asked how participation in the URE had influenced their career goals, over one third of the interns indicated it helped them to clarify their career goals. For about 22% of the interns, the URE strengthened their preexisting interest in a research science career. Yet, for an equal number, the URE decreased their interest in a research science career. These open-ended data were supported by interns' responses to the two close-ended questions that asked whether the internship had helped them to decide to pursue a career in research (44% indicated "yes") and to decide against a career in research (33%). Like Seymour et al. (2004), we found little support from either the open-ended or close-ended data to confirm claims that UREs can prompt students to suddenly "choose" a research science career in the absence of preexisting inclinations toward that career. On the other hand, our data point to the significant impact that UREs have in broadening students' outlooks on careers, in helping them identify particular areas of science they enjoy, and in helping a limited number of students rule out careers in research science.

Gender Differences

Few gender differences emerged in this study. Men and women did not differ with respect to what they identified as the most disappointing and frustrating aspects of the URE. Similarly, they generally did not differ in their perceptions of the most personally beneficial and satisfying aspects of the internship, although significantly more women than men did mention gains in perceived self-efficacy. The general absence of gender differences is similar to findings reported previously by Kardash (2000) and Lopatto (2004) regarding other aspects of UREs.

The most striking gender differences that did emerge in our study involved career plans and self-efficacy and independence. When asked about the extent to which the URE increased or decreased their self-confidence in terms of becoming successful research scientists, men's confidence ratings were significantly higher than women's. When asked how the URE influenced their career plans, more than four times as many women as men indicated it had decreased the likelihood that they would choose a career in research science.

At the same time, significantly more women than men indicated that the URE had opened their eyes to new career possibilities. Could this change in career plans have been due to more women experiencing declines in self-efficacy as a result of their participation in the URE? On the one hand—again in response to the question of how the URE had affected their career plans—significantly more men than women mentioned that participation in the URE had enhanced their sense of self-efficacy.

On the other hand, other evidence indicates that the URE played a very important role in increasing women's sense of self-efficacy. When asked to list the most beneficial and satisfying aspects of the URE, significantly more women than men mentioned gains in perceived self-efficacy and in their ability to think and work independently. Moreover, men and women did not differ significantly in their self-ratings of their ability to be successful research scientists at either the beginning or the end of the URE. Thus, although it seems that the URE might have discouraged more women than men from pursuing a graduate career in the research sciences, the reasons for this effect are much less clear. One possible reason might be found in the fact that significantly fewer women than men rated the URE as "exceptionally challenging and stimulating." Another reason may be that specific negative events occurring during the URE discouraged more women than men from pursuing research science careers. Data from another study that specifically addresses that possibility are currently being analyzed.

ACKNOWLEDGMENT

This research was sponsored by the National Science Foundation Recognition Award for the Integration of Research and Education (Award STI-96-20032).

NOTES

1. Not all open-ended questions were asked each semester, and thus the total possible N for each question differs. The possible numbers of interns who could choose to answer each question were: Question 1, 154 interns; Question 2, 131 interns; and Question 3, 131 interns.

2. Some interns skipped items on either the beginning or end of URE surveys. Other students completed the beginning of the URE survey, but not the end of the URE survey, whereas other students did the opposite. Thus the Ns for each analysis differ.

3. Fisher's Exact Test, $p = .014$, two-sided.

4. Chi-square analysis, $\chi^2 (1) = 10.06$, $p < .01$.

5. Chi-square analysis, χ^2 (1) = 11.19, $p < .001$.

6. Chi-square analysis, χ^2 (1) = 3.16, $p = .075$.

7. These data were entered into a 2 Gender × 2 Time of Rating (beginning vs. end of the URE) × 4 Item mixed-model ANOVA. The ANOVA yielded significant main effects for time of rating, F (1,131) = 14.19, $p < .001$ (eta squared = .10); and item, F (2.23, 292.16) = 39.55, $p < .001$ (eta squared = .23); and a significant time of rating × item interaction, F (2.75, 359.94) = 12.88, $p < .05$ (eta squared = .02). (Because Mauchy's test of sphericity indicated that the assumption of sphericity of the variance-covariance matrix was untenable, the Greenhouse-Geisser correction was used to adjust the degrees of freedom.) The time of rating × item interaction was followed up with tests of simple main effects.

8. Independent samples t-tests, t (132) = 3.09, $p < .01$, and t (132) = 4.23, $p < .001$, for the ability and interest ratings, respectively.

9. For motivation and desire, $p = .08$ and $p = .07$, respectively.

10. Independent samples t-test, t (146) = 2.10, $p < .05$.

11. Chi-square analysis, χ^2 (1) = 11.12, $p < .001$.

12. Data were entered into a 2 Gender × 3 Rating chi-square analysis, χ^2 (2) = 10.26, $p < .01$

REFERENCES

Bauer, K. W., & Bennett, J. S. (2003). Alumni perceptions used to assess undergraduate research experience. *Journal of Higher Education, 74*(2), 210–230.

Berg, B. (1998). *Qualitative research methods for the social sciences* (3rd ed.). Boston: Allyn & Bacon.

Brickhouse, N. W. (2001). Embodying science: A feminist perspective on learning. *Journal of Research in Science Teaching, 38*, 282–295.

Cronin, C., & Roger, A. (1999). Theorizing progress: Women in science, engineering, and technology in higher education. *Journal of Research in Science Teaching, 36*, 637–661.

Davis, K. S. (2001). "Peripheral and subversive": Women making connections and challenging the boundaries of the science community. *Science Education, 85*, 368–409.

Eccles (Parsons), J. S. (1984). Sex differences in mathematics participation. In M. Steinkamp & M. Maeher (Eds.), *Women in science.* Greenwich, CT: JAI Press.

Hunter, A.-B., Laursen, S. L., & Seymour, E. (2007). Becoming a scientist: The role of undergraduate research in students' cognitive, personal, and professional development. *Science Education, 91*, 36–74.

Kardash, C. M. (2000). Evaluation of an undergraduate research experience: Perceptions of undergraduate interns and their faculty mentors. *Journal of Educational Psychology, 92*, 191–201.

Kardash, C. M., & Wallace, M. (2001). The Perceptions of Science Classes survey: What undergraduate science reform efforts really need to address. *Journal of Educational Psychology, 93*, 199–210.

Kardash, C. M., Wallace, M., & Blockus, L. (2008). Science undergraduates' perceptions of learning from undergraduate research experiences. In R. Miller, R. F. Rycek, E. Balcetis, S. T. Barney, B. C. Beins, S. R. Burns, R. Smith, & M. E. Ware (Eds.), *Developing, promoting, and sustaining the undergraduate research experience in psychology* (pp. 258–263). Retrieved February 26, 2008, from http://teachpsych.org/resources/e-books/ur2008/ur2008.php

Lopatto, D. (2004). Survey of Undergraduate Research Experiences (SURE): First findings. *Cell Biology Education, 3,* 270–277.

Rosser, S. V. (1990). *Female-friendly science: Applying women's studies methods and theories to attract students.* New York: Pergamon Press.

Seymour, E., & Hewitt, N. M. (1997). *Talking about leaving: Why undergraduates leave the sciences.* Boulder, CO: Westview Press.

Seymour, E., Hunter, A.-B., Laursen, S. L., & DeAntoni, T. (2004). Establishing the benefits of research experiences for undergraduates: First findings from a three-year study. *Science Education, 88*(4), 493–534.

Strauss, A., & Corbin, J. (1998). *Basics of qualitative research: Techniques and procedures for developing grounded theory* (2nd ed.). Thousand Oaks, CA: Sage.

Zydney, A. L., Bennett, J. S., Shahid, A., & Bauer, K. W. (2002). Impact of undergraduate research experience in engineering. *Journal of Engineering Education, 91*(2), 151–157.

Transcending Deficits and Differences Through Undergraduate Research

Ashley Campbell and Gerald D. Skoog

> The price of advancement for women in science, perhaps, is simi-
> lar to the price of liberty—eternal vigilance—and action. Talent,
> from every source and from all sources, is imperative for the in-
> novation which gives us the ability to resolve the 21st century
> challenges which are unfolding. And, it may well be that recent
> ire over the notion that women do not possess the innate ability
> to do science has raised the issue to hyperconsciousness, and
> that which may well augur change. It cannot hurt to have bright
> women, at all levels, challenged to rise to their innate talent.
> —Shirley Ann Jackson, speech at Smith College

DEFICITS AND DIFFERENCES

From their study Project Access, Sonnert and Holton (1995) developed two models to identify and differentiate between barriers that impede the progress and
careers of women in science. The *deficit model* proposed that "women as a group
receive fewer chances and opportunities in careers; and collectively have worse
career outcomes" (p. 2), whereas the *difference model* "emphasizes deep-rooted
differences in the outlook and goals of women and men" (p. 3). Within the difference model, Sonnert and Holton differentiated between *structural obstacles*, which
are "barriers that exist as a feature of the social system of science," and *internal
obstacles*, which are "barriers that exist in the form of women's attitudes and
values" (p. 6). In considering informal factors inherent to the difference model,

the authors concluded, "women have less access to strategic resources, such as social networks, which are essential for career success" (p. 2). They identified the differences in the socialization of men and women, the tendency to identify science as a male field, and deep-seated epistemological gender differences as three categories of culturally determined differences between men and women that shape the difference model. These and other factors related to this model may indirectly affect women by influencing their decisions not to pursue a science career. Sonnert and Holton concluded that policies aimed at removing barriers inherent to the deficit model are geared toward helping women "become more successful under the current rules of the game" whereas policy initiatives concerned with the difference model aim at "changing the rules themselves" (p. 189).

Much public discussion ensued regarding the status of women in science following the January 2005 comments made by Lawrence Summers, then president of Harvard University, in reference to the inherent differences between men and women in science. As a result, in April 2005 Elizabeth Spelke and Steven Pinker participated in a debate titled "The Science of Gender and Science" (Edge Foundation, 2005). While Spelke cited discrimination and social forces as primary reasons for fewer women scientists, Pinker stated that intrinsic forces play a larger role. Spelke's views most align with the deficit model; Pinker's views tend to conform to the difference model. Summers' comments actually opened up channels of communication about existing and needed program and policy initiatives for increasing the representation of women in science. The identification of persistent barriers and the characteristics of best practices are necessary to inform the design and implementation of needed programs.

A STUDY OF AN UNDERGRADUATE RESEARCH PROGRAM

In 1992 the Texas Tech University/Howard Hughes Medical Institute (TTU/HHMI) program was established with the support of the Undergraduate Biological Sciences program of the Howard Hughes Medical Institute (HHMI). One of the specific goals of the TTU/HHMI program in Phases I and II (1992–1998) was to increase participation by women and minorities in the sciences. Of the Texas Tech University HHMI grant monies, roughly 59% fund the Student Development and Broadening Access to Science component. This component funds research scholars, who work 20 hours per week in research laboratories during the academic year and 40 hours per week during the summer. After students who apply to the program are accepted, they choose a mentor from over 100 faculty members at Texas Tech University and Texas Tech University Health Sciences Center. Scholars make a commitment from the onset of their involvement with the TTU/HHMI program to a specific lab. Since 1992, the program has supported the research efforts of over 350 students.

We conducted a study to determine if the TTU/HHMI program prepared female scholars to overcome internal and external barriers commonly cited in the literature, such as bias, access, and self-efficacy concerns. This research was designed to identify barriers that existed in graduate programs and ascertain whether the undergraduate experience helped the females circumvent the barriers. The questions guiding the research were: (1) How did the experiences of females in the TTU/HHMI undergraduate research program prepare them for a career in science? and (2) What experiences of females in the TTU/HHMI undergraduate research program were important in eliminating or alleviating the barriers women in science often encounter?

METHODS

Qualitative interview questions were written by the first author based on previous data collected from HHMI scholars. The interview questions then underwent expert review by a team of three education professors at Texas Tech University. A pool of potential interviewees was identified using the existing biographical data in the TTU/HHMI database. Individuals in this pool who were pursuing a doctorate in the biological sciences were selected to participate in the interviews.

The purpose of the interview was to allow each woman to elaborate on her personal experiences. The interviews were open-ended with the goal of gaining detailed insight into how the TTU/HHMI program impacted each of their careers. Once female scholars began to provide similar answers over the range of questions and a trend was established, interviews were not scheduled with additional female scholars. Hence, the exact number of female scholars interviewed was determined by the data collection.

Seven female scholars were interviewed who had not yet completed their PhD programs; three of them expected to graduate within the year. The female scholars were dispersed geographically—three in the North and four in the South. The women, who are identified by pseudonyms, were Lori, Carol, Tracy, Joan, Rachel, Liz, and Nicole. Each female scholar interview was conducted by telephone. Interviews were recorded and then transcribed. The first author analyzed the transcripts. This analysis was confirmed by the expert review team that had reviewed the interview questions.

RESULTS AND DISCUSSION

Analysis of the interview transcripts indicated that the research experience, the support and interaction with the mentor, a sense of increased self-confidence, and the awareness of the time commitment required for success contributed to their success in pursuing graduate work in science.

Research experiences and mentor relationships were important in preparing these women for a career in science. Lori's observation that "doing research allows you to see what the whole research field is like, something you definitely cannot get a feel for from just being in classes and taking lab classes" exemplified the experiences of the group. Joan considered the undergraduate research experience to be an "inherent encouragement for a career in science." Her mentor relationship was so successful that she made the decision to continue working with her mentor to obtain a master's degree. Carol also spoke of the support she received from her mentor and the importance of his counsel and encouragement during the undergraduate years. Nicole developed a love for scientific research because of the research experience she gained in the TTU/HHMI program. The program helped the female scholars by increasing their confidence and their level of interest in science.

The interview transcripts also revealed that the female scholars' involvement in research laboratories helped them become more resilient, and thus more able to deal with the failures and setbacks that are a part of the culture of a research lab. For example, female scholars noted that they had to deal with many disappointments and learn that research results were not immediate. Joan noted, "Science is all about failures, and as an undergraduate scholar, I had more than my fair share." She added, "You really get the whole scientific process hard-wired into your brain. For every success, there are at least 10 failures."

The frequency of references from each interview was recorded (see Table 10.1). All female scholars made references to the positive impact of the undergraduate research experience and the mentor to their career goals. Six of the female scholars cited the support and interactions from the program as factors contributing to their success.

The interviews substantiated Eisenhart and Finkel's (1998) claim that in terms of time commitment graduate study in science is "greedy." Some of these difficulties relate to family issues. The women interviewed were in the traditional childbearing phase of their lives. The two female scholars with children, Liz and Nicole, noted the difficulties that resulted from the excessive time demands from their research. In addition, Rachel noted, "Some people do not think women should have families and shouldn't spend that much time at home." Liz noted that the head of her department insisted, "Gender issues have no place in the work environment." She also reported, "My advisor told me that I needed to apologize to him for putting my family first, and that if I couldn't do that, then I'd have to leave." Even though Nicole had considerable talent and was accepted by every graduate program to which she applied, she was effectively forced to take a leave of absence from graduate school when she became pregnant. Essentially, Nicole was told she could no longer work in the lab she had chosen if she went forward with

Table 10.1. Number of theme references from interviews:
Key program factors

Theme	Lori	Carol	Tracy	Joan	Rachel	Liz	Nicole
Research experience	3	5	2	4	2	4	1
Mentor	3	3	2	2	1	2	1
Support and interactions	3	1	4	0	2	1	1

her pregnancy. Because of the passion that she developed for research as an under-graduate, she planned to eventually return to graduate school. Tracy shared that it was "hard to find a balance between how many hours you should spend at school and at the same time wanting to spend time at home." Joan ultimately dropped out of her doctoral program because of the time demands that resulted in the lack of balance in her life.

Three of the seven female scholars (Lori, Tracy, and Joan) reported that they had not encountered barriers to their career. Rachel stated, "Science is a tough career to go into because of the time demands." However, she noted that the "posi-tive reinforcement you get from doing a good job or traveling to places and learn-ing new things act as positive influences." Joan felt that barriers were "usually a problem of perception." She went on to suggest "the caliber of your science, of your work should stand up, and if it doesn't I see calling the 'I'm a woman, and you're treating me unfairly' as kind of a crutch."

Overall, responses of the female scholars interviewed provided evidence that the undergraduate research program had given them a significant jump-start in their careers, which could have catapulted them over barriers that many women encounter as they pursue graduate work. In particular, the data from this study provided evidence that research experience and mentoring opportunities made a significant impact on the career paths of these women. Self-confidence and the importance of support and interactions with others in the field were helpful in preparing these women to meet the challenges associated with their responsibili-ties in research labs during their graduate studies.

CONCLUSIONS

Data in this study supported the premise that the Howard Hughes Medical Insti-tute Undergraduate Biological Sciences grants program and similar programs which provide undergraduate women experiences and mentoring in a research laboratory have the potential to facilitate the success rate of women pursuing careers in science. Interviews confirm that these women experienced science differently in research laboratories than in classrooms. The research experience was a critical factor in building confidence in their ability to be successful in a science career. Overall data from this study provided evidence that the program with its emphasis on research experiences and mentoring made a large impact on the career paths of scholars. The data from this study also are consistent with the recent analysis of several undergraduate research programs that concluded that student confidence, understanding, and awareness of what graduate school is like increased in these programs (Russell, Chapter 4; Russell, Hancock, & McCollough, 2007).

Sue Rosser (2003) concluded that "isolation, lack of mentoring, stereotypes about women's performance, and difficulty in gaining credibility among male peers and administrators" persist as a result of the scarcity of women in science and engineering. There is a growing recognition of the importance of early and continuous involvement of females in science-related activities and research during all stages of their education and careers. A report from the National Council for Research on Women (NCRW) stated "supportive mentors, role models and networks have been shown to be helpful beginning at early educational levels and continuing throughout a woman's scientific career" (Basch, 2001, p. 12). These and other conclusions indicate the policies and practices that have the potential to ease and eliminate barriers that impede women's access to science must be given more support.

REFERENCES

Basch, L. (2001). Preface. In M. Thom, *Balancing the equation: Where are women and girls in science, engineering, and technology?* (pp. 10–13). New York: National Council for Research on Women.

Edge Foundation. (2005, May 10). *The science of gender and science, Pinker vs. Spelke: A debate.* Retrieved February 1, 2006, from http://www.edge.org/documents/archive/edge160.html#d

Eisenhart, M. A., & Finkel, E. (1998). *Women's science.* Chicago: University of Chicago Press.

Rosser, S. V. (2003, July/August). Attracting and retaining women in science and engineering, *Academe 89*(4), 24–28. Retrieved March 16, 2006 from www.aaup.org/AAUP/pubsres/academe/2003/JA/Feat/Ross.htm

Russell, S. H., Hancock, M. P., & McCollough, J. (2007). Benefits of undergraduate research experience. *Science, 316*(5824), 548–549.

Sonnert, G., & Holton, G. (1995). *Who succeeds in science? The gender dimension.* New Brunswick, NJ: Rutgers University Press.

Looking Back and Looking Forward

Alumni Perspectives on Undergraduate Research

INTRODUCTION, by Robin Henne

THERE ARE numerous methods for quantitatively evaluating the impact of undergraduate research on the lives of students. However, these tools result in a loss of the depth, scope, and power of individuals' personal perspectives on their own experiences. This chapter is a collage of six personal narratives contributed by alumni TTU/HHMI Fellows who conducted scientific research as undergraduate students supported by the Texas Tech University/Howard Hughes Medical Institute Science Education Program. The fellows have unique personal perspectives concerning the importance of long-term undergraduate research on their education and scientific growth. Their perspectives vary due to the span of time since graduation, their research topics, their experiences in their laboratories, their interests in science, and how the experience shaped their future.

When asked to compose their narratives, the alumni fellows were prompted to reflect on several topics: (1) the experiences in their lives that sparked their interests in scientific research; (2) their TTU/HHMI research project, along with their undergraduate experiences; (3) how undergraduate research affected their undergraduate education, graduate education, and plans for their future; and (4) their current research interests and how their experiences in undergraduate research led them to where they are now.

The narratives below have received only minor changes throughout the editing process, in order to preserve their authors' thoughts. The narratives have been ordered starting from the most recent graduation date, to make it evident how undergraduate research has immediate effects and continues to have long-term benefits in the lives of students. These narratives reveal the importance of undergraduate research in the lives of future scientists through the unique perspective of personal reflections. There are common themes that are expressed through the narratives that highlight the life-altering, inspiring, and long-term effects of the undergraduate research experience. All of the alumni fellows agree that their experience in undergraduate research was a cornerstone of their undergraduate education and an invaluable foundation for their futures.

"THE BEAUTY OF MOLECULAR BIOLOGY"

William Henne, Graduate Student

I ALWAYS liked science. Not just science class, the science magazines, and those TV nature specials, but the *feeling* of science. It made sense, and I understood *why* it made sense from an early age. Furthermore, my only contact with actual scientists (on TV or in the movies) showed them to be passionate about their profession. It was clear that they enjoyed their work, and saw beauty where most saw endless numbers and test tubes. Most of all, going to work filled them with a sense of purpose. I think that desire for purpose—to do something that could help the world as a whole, not just patients in a hospital or clients in an office—drove me, as high school graduation loomed closer, to consider an undergraduate education in the natural sciences.

My AP Biology teacher was also instrumental in this decision. Miss Hale, the stereotypical tomboy alpha who greeted you in class with a cheerful "Welcome to H-a-e-l-l!" was my first biology mentor. Enrolling in her AP Biology class as a senior, I was not sure what to expect. She seemed more apt to supervise the predator exhibit at the zoo than to educate 30 high school seniors on the Krebs cycle (she did in fact care for animals, as our classroom was an animal rehabilitation center, filled with abused parrots, lizards, and even a prairie dog). However, she soon proved an excellent and caring instructor. But it was again the passion for her work—evident when she hiked with us on wilderness trips to teach forest ecology, or seen when we ignited controversy by debating stem cell research—from which I learned the most. She loved biology, and loved to show others its beauty.

Corny as it sounds, it was when I was studying for one of her infamous exams that I experienced my first epiphany about the beauty of molecular biology. I was studying the rules of genetic codons and examining a schematic of the double helix, when I had an "enlightened moment." Not only did all the rules make perfect sense, but the *beauty* of the system—a system derived by nature billions of years ago and selectively preserved by mechanisms I was only beginning to discover—that captured me. I think I fell in love with molecular biology at that moment. It held that "secret of life" mystique that novelists and movie scripters try to craft into their bestsellers, but this phenomenon was real!

By my last semester of high school, I knew I wanted to study biology. I only needed a college at which to study it.

My girlfriend at the time (now my wife) and I toured several Texas schools, searching for a strong undergraduate biology program to "turn us into scientists." We were not sure what constituted such a program, or even which questions to ask the university faculty, but we will never regret our trip to Texas Tech. There the already flourishing TTU/HHMI program received us with warm welcomes and straight answers. We learned that the undergraduate biology curricula at Texas Tech was considered exceptional, but even more so was the opportunity to experience undergraduate research. From conducting actual laboratory research, you could decide if you wanted to pursue it as a career, as well as gain the experience needed to enter into competitive graduate programs. With these opportunities, Robin and I knew immediately that Texas Tech would be our undergraduate home.

We actually began our research adventure the summer before our undergraduate curricula began, as we were accepted into a Texas Tech summer program called Clark Scholars, designed to expose young minds to academic research. Little did I know, but my assigned lab would significantly shape my career interests. As a Clark Scholar, the neurophysiologist Dr. Jean Strahlendorf would be my second great mentor.

Under Dr. J (as her staff and students affectionately call her) my passion for molecular biology matured and acquired definition as my interest in neurobiology emerged. I studied mechanisms of programmed cell death in the brain, specifically those from bouts of excitotoxicity, often caused by massive strokes or chemical warfare. During excitotoxic events, neurons become stressed and release massive amounts of neurotransmitter into their local environments. For reasons still not completely understood, this large-scale neurotransmitter release proves pathogenic to many neurons, and the neurons subsequently activate genetically programmed mechanisms of cell death as a response to the stress. The key players of these mechanisms are specific proteins, many of which are both necessary and sufficient to cause programmed cell death. Therefore, I studied the individual proteins within these excitotoxicity-stressed neurons with the intention that, if we can properly regulate them, we can create therapies to reduce or prevent the damaging effects of stroke and other neurodegenerative diseases. My research was fruitful, and with the help of the TTU/HHMI travel funds, I had the opportunity to present it at three international and eight state or local scientific conferences. I was also author on three academic publications, including a first author paper, before my undergraduate degree was even complete.

By the end of my undergraduate career, I was accepted into several graduate programs, but choose to begin PhD research at the MRC Laboratory of Molecular

Biology, part of the University of Cambridge. I am currently in Harvey McMahon's lab, doing research on lipid membrane interacting proteins. Specifically, I am studying protein domains that can induce and stabilize membrane curvature. This is important in processes like endocytosis and exocytosis, where vesicles inside the cell must deform to allow fusion and fission with the plasma membrane. It is a natural extension of my undergraduate research, which focused on neurotransmitter release in neurons, since neurotransmitters are the chief vesicle cargo in neurons. The research has been fruitful—in 18 months I have solved the X-ray crystal structure of a novel membrane bending protein domain, called the F-BAR domain, and published a paper in the journal *Structure*.

My experience with undergraduate research was critical to my acceptance into a competitive graduate program for two reasons: (1) It provided the research experience highly sought after in applicants, and (2) it exposed me to the emerging "hot topics" of the neurobiological world. I see neuroscience as one of the dominant scientific endeavors of the twenty-first century, lying at the crossroads of controversial issues in medicine, ethics, and even philosophy. To receive firsthand experience in such a field at a young age is priceless. It has laid a firm foundation that I hope to build upon as I seek a leadership position in this field. Likewise, undergraduate research prepared me for a rigorous PhD program like that offered at the University of Cambridge, which allows students to complete their PhD in 3–4 years. The demands on students are exceptional in this environment, and I cannot see how I would have survived this program without substantial undergraduate research experience. In closing, science is definitely a profession of passion, and I will be forever grateful that I found that passionate sense of purpose because of my early research opportunities.

"THE VASTNESS OF THE FIELD OF SCIENTIFIC RESEARCH"

Robin Henne, Research Grants Officer

IN GRADE SCHOOL my favorite subjects to study were math and science. I enjoyed the logical principles, the ability to solve problems, and the factual basis of the subjects. Throughout my early years, my dreams for the future switched between two jobs: I always imagined myself as either an astronaut or a teacher. In ninth grade, I became enamored with the subject of biology. I loved the study of life, the ability to understand how the world functioned from the molecular basis to the complex ecology of the world. My passion continued to grow through high school. During my junior year in high school, I began to research colleges to decide where I would continue my education. I knew that I wanted to study biology in college because my passion for the subject had not subsided.

Like most high school students, I assumed that with a biology degree I could either teach in a high school or continue on to medical school. As I toured Texas Tech University, I was introduced to the TTU/HHMI program. The program offers students the ability to conduct long-term undergraduate research in laboratories mentored by leading scientists. During the tour a current TTU/HHMI Fellow showed me a culture of breast cancer cells that they were using to study the effects of pharmaceuticals on the growth or death of the cells. I was very impressed. I was also informed of the Clark Scholars program, which brings high school students to the TTU campus for a summer and places them in faculty research labs. I knew instantly that I wanted to attend Texas Tech University and participate in both the Clark Scholars Program and the TTU/HHMI program. Before the tour, I had no idea that research was even possible for biology majors; following the tour, I was convinced that research was what I wanted to do for my career.

During my senior year of high school I applied for admission to Texas Tech University and the summer Clark Scholars Program. I was accepted to both. Following my graduation from high school, I began research in the Texas Tech University Health Sciences Center (TTUHSC) Department of Microbiology and Immunology under the mentorship of Dr. Joe Fralick. That summer was the best summer of my life. I learned more in that summer than I have at any other point in my life. My eyes were opened to the vastness of the field of scientific research.

I transferred directly from the Clark Scholars program into the TTU/HHMI program as I began my freshman year of college. During my freshman year, I enrolled in the university-required courses and honors chemistry. In the following summer, I attended the Molecular Genetics of Bacteria and Phage Conference in Cold Spring Harbor, New York. I was surprised to discover that my poster abstract was selected for an oral presentation in one of the seminar series. Therefore, as a sophomore in college without any college biology, I gave an oral presentation to an auditorium full of international experts.

My research as an undergraduate focused on antibiotic resistance in bacteria. The emergence of antibiotic resistant bacteria is a serious concern for modern medicine. The antibiotics that have been used to easily kill bacteria in the past are no longer working. There are many ways that bacteria become resistant to antibiotics, and one of those mechanisms is physically pumping antibiotics out of the cell via a multidrug-resistant efflux pump. I studied one such pump from the bacteria *Vibrio cholerae*, which causes cholera, a severe and often fatal diarrheal infection. During my 2 years of research. I was able to show that (1) the genes that make the proteins of the pump are transcribed together at the same time, (2) the regulatory protein functions as a negative regulator, and (3) the regulator binds to a specific portion of DNA upstream of the pump genes.

I have presented my research at one national conference, two state conferences, and twelve local conferences. I received First Place in the Undergraduate

Division of the TTUHSC Student Research Days Conference in both 2002 and 2003. I am also the first author on an article published in the *Journal of Bacteriology* entitled "Characterization of the *Vibrio cholerae vceCAB* Multiple-Drug Resistance Efflux Operon in *Escherichia coli*."

I thoroughly enjoyed my experiences in research. My undergraduate research molded my way of thinking into that of a scientist. It has enhanced my undergraduate education beyond that of traditional classes with lectures. I learned how to ask questions, design experiments, analyze data, and read scientific papers. I understood information on a level far beyond memorization: I could apply the information. I absolutely loved my research, however, it was not my passion. I was frustrated by the obstacles and I became bored with the protocols. I discovered through my research that I would rather know and learn about science on a broad scope than become an expert in only one area. I turned my attention toward science teaching.

Throughout my training in science education, I loved the feeling of excitement and pride after watching someone's "lightbulb turn on." I discovered the challenges of making science interesting for students who are uninterested. It was the biggest challenge of my life but also the most rewarding.

Upon my move to Cambridge, England, I was unsuccessful in my attempt to find teaching jobs due to UK/USA teaching certification inconsistencies. I was delighted to accept a position as a Research Grants Officer for the Alzheimer's Research Trust. The Alzheimer's Research Trust is the leading UK charity for medical research into Alzheimer's disease and related dementias. The position suits my personality and training perfectly. I utilize my research experience when reading and interpreting grant applications and progress reports. I utilize my teaching experience when converting the scientific reports into lay terminology so that we can inform our donors how their money has funded essential scientific research.

My experiences in undergraduate research have molded who I am today. I think scientifically. My college classes were a breeze because I could understand and apply the information rather than memorizing it. It gave me the opportunity to explore the possibility of becoming a research scientist and led me to my passion of helping to improve society as a liaison between scientists and the public.

"THE POWER OF DNA"

Wyatt McMahon, Postdoctoral Fellow

EDUCATING TOMORROW'S scientists is key to maintaining America's position at the forefront of the scientific and, therefore, economic world. One method of learning how to create new scientists involves understanding how today's scientists were formed. As a postdoc in plant and soil science, I now have the opportunity to look back on my formative scientific years and reflect on what brought me to where I am. In order to help others understand what is important in developing a scientist, I have enumerated the steps that drew me toward a career in science. It is my hope that describing these moments will give investigators perspective on how a student becomes a scientist.

Children are constantly asked what they want to be when they grow up. From an early age, I knew that I always wanted to contribute something to society. My father was very involved in projects that improved the city in which I was born. I recognized his dedication toward building a greater community, and as a youth I volunteered my time and efforts to clearing snow from sidewalks for the elderly, raising money for the poor, and building houses for the homeless. Such activities made me feel like I had made a difference to someone. Thus, when people asked me what I wanted to be, I realized that I wanted to help improve society, but I was not sure how.

I first began to consider a career in science as a teenager when my class went to the FBI building in Washington, D.C. Inside, I saw the forensics department, where scientists were using DNA to differentiate between suspects. If DNA from blood, semen, or a single hair was found at a crime scene, this DNA could be compared to DNA sequences from potential suspects for a crime. It was explained to me that the differences between individuals is largely due to the differences in the genes each individual carries. These scientists used the DNA found at a crime scene to determine which suspect was at the scene of the crime, thereby providing potent evidence toward convicting someone of a crime. This experience was important in my becoming a scientist because it taught me not only about the power of DNA, but about the variability between people, such that even small differences in DNA sequence could differentiate between individuals. I became fascinated with the power of DNA, and how I could wield that power toward the betterment of society.

The second moment that directed me toward biological research came the following school year, when a biology teacher taught me that while differences between people were found mainly at the level of DNA, every cell in an individual's body contains (mostly) the same DNA. Thus every cell in every tissue in the body contains essentially the same genes; however, only cells in the iris express the gene for colored muscle (i.e., eye color). Although I later learned that eye color is determined by a much more complicated process, the concept was clear: While individuals can be distinguished by the DNA they have in their cells, tissues are distinguished by the genes they express. Each tissue has a unique gene expression profile. Thus the reason the brain is responsible for thought and observation is because of the genes it expresses. I realized then that gene expression was a key process in determining a healthy individual.

After graduating from high school, I moved to Waco, Texas, to attend Baylor University because it had a reputation as being a good university for studying biology. Here was the third instance that suggested I should become a biological researcher. In my freshman biology classes, I learned that diseased tissues are often diseased because they express their genes incorrectly. They either express a gene they should not, or they do not express a gene they should. In particular, viral infections cause symptoms because of the genes expressed by the virus, and cancer is the result of abnormal gene expression. Therefore, it was during my college education that I began a deeper understanding of gene expression, and the importance it plays in maintaining health. With my freshman year at college under my belt, I decided to look into a career studying how genes were expressed, and thus began my career as a researcher.

Baylor offered little in the way of undergraduate research opportunities, and I therefore returned home to Lubbock, Texas, during the summers and joined the TTU/HHMI program. I began working in Dr. Clinton MacDonald's laboratory. He was interested in polyadenylation, an essential process in gene expression. Without polyadenylation, genes are not expressed, and aberrant polyadenylation has been shown to cause diseases of the blood, and has been implicated in maintaining a healthy immune system and fertility in men. This was the beginning of my undergraduate research and my introduction to life as a scientist.

For the rest of my tenure at college, I spent the school year at Baylor, taking courses in genetics, molecular biology, chemistry, and physics, all aimed at learning more about how genes are expressed. During the summers, I returned to Lubbock and the TTU/HHMI summer program, where I continued my research into polyadenylation. Additionally, I began to contribute to the understanding of gene expression processes. While I did not completely understand what impact I was having, I believed that working in a research laboratory was more helpful to society than what many of my friends were doing during their summer jobs. Therefore, not only was I following my passion of understanding gene expression, but I was also helping society through my studies. With hindsight, I see that the projects I was involved in were not changing the world, but they were moving science forward and moving me closer to a career in science.

My first project was to study a portion of a protein (called a *domain*) involved in polyadenylation. Preliminary studies suggested that this domain was involved in "measuring" the distances in various steps in polyadenylation. My project was to purify this domain and then send it to collaborators who would study its structure. I learned a great deal in this first project because I was unable to purify this domain. I learned how frustrating science can sometimes be and how not all research can yield a result. However, we eventually had the domain synthesized and analyzed by a machine. This experience taught me that not everything in science is finished the way one hopes. Rather, an imaginative mind and a great deal of patience are necessary for a real contribution to be made. But, with my first research article in press, I had my first taste of success and was eager for more.

My second project as an undergraduate researcher had larger implications. At the time, our laboratory had noticed that cells that give rise to sperm—called *male germ cells*—carried out polyadenylation differently than did other cells. These differences suggested that there was another protein involved in polyadenylation in male germ cells that was absent from other cells. My project was to better understand some of the tools that we were using to study polyadenylation, and I did an experiment that indirectly led to the discovery of a protein found only in male germ cells, which appeared to be involved in polyadenylation. The excitement this generated also taught me a great deal. I learned that there is often a little bit of luck involved in any great discovery, but that one can only take advantage of luck by working hard. I had done an experiment with one purpose, but because I worked hard and paid attention to the results, I was able to make a significant contribution to gene expression research. With this discovery, I coauthored my second paper and finally made a real contribution to science and society.

After completing my college degree (BS in Biology from Baylor University), I enrolled in a PhD program at the University of Texas Health Sciences Center at San Antonio. My years as an undergraduate researcher became invaluable here as the program was very demanding. My experiences had taught me much about how science was conducted, and I therefore had an academic advantage over many of my classmates.

I completed my first year of graduate school and joined a laboratory studying a disease that was the result of aberrant gene expression. Individuals with this disease did not express a normal copy of a gene involved in DNA damage repair. As a result, these patients suffered from maladies that included lung infections, loss of muscle control, and cancer. My project was to express a normal copy of this gene in cells from these patients and see whether it alleviated the symptoms of this disease. The project was demanding and important, and my previous experiences as an undergraduate researcher were invaluable. Many experiments I undertook failed, but I never quit trying because I believed that hard work would result in a great discovery. Sure enough, within a year I had successfully expressed the normal copy of that gene in cells from patients and alleviated their symptoms. I wrote a third paper and was invited to speak at a San Antonio Cancer Institute meeting, and began to feel that I could make a real impact on the world as a scientist.

Despite early successes in San Antonio, I understood that the faculty at Texas Tech University Health Sciences Center in Lubbock, where I had done my undergraduate research, were more involved in their students' education than the faculty in San Antonio. I therefore chose to return to Dr. Clinton MacDonald's laboratory as a PhD student, again studying polyadenylation.

Upon my return, I was fortunate enough to get an exciting project. The protein I helped discover as an undergraduate appeared to be involved in polyadenylation, but there had never been a direct test of this. It therefore became my project to test whether this protein really was involved in polyadenylation. After 5 years in the laboratory, I believe I have compiled enough data to say that our protein is involved in polyadenylation.

I began my career in science wanting to serve society, as well as satisfy my curiosity for how gene expression contributes to the health of an individual. As I have progressed through my studies, I have learned how to use my newfound skills to achieve both goals. As of now, my career is moving toward understanding the viruses and bacteria that could be used in a biological attack on the United States, by working in a laboratory dedicated to biological defense. Understanding the genes these organisms express will be crucial in developing fast, inexpensive treatments for the diseases they cause, thereby diminishing any casualties caused by such an attack. I will therefore continue to work to serve humankind as I continue my studies in gene expression. And I feel confident that my earliest experiences— from my father's dedication to the city to my trip to the FBI building—formed my direction. I am looking forward to a long and happy career using science to help serve the public.

"A SENSE THAT THERE WERE NO LIMITATIONS TO WHAT I COULD DO AS A GRADUATE STUDENT"

Susan Harrell Yee, NHEERL Postdoctoral Research Fellow

WHEN I FIRST started as a freshman at Texas Tech University, I chose environmental engineering as my major. It seemed a wise decision: I liked math and I liked ecology, and environmental engineering seemed to be a logical combination of the two. But after a single day, I knew the engineering route was not for me. I enjoyed biology and math as interesting sciences in and of themselves, not merely tools you can apply toward engineering. So I changed my major to pure math with a biology minor. My instincts told me to stick with classes I enjoyed, although I was still oblivious to what career I could find that would combine the two.

Luckily, the teaching assistant for my biology course saw more potential in me than I saw in myself. He said math skills are an enormous and uncommon asset in the biological sciences, even in ecology. He encouraged me to work as an undergraduate researcher for his own master's advisor, Dr. Michael Willig. I applied for the TTU/HHMI program in the spring of my freshman year. I had zero experience doing actual scientific research, aside from a few biology labs learning the basics of hypothesis testing, and had no idea what to expect. The reality of a career in science was a totally foreign concept. Dr. Willig's first task for me was to begin helping a PhD student, Dianne Hall, with her research. Dianne was sampling playa lakes in West Texas to understand how the surrounding land use (agriculture, rangeland, or conservation protected) affected invertebrate communities in the lakes. So my very first experience as a young ecologist was slogging through a foot of mud in the middle of a lake wearing a pair of oversized wading pants, in order to collect invertebrates. But it was fun and interesting, and I was getting paid to do it! So I spent my undergraduate career leading dual lives as a math student and field ecologist.

I soon went on to work on some of my own projects. In a project similar in concept to Dianne's, I took water samples from playa lakes to investigate how the surrounding land use affects the bacterial community. I presented this research at several scientific meetings, including Sigma Xi Research Days at Texas Tech and the annual meeting of the Southwestern Association of Naturalists. I won awards for First Place student poster at both meetings. I also presented this work at the annual meeting of the Ecological Society of America. This is a major meeting attended by more than a thousand ecologists, and I had the opportunity to meet several eminent scientists and fellow students, as well as learning about current research. Being able to interact with other scientists and discuss each others' research is a necessary skill in a scientific career, and the TTU/HHMI program certainly encouraged participation in meetings.

In another project, I established playa microcosms in a greenhouse to study the invertebrate community. I removed an opportunistic predator, tadpole shrimp, from half of the microcosms to determine how this species affects the invertebrate community. Counterintuitively, we found the presence of this predator actually had a positive effect on many invertebrate species, as its foraging activities stirred up sediment, and encouraged buried invertebrate eggs to hatch. Dr. Willig encouraged me to write up this research as a manuscript for publication, another necessary skill to survive as a scientist. This process involves analyzing data, creating graphs, organizing, reading similar research, writing, rewriting, choosing a journal, submitting, rewriting, resubmitting. It is a tough process for anyone to go through, but getting early practice at it has certainly given me an edge in graduate school and my current postdoctoral position.

I am most grateful to the TTU/HHMI program for giving me the opportunity to conduct research in Puerto Rico for two summers. Dr. Willig monitored snails and other invertebrates as part of the Long-Term Ecological Research program at El Verde Field Station. This provides valuable long-term data which can be used, in part, to assess forest recovery after hurricanes. In addition to helping a graduate student with his PhD research assessing invertebrate diversity in water-filled heliconia bracts, I conducted my own research project examining whether light gaps in the forest canopy led to increased herbivory on understory plants.

I enjoyed my undergraduate research enough that I was willing to continue my scientific career by entering graduate school. I wanted to continue doing experimental ecology, but strengthen my skills by learning mathematical modeling.

I got my master's degree in mathematics at the University of Tennessee with a purely theoretical project modeling how the spatial distribution of predators affects the interaction with their prey, but I missed doing the empirical research I had enjoyed as an undergraduate. For my PhD at the University of Chicago, I was determined to find a project combining experimental research with mathematical modeling. For my dissertation research, I developed a novel technique for fitting complex stochastic spatial models to spatial and temporal data, in order to delineate what biological mechanisms are important in explaining observed dynamics in an ant-treehopper mutualism. I also used system-specific models to interpret experimental data that I collected assessing the roles of treehopper movement and spatial distribution on survival.

I currently have my dream job as an NHEERL Postdoctoral Fellow with the United States Environmental Protection Agency. I am using my modeling skills to investigate the influence of environmental factors on bleaching and disease susceptibility of corals, and to develop spatially explicit methods for risk assessment of fish populations. The TTU/HHMI program was a pivotal first step in what is turning out to be a promising and enjoyable career as an ecologist.

My experience as a TTU/HHMI undergraduate researcher provided me with invaluable experiences as a scientist. When students enter graduate school, one of the major setbacks is just learning how to be a graduate student and a scientist. Undergraduate research allows a new graduate student to hit the floor running. I already had experience in reading the primary literature, finding and designing a project, analyzing data, organizing results into a presentation, and writing up a manuscript for publication. This gave me a great deal of confidence as I entered graduate school, where it is easy for new students to feel insecure, intimidated, and overwhelmed. Also, because I had done a variety of projects and traveling as an undergraduate, I had the sense that there were no limitations to what I could do as a graduate student. Most important, I made valuable contacts and friends as an undergraduate student that continue to be my research colleagues even today, 10 years later.

"THE OPPORTUNITY TO PERFORM UNIQUE RESEARCH WITH A POTENTIALLY DANGEROUS ORGANISM"

Trevor Brasel, Laboratory Supervisor

"DANS LES CHAMPS de l'observation le hasard ne favorise que les esprits prepares" (In matters of observation chance favors only the prepared mind). These are the words of one of the great pioneers of microbiology, Louis Pasteur (1822–1895), when he was installed as professor and dean of a newly created Faculty of Sciences at Lille in France. The words turned out to be serendipitous in that they were spoken well before any of the discoveries for which Pasteur is best known were made. At the time, Pasteur was a chemist researching the intricacies of tartaric acid, a compound found in cream of tartar and Rochelle salt (used to silver mirrors)—indeed, not the most monumental of tasks. The region of France where Pasteur took his position was well known for its breweries and distilleries in which alcohol was produced from beet root sugar. At the time, it was thought that fermentation was purely a chemical process. An owner who obtained low product yields would logically ask the help of a local chemist to attempt to solve the problem. Pasteur was approached and agreed to try to determine why sugar was converted into alcohol in some vats, but was converted to acid in others. This chance encounter turned Pasteur's attention from tartaric acid research to the process of fermentation. Louis Pasteur's observations and experimentation convinced him that living organisms were responsible for fermentation, a conclusion that led to the development of a brand new microbiological field of inquiry for which he is renowned.

Like Pasteur, it would seem that chance and a prepared mind have led me to where I am today. I am a microbiologist specializing in the fields of aerosol science and biodefense research. Ever since I was a young boy, I desired to become a scientist (an astronaut or president of the United States were my next choices). The term *scientist* sounded prestigious to me at the time, but honestly, I was naive in all aspects of a scientist's responsibilities and did not have the slightest realization of how important this work can be. My interest in the biological sciences peaked when I began my high school education. My ninth-grade biology teacher, Mr. MacAllen, would always make class interesting with his imaginative stories and demonstrations. I can still remember a story in which he became the unfortunate victim of an octopus's tentacles while doing research for his master's thesis. Probably not so funny to Mr. Mac at the time, but we students could not help but laugh out loud. As I continued my high school career, I enrolled in as many science classes, particularly biology, as I could. I came to realize that the world of biology was far more intricate and exciting than I had realized. It was a field with seemingly endless opportunity and one in which I wanted to be involved.

I graduated from high school as an honors student in 1996. I was in the top 3% of my class of 550 students and thought I knew everything. After a non-challenging year in junior college (to complete my basic course requirements), I was accepted to Texas Tech University. I decided to major in cell and molecular biology primarily because of the title I could receive; how cool would it be to become a Cell and Molecular Biologist? It was during my first year at Tech that I came to realize how intricate biology could be and how little I knew. I will not go into detail about my academic career at the time, but it was certainly subpar. I simply was not enjoying the courses associated with my major. However, any mention of bacteria (DNA replication therein for instance) greatly peaked my interest. I was so fascinated at how such a simple organism could be so complicated. Moreover, I was amazed at how bacteria and other microbes were able to adapt and evade mankind's best attempts at defeating them. On a whim, I changed my major to Microbiology. Sure, it was going to set me back a semester, but I had a feeling it would be worthwhile.

My college education started to improve from the moment I modified my degree plan. My classes were much more enjoyable and my grade point average vastly improved. I made many new friends who were always willing to discuss current matters in microbiology and other fields of science. One chance encounter led to friendships with two members of the TTU/HHMI program. They advised me to apply to the program and, to this day, I am thankful that I took their advice. I applied to TTU/HHMI in the fall of 1998. I remember the interview well. Unfortunately, my past academic mishaps came back to haunt me. I was certain that I would not be accepted to the prestigious program. In fact, the next semester, as decisions were being made, I received a phone call from Julie Isom (the TTU/HHMI Associate Program Director) saying that I was not accepted. From the little that she knew about me, Julie seemed to understand my personality quite well, and as it turned out she was joking. I am usually the one to play such tricks on people, but I was more than obliged to have such a turn of play. Julie told me that it was my passion for the field of microbiology that convinced the program to accept me. I was sincerely thankful and could not wait to get started in my new scientific endeavors.

My first interview was with Dr. David Straus in the Department of Microbiology and Immunology at Texas Tech University Health Sciences Center. TTU/HHMI normally requests that new Fellows interview five different professors, but I only needed one. Dr. Straus's research involving mold-contaminated indoor environments and the phenomenon known as "sick building syndrome" (SBS) was completely foreign to me and something that I desired to explore further. Beginning in the summer of 1999, I worked as a TTU/HHMI Undergraduate Research Fellow in the laboratory of Dr. Straus until I completed my bachelor's degree in microbiology in May of 2000. Though only a Fellow for one year, my knowledge of practical research science vastly matured. Studying in a classroom is one thing; devising experiments and carrying them out is distinctively another. I learned from my mistakes and, believe me, they were numerous. To this day, I believe that one cannot fully understand science without being intimately involved. My project as a TTU/HHMI Fellow was concerned with the isolation and characterization of a proteolytic enzyme produced by a fungus commonly found in water-damaged buildings, *Penicillium chrysogenum*. We hypothesized that this protease was the cause of certain allergic responses experienced by people in such environments. At the conclusion of my undergraduate tenure in the lab, a graduate student continued the research for his doctoral thesis. The work was significant and was presented at numerous national meetings and has since been published in several peer-reviewed journal articles.

My experience as a TTU/HHMI undergraduate researcher was thoroughly enjoyable. Because of this, I wanted to continue work in the laboratory of Dr. Straus and thus applied for graduate school at the Health Sciences Center. No doubt, my status as a TTU/HHMI Fellow reflected well upon my character as an individual with a potential successful future in research science. I was accepted into graduate school shortly after my graduation in 2000. My research shifted from studying the allergenic properties of *P. chrysogenum* to characterizing toxin production by *Stachybotrys chartarum*. This was an exciting transformation for me because I now had the opportunity to perform unique research with a potentially dangerous organism. *S. chartarum* is known to produce many potent mycotoxins (known as trichothecenes) and is thought to play a major role in SBS. My dissertation work was concerned with the collection and detection of airborne trichothecene mycotoxins in buildings contaminated with *S. chartarum*. This area of research was considered a "hot topic" and throughout my career as a graduate student, I met many prestigious individuals, worked in various settings outside of Lubbock, and presented at numerous national meetings including podium presentations in front of large audiences. My research was praised by several key individuals in the field—talk about a confidence booster. When people begin to recognize and commend your work, it really makes you feel like your research is worthwhile and that you are indeed a capable scientist. Though I had many grueling hours in biohazard suits, I successfully completed my project and graduated with a PhD in medical microbiology in December of 2004. From my 5 years at the Health Sciences Center, I was able to publish three first author manuscripts and six co-authorships in peer-reviewed journals. I have been told by many people that this was an unusual feat for graduate students and something of which to be proud—and I am.

So how in the world did I switch from studying mold to doing research in aerosol science and biological defense? It was the tragedies of September 11, 2001, and the ensuing anthrax letters in the Washington, D.C., area that made abundantly clear to me that the United States was not prepared for terrorist attacks, particularly those involving biological organisms. Biological defense research had always been one of my passions. I even remember discussing this in my TTU/HHMI interview. As much as we know about microbiology, we know very little about how to prevent attacks with dangerous microbes. By chance, at one of the American Society for Microbiology meetings, I came upon an opening for a postdoctoral position under the Defense Threat Reduction Agency (DTRA). One project involved the development of a new bioaerosol sampler for potentially dangerous microbes. My broad knowledge of aerosol samplers and experience with dangerous microbes was perfect for the position. Furthermore, *S. chartarum* was going to be used as a test organism. There was a twist though—I would have to spend half of my time in Russian laboratories. Personally, I found this to be an exciting opportunity. What better way to get involved in biodefense research than by working side-by-side with Russian scientists who played major roles in the massive biological weapons program of the former Soviet Union? My wife thought otherwise. After much discussion, however, my wife and I decided this would be best for our future and I took the job. I began work in 2005, immediately after finishing the exhausting task of writing my dissertation. The project was contracted by DTRA through Lovelace Respiratory Research Institute in Albuquerque, New Mexico. Though immensely different from Lubbock, Albuquerque is a culturally unique city rich in science and opportunity. I am happy with the decisions I have made in my career and look forward to what chance will offer me in the future.

I can never fully thank TTU/HHMI for all they have given me, but I will always do my best by keeping a prepared mind and performing science to the best of my ability. My scientific career has evolved into what I set out to become those many years ago in Mr. Mac's biology class. To this day, I continue to interact with TTU/HHMI whenever possible, be it through a simple "hello, how are you" e-mail or by presenting my experiences to new undergraduate Fellows. I often find myself bragging about the program and explaining the benefits of undergraduate research to Lovelace employees, particularly those initiating their scientific career. As cliché as it may sound, I can honestly say that I would not be where I am today without my undergraduate research experiences and TTU/HHMI. I can only imagine what the future holds.

"AN INVALUABLE EXPERIENCE AT SUCH AN EARLY PART OF MY CAREER"

Natasha J. Mehdiabadi, NSF Postdoctoral Research Fellow

EFFECTIVE TEACHERS are important role models. I learned this firsthand when I was enrolled in a biology class during my sophomore year at Texas Tech University. I was an undecided major at the time, but things were soon to change. Dr. Mark McGinley was the professor, and his enthusiasm for the course material was contagious. I found myself wanting to learn more about ecology, evolution, and behavior. I not only read the book and notes associated with the course, but I also met Dr. McGinley regularly during his office hours to talk with him about what I had learned and to ask him questions that had intrigued me. When he recognized my genuine interest in the course, he encouraged me to get involved in scientific research.

At that time, it was the inaugural year of the TTU/HHMI program, and I was fortunate to become one of the first recipients of a fellowship. Dr. McGinley and I began brainstorming for potential projects in plant community ecology (his area of research expertise). I immediately got a taste for research life—exploring ideas, reading the literature, testing hypotheses, and devising an appropriate experimental design to test those hypotheses. It was clear that research was very hard work, but I was invested in this experience and was having the time of my life.

I began working on a project that examined the effects of soil nutrient content and the microbial community on seedling growth of the grass species, *Schizachyrium scoparium*. This grass species was native to the area, and little was known about the independent and interactive effects of these variables on plant growth. With the culmination of this project, I was given an opportunity to present this work at the meetings of the American Association for the Advancement of Science and the Ecological Society of America. To learn how to effectively communicate my work to an audience was an invaluable experience at such an early part of my career.

Another project that I performed during my TTU/HHMI undergraduate research experience was investigating the effects of animal-generated disturbances on seedling growth of several grass species in a sand shinnery oak system. One of the animal-generated disturbances that had the most significant effects on plant growth was harvester ant mounds. These results intrigued me, so I went to the library to find out what previous work had been done on harvester ants. I found many journal articles by Dr. Deborah Gordon, a professor at Stanford University. At this time, I was about to graduate from Texas Tech, and I realized that I wanted to continue on with research because of my life-changing TTU/HHMI experience. As a result of my newfound interest in harvester ants, I applied to work on a master's degree with Dr. Gordon at Stanford and was accepted in the fall of 1996.

There is no doubt in my mind—my TTU/HHMI experience was my ticket into graduate school. To have gained research experience during my undergraduate years was quite rare at that time, and the experience set me apart from others. In addition, I showed that I was capable of generating my own funding, which is essential in academia.

I had a fairly smooth transition from undergraduate to graduate school. Because I already knew what research entailed, I was ahead of most other graduate students. I already knew how to go about finding a research question. I already knew how to come up with the best experimental design to test a hypothesis. I already knew how to work diligently every day on a research project. I already knew how to analyze and interpret results. I already knew all of these things because of my TTU/HHMI undergraduate research experience.

During my master's work, I continued with my general interests in the ecology and evolution of social interactions. I examined how an ant's tendency to perform a certain task was related to its brief encounters with others. This work demonstrated that brief antennal contacts might be an important cue for allowing ants to respond to changing conditions and to perceive the behaviors of others so that the society can function and survive. Dr. Gordon and I published this work in one of the leading journals of the field, *Behavioral Ecology and Sociobiology*.

After receiving my master's degree in just one year, I knew that I was ready for the next step: a PhD. Because I wanted to continue studying the ecology and evolution of social interactions by using ants as a model system, I applied to several PhD programs around the country. It was evident that my TTU/HHMI experience combined with my master's work gave me the opportunity to get a PhD at one of the best programs in the nation: the University of Texas at Austin.

For my dissertation, I examined the costs and benefits of antagonistic and mutualistic interactions between ants and their symbionts. My work with Dr. Larry Gilbert and Dr. Ulrich Mueller led me to gain greater depth and knowledge in my study of social interactions, which initially began during my TTU/HHMI undergraduate research experience.

Currently I am an NSF postdoctoral fellow at Rice University with Dr. Joan Strassmann and Dr. David Queller. My research program still centers on the evolution of cooperation and conflict; however, I now use a new model system (a social microbe in addition to ants) and a new level of analysis (molecular work in addition to fieldwork) to investigate this fundamental question in evolutionary biology.

As I begin the process of applying for tenure-track positions, I reflect fondly on my past research experiences. I would not have found my "dream job" if it were not for my undergraduate research mentor and TTU/HHMI. As I get closer to achieving my ultimate career goal of becoming a university professor, I look forward to becoming a mentor like Dr. McGinley and to giving back to an outstanding program that changed my life.

ACKNOWLEDGMENTS

The authors of these narratives would like to thank the Texas Tech University Howard Hughes Medical Institute Science Education Program for funding, but more importantly for the experience, guidance, and mentorship that has shaped our careers.

CHAPTER 12

A Brief History of Undergraduate Research, with Consideration of Its Alternative Futures

Richard L. Blanton

UNDERGRADUATE RESEARCH has traditionally been an informal cottage industry of individual arrangements between students and professors, plus a network of federally funded summer research opportunities (e.g., the Summer Undergraduate Laboratory Internships at the various Department of Energy National Laboratories; the Research Experiences for Undergraduates sites funded by the National Science Foundation). The cottage industry is alive and well, but in recent years undergraduate research has developed into a movement, as manifested by the signs of institutionalization: organized undergraduate research programs, offices of undergraduate research, high-level administrative positions dedicated to undergraduate research, undergraduate research journals, undergraduate research symposia, and societies dedicated to undergraduate research (e.g., CUR—the Council on Undergraduate Research, founded in 1978; NCUR—National Conferences on Undergraduate Research, founded in 1987). Groups of undergraduate researchers descend upon state capitols, displaying their work at "Research in the Capitol" events around the country. Undergraduate research has become the topic of scholarly studies presented at national meetings (e.g., the Reinvention Center national and regional conferences; the "Student as Scholar: Undergraduate Research and Creative Practice" conference sponsored in 2007 by AAC&U, the Association of American Colleges and Universities). Serious efforts began to be made to evaluate the impact of undergraduate research programs (reviewed in Seymour, Hunter, Laursen, & Deantoni, 2004; see also Hunter, Laursen, & Seymour, 2006; Lopatto, 2004; Russell, Hancock, & McCullough, 2007; and the chapters in this volume).

In this chapter, I explore the questions of why an undergraduate research movement occurred, how that movement has affected the traditional undergraduate research experience, and what kinds of future developments we can expect for undergraduate research. To begin, I will set a historic context for undergraduate research.

A BRIEF HISTORY OF UNDERGRADUATE RESEARCH

A comprehensive history of undergraduate research has not yet been written. Instead, we must rely upon biographies and memoirs to build a picture of undergraduate research over the years. A cursory review of selected scientific biographies and memoirs reveals undergraduate research to have a long history. In fact, it may be that undergraduate research has occurred for as long as there have been undergraduates. Consider Isaac Newton, undergraduate at Trinity College, Cambridge University, from 1661–1665. Working independently as an undergraduate student, he discovered the generalized binomial theorem, made initial insights into mechanics, and laid the groundwork for the 18 months following the receipt of his undergraduate degree, when he discovered calculus, the law of gravity, and the principles of optics (Westfall, 1980).

Consider Charles Darwin, initially an undergraduate at the University of Edinburgh, 1825–1827, where he engaged in extensive independent collecting expeditions, presented original results to the Plinian Society (a group of undergraduates interested in natural history and antiquarian research), and even encountered professional jealousy from his research mentor, who published Darwin's original observations without attribution or acknowledgment of his contribution (Browne, 1995). Darwin transferred to Christ's College, Cambridge University, where he pursued undergraduate studies from 1828–1831, continuing his avid field collecting (including supplying specimens to experts) and being integrated into the intellectual community by his mentor, John Stevens Henslow (Browne, 1995).

Thomas Hunt Morgan welcomed Columbia University undergraduates Calvin B. Bridges, Alfred Henry Sturtevant, and H. J. Muller into his laboratory in 1910. Thus was born the legendary "fly room" and modern genetics. Morgan guided all three to their PhDs, and in 1915 shared with them the authorship of *The Mechanism of Mendelian Heredity* (Allen, 1978).

Dorothy Crowfoot Hodgkin had a childhood fascination with patterns (including those of the mosaics uncovered by her archeologist parents in the Middle East), chemistry, and crystals. As an undergraduate, she spent a research summer in Heidelberg and began her research using X-ray crystallography while an undergraduate at Sommerville College, Oxford University (Ferry, 1998; Nobel Foundation, 1972).

Rita Levi-Montalcini worked on several research projects as an undergraduate medical student with the histologist Giuseppe Levi (Levi-Montalcini, 1988; McGrayne, 1998). Richard Feynmann published two scientific papers before receiving his bachelor's degree from MIT in 1939; the second paper, "Forces and Stresses in Molecules," lives on as the Hellman-Feynmann Theorem (Gribbin & Gribbin, 1997). John Tyler Bonner's long and productive career of research involving the cellular slime mold *Dictyostelium discoideum* began with two years of undergraduate research on that organism (Bonner, 2002). Edward O. Wilson engaged in research from his first days on the campus of the University of Alabama in 1946. His expertise with ants led to a temporary leave of absence from his undergraduate studies to accept a 4-month appointment with the Alabama Department of Conservation to study fire ants and their impact upon the environment, yielding a report with original findings on those ants (Wilson, 1994).

The autobiographies provided by most Nobel Laureates until 2005 provide useful sources for identifying undergraduate research involvement. A review by this author of all the autobiographies for the period 1996–2005 revealed that 9 of 26 chemistry, 8 of 22 physiology or medicine, and 14 of 27 physics Nobel Laureates described having been involved in undergraduate research (Nobel Foundation, 2007).

Studies of the accomplishments of women scientists provide another opportunity to detect the influence of undergraduate research experiences. Of 15 female Nobel laureates and "near-laureates" (as defined by McGrayne, 1988), three are described as having engaged in undergraduate research (McGrayne, 1998). A study of female members of the National Academy of Sciences concluded that "hands-on experience in a research laboratory at an early stage persuaded many women to become scientists" (Wasserman, 2000, p. 176). However, only 4 of the 26 women profiled actually described having formative undergraduate research experiences. In two other compendia of profiles of women scientists, zero of 10 (Yount, 1994) and 2 of 23 (Reynolds, 1999) include an undergraduate research experience.

This brief survey of scientific biographies and memoirs reveals that undergraduate research experiences are common (but by no means universal) in the backgrounds of prominent scientists, many of whom cite those experiences as being formative. With the exception of Newton's extraordinary achievements, the undergraduate research experiences described by and for these scientists are typical. For some, it was the natural extension of an already well-developed enthusiasm; others were drawn to research by a particularly effective course, still others as an escape from an ineffective curriculum. For many, their undergraduate research experience occupied most if not all of their undergraduate years. For others, the research came as a natural part of their curriculum, necessary for a senior honors thesis or honors degree. Only a few mention making discoveries that resulted in publications. A small number worked independently (with varying levels of supervision); most were members of research groups. Some cite the importance of the experience in introducing them to the culture of science.

In only two instances were formal undergraduate research programs identified, but this is likely due to the relative youth of such programs and the seniority of the scientists in the sources that were consulted. Robert Richardson, 1996 Nobel Laureate in Physics, cited in his Nobel autobiography the formative experience of a summer research internship at the National Bureau of Standards (Frängsmyr, 1997). Mary K. Gaillard, theoretical physicist and member of the National Academy of Science, stated that a summer research experience at the Brookhaven National Laboratory "is what really got me into physics" (Wasserman, 2000). By searching further back into the Nobel autobiographies we can find that Thomas Cech, 1989 Nobel Laureate in Chemistry, identified summer undergraduate research at the Argonne and Lawrence Berkeley National Laboratories (Frängsmyr, 1990) as being responsible for motivating him to pursue a research career.

The conclusion from this brief historical review is that undergraduate research has a long and rich history with significant (albeit self-reported) impact upon the careers of scientists. The vast majority of these experiences were within the context of the "cottage industry," individual students finding ways to connect to an ongoing research enterprise. If undergraduate research has existed for so long, what catalyzed the recent development of an undergraduate research movement?

ORIGINS OF THE UNDERGRADUATE RESEARCH MOVEMENT

What were the motivating factors for the undergraduate research movement? One was the Boyer Commission report (Boyer Commission on Educating Undergraduates in the Research University, 1998), which recommended that research universities involve more undergraduates in the research programs of faculty members. Another was the grant competitions sponsored by the Undergraduate Biological Sciences Education Program of the Howard Hughes Medical Institute (HHMI). Many institutions proposed to meet HHMI's goal of broadening access to science by developing undergraduate research programs that sought to involve more women and members of underrepresented minority groups in the sciences. Further motivation was provided by the increased emphasis on the integration of research and education by the National Science Foundation, underscored by the special one-time competitions in 1997 for Recognition Awards for the Integration of Research and Education (RAIRE) and in 1998 for Awards for the Integration of Research and Education (AIRE), and always present in the "broadened impacts" criterion applied in all grant reviews.

The grant programs may explain the initiation of many new formalized undergraduate research programs, but the institutionalization of undergraduate research (offices of undergraduate research, administrative positions, institutional funding of undergraduate research programs) was driven by the perceived benefits of these programs for the institution and students. To illustrate, I will describe the history of the development of the HHMI-sponsored undergraduate research program at Texas Tech University. The effect of the program on its participants can be read in the chapters by Henne et al. (Chapter 11) and Campbell and Skoog (Chapter 10), which present the stories of just six and seven, respectively, of the 372 students who have been supported by the program.

Texas Tech was first invited to submit an application to the 1992 competition of the HHMI's Undergraduate Biological Sciences Education Program. The timing of the invitation was ideal, because the Department of Biological Sciences had been transformed by the hiring of 17 new, research-active faculty members over the period of 1986–1990. However, the department's long-standing tradition of effective teaching and faculty involvement with undergraduates remained intact. There were abundant opportunities for undergraduates to pursue research, not only in the Department of Biological Sciences, but with life sciences researchers located in the Department of Chemistry and Biochemistry, Department of Physics, various departments in the Colleges of Agriculture and Engineering, and in the Texas Tech University Health Sciences Center. The life sciences majors included a high percentage of females and a growing population of Hispanic students.

As we designed our proposal, we documented a long history of undergraduate involvement in research, but noted that many of those experiences were short term and late in the academic careers of the students. We decided that our greatest need was to have a program that would enable early involvement in research and would provide a continuous, year-round research experience. Our goal was to give students the opportunity to become fully integrated into a research team and to pursue a project to the point of presentation and publication. Our reasoning was that we would present the participating students with a more realistic research experience and, by involving them earlier in their careers, would maximize the chances that the experience would impact their career decision. Furthermore, we reasoned that integration into a research group and an early, long-term research experience would provide a supportive environment and motivating experience for women and members of underrepresented minority groups.

Texas Tech was awarded its first HHMI grant in 1992 and received subsequent awards in 1994, 1998, 2002, and 2006. As we had anticipated, the grants provided a diverse group of Texas Tech students with long-term, continuous research experiences. However, there were unanticipated consequences that led to significant institutional support of our program. For example, we found that the formal undergraduate research programs conferred a competitive advantage on our institution. We began to see students declining offers from nationally prestigious institutions in favor of attending Texas Tech because of our HHMI-funded undergraduate research program and its promise of early involvement and continuous support. Texas Tech moved from being the "safe," or backup, institution for many applicants interested in biology to their primary choice.

The program conferred prestige. In a state where the flagship state institutions in Austin and College Station rule most things, it was particularly sweet when Texas Tech ranked first among all Texas institutions (public and private) in cumulative HHMI education funding and, in fact, for a time was the only institution in Texas to have an active HHMI education grant. Prior to the HHMI grants, Texas Tech had one Goldwater scholar; since the first HHMI grant to date, there have been 27 (22 of them TTU/HHMI participants). Additional prestige accrued from our Gates-Cambridge scholars, numerous student research awards at national meetings, students as authors on papers in prestigious journals, and student matriculations at prestigious graduate institutions. Senior administrators recognized the contributions that had been made by the program and began to dedicate significant institutional funds to the program, provided it with state-funded staff positions, and assigned it increased amounts of space. The university-level Center for the Integration of Science Education and Research was established to provide institutional context for the program.

Texas Tech and its students were not alone in experiencing these and other benefits of a formal undergraduate research program. In what is perhaps the ultimate endorsement of a trend in higher education in these sad times, undergraduate research began to be featured in the annual *US News and World Report* rankings publication. Recently, it has been featured in the *Chronicle of Higher Education* (Guterman, 2007) and *Science* (Mervis, 2007).

Because undergraduate research mattered in the competition for top students, it could no longer be left to chance, but required administrative guidance and support, Web-based databases of research opportunities, and institutional funds for undergraduate research stipends. The formal efforts are as diverse as the institutions hosting them. Some operate mostly as resource centers, providing guidance and information on opportunities at the home campus and elsewhere. Some are limited to summer opportunities, others to academic year opportunities. Some are early involvement, long-term support programs. Programs may offer stipends that compete favorably with part-time jobs during the academic year or full-time summer jobs, or they may offer token stipends, or even no stipends. Some have substantial infrastructure, with several staff members, support funds for travel and student camaraderie events, and large pools of money for student stipends. Some target women, others members of minority groups underrepresented in the sciences. Some address specific university goals, such as retention. Some operate as bridge programs, providing research experiences the summer prior to matriculation in the university or college. Some academic year and most summer programs operate as living-learning programs, with the research students living together in a university residence hall. In the midst of the formal undergraduate research programs, it should be noted that the long-standing tradition in undergraduate research of individual arrangements between students and mentors still persists.

The increased emphasis upon and institutionalization of undergraduate research are mostly to be celebrated. However, they bring their own challenges, addressed in the next section.

CHALLENGES PRESENTED BY THE UNDERGRADUATE RESEARCH MOVEMENT

The challenges presented by the undergraduate research movement include (1) the challenge of assessment, (2) the challenge of authenticity, (3) the challenge of increased expectations, and (4) the challenge of sustainability.

The Challenge of Assessment

Formal programs supported by institutional or grant funds are expected to demonstrate their effectiveness to justify continued funding. Most programs perform some kind of assessment, and some of those studies have been published, although for various reasons most of them are of limited utility in establishing the benefits of undergraduate research (Seymour et al., 2004). The challenges to effective assessment of programs are discussed in this volume by Locks and Gregerman (Chapter 2), Bauer and Bennett (Chapter 5), Lopatto (Chapter 6), and Hunter et al. (Chapter 7). There are the challenges of small sample sizes, inadequacy of instruments, costs of evaluation studies, and lack of appropriate control groups. A key question is, What are the desired outcomes for a program? At the University of Michigan, the formal undergraduate research program was seen as a mechanism for retention of underrepresented minority students, and its demonstrated success in student retention led to further institutional support for the program (Locks & Gregerman, Chap-ter 2). At the University of Delaware, a multifaceted approach was used, involving surveys of current students, alumni, and faculty, and a longitudinal study of a group of undergraduates, which together yielded insights into the value of undergraduate research (Bauer & Bennett, Chapter 5). Another approach is that of Kardash et al. (Chapter 9), who approach not only the question of gains from undergraduate research, but also disappointments, that is, the negative effects of the experience and what might be done to help address those in a program.

Hunter et al. (Chapter 7) argue that "to focus on institutional and extrinsic measures of success for undergraduate research, rather than on students' personal, intellectual, and professional growth, is missing the point." Their study joins those of Lopatto (Chapter 6; Lopatto, 2004), Taraban et al. (Chapter 8), and Russell (Chapter 4; Russell et al., 2007), in featuring larger sample sizes (very large in the case of Russell), involving multiple institutions, and focusing on specific gains made by the students. The studies reaffirm the benefits of undergraduate research experiences. Each provides insights into what makes for effective experiences: Russell (Chapter 4; Russell et al., 2007) identified length of experience as a key factor and the importance of the experience in graduate school and career decisions. She also determined that requiring research experiences would be counterproductive. Hunter et al. (Chapter 7) found that students emphasized personal–professional transitions as gains, as did their advisors, who also stressed socialization as one of the students' gains. Lopatto (Chapter 6; Lopatto, 2004) found gains in skills, self-confidence, professional plans, and active learning. Taraban et al. (Chapter 8) found that the length and intensity of the research experience were key influences on the factors measured by their undergraduate research questionnaire (categorized as academic mindset, research mindset, research methods, faculty support, and peer support). They also developed a uniform instrument that could be useful for long-term evaluation of undergraduate research experiences.

Of course, it is comforting that these large-scale studies confirmed the benefits of undergraduate research, and together they provide insights into critical factors in success. However, most of the studies group together students with widely varying experiences in terms of time (summer-only versus academic year versus year-round; short-term and long-term experiences), institution (liberal arts colleges, major research universities, other research organizations), and level of student. Russell (Chapter 4; Russell et al., 2007) provides some data on sponsored (i.e., participating in a formal program) and nonsponsored (i.e., in an individual arrangement) research students, but one aspect of the evaluation challenge is even knowing which students are participating in undergraduate research, particularly those in "nonsponsored" situations.

Although it is true that what matters in the end is student growth, it is important to address questions about the programs themselves. For example, it would be helpful to know that the cost of formal programs is justified in terms of their contribution to student growth, to identify the essential elements in order to focus program resources on those elements, and to identify shortcomings that should be addressed (quality of mentoring is a common concern). Should we advise students to engage in long-term projects in the same laboratory, or is a diversity of experiences more effective? How can we better match students and mentors? How can we enable students to make more informed choices concerning research areas? When is the best time to start a research experience? Should research experiences be progressive, that is, start with a research methods course, proceed to a group project, and then proceed to the individual laboratory? None of these studies found that undergraduate research draws students to careers in science (instead, they found that the programs confirmed a preexisting inclination, or actually led students to conclude that they did not wish to pursue a research career), and yet those of us who have run such programs have supported students who had not previously considered research and from their participation in the program decided to do so. What role can formal programs play in attracting to research careers women and members of underrepresented minority groups?

Another key question is the relationship of formal programs to the prior and ongoing informal program (i.e., the individual arrangements of Russell's "non-sponsored" researchers). Are the formal programs recruiting new students to the pool of potential researchers, or are they supporting students who would have found a way to do research anyway? Are they increasing the number of research students? Are faculty members redirecting student support funds on research grants to other grant purposes given the availability of undergraduate research program funds?

The Challenge of Authenticity

The central goal of the TTU/HHMI program was integration of students into faculty-led research groups. The desired outcome was first of all a transformative experience for the student, but close behind was that the students see the project through to the point of publication and presentation. These publications were to be in scholarly peer-reviewed journals, and the presentations were to be at the regional, national, and international meetings of the discipline. In this model, undergraduate research is an integral part of the disciplinary research enterprise. To date, TTU/HHMI students have been authors on 74 papers in peer-reviewed scientific journals and over 284 abstracts for presentations at scientific meetings.

One characteristic of the undergraduate research movement is the proliferation of undergraduate research journals and undergraduate research symposia. Do these create the impression that undergraduate research is something separate from the research enterprises of the respective disciplines? Are they expensive and distracting uses of resources? Or are they useful intermediary points for presentation and publication? It has been argued that undergraduate research journals offer undergraduates unique opportunities to participate as reviewers (not just authors) in the peer-review process and provide avenues for exploring potential careers in scientific publishing (Ali et al., 2007; Carlson, 2006).

North Carolina State University (my present affiliation) serves as an example of the proliferation of undergraduate research symposia. The university has two campuswide undergraduate research symposia per year and hosted for the second time in fall 2006 a statewide undergraduate research symposium. In spring 2007, the second ACC undergraduate research symposium was held at the University of Virginia. In addition to the four undergraduate research symposia, undergraduates can present their work at a "Research in the Capitol" event in alternate years; the national symposia hosted by Sigma Xi, the National Collegiate Honors Council, NCUR, and CUR; the regional symposia by those and related organizations; and the undergraduate research symposium sponsored by the North Carolina Academy of Sciences. Should limited travel and event funds be used for these undergraduate-specific events, or should a program concentrate on enabling students to present at major national meetings (e.g., the Society of Neuroscience, the American Society of Plant Biologists)?

The Challenge of Increased Expectations

If undergraduate research confers benefits, then you can predict that an administrator will declare that all students should thereby participate. At the College of Wooster, Reed College, and many other liberal arts colleges, this occurs through the mechanism of requiring a senior thesis of all graduates. It occurs or comes close to occurring at some major research universities, examples including MIT and CalTech (Merkel, 2001). However, it would seem nothing could destroy undergraduate research more effectively than requiring it of students, a point confirmed by Russell (Chapter 4; Russell et al., 2007). A more reasonable suggestion would be to seek to introduce key elements of research into the undergraduate curriculum, such as inquiry-guided learning and research-based courses. The idea of a continuum of research experiences is addressed elsewhere in this volume (Trosset et al., Chapter 3; Taraban et al., Chapter 8).

Another source of increased expectations for undergraduate research derives from the perceived competitive advantage and prestige conferred by undergraduate research programs. To keep competitive for top science students, liberal arts colleges are increasing their expectations of faculty sponsorship of undergraduate research students. This increasing research focus is changing the nature of the liberal arts college enterprise, and not necessarily for the better. As Mitchell Malachowski (2006) of the University of San Diego writes, "Could our institutions become the functional equivalents of research universities without the graduate students?" (p. 27). Liberal arts colleges are the institutions of baccalaureate origin for a disproportionate number of PhDs in the sciences (Cech, 1999). It would be a pity for them to sacrifice their essence which, after all, led to their long history of success in preparing students for postgraduate careers in the sciences.

The Challenge of Sustainability

The greatest challenge for undergraduate research programs is that of sustainability. Although undergraduate research may have been institutionalized to some degree, that often means only support of a coordinating office, with the vast majority of programs still heavily dependent upon grant funds for student salaries/stipends and research travel. Even the institutional funds may prove to be ephemeral, given the likelihood in times of financial stringency that "extras" such as undergraduate research would be primary targets for budget cuts. This is why effective evaluation is so critical, not only to provide evidence to administrators of the value of an undergraduate research program, but also to focus the resources dedicated to undergraduate research to the aspects of the program that best promote student growth.

Given the benefits to the institution and its students, undergraduate research programs should be high-priority development targets, and some programs, such as the Meyerhoff Scholars at the University of Maryland–Baltimore County, are endowed (Summers & Hrabowski, 2006). But most programs will not join these fortunate ranks, or they may join them only partially and still need to consider how to keep the rest of the operation going.

The challenge becomes even greater if we consider the sobering analysis of the situation in which institutions of higher education find themselves provided by Alan Guskin and Mary Marcy, co-directors of the Project on the Future of Higher Education at Antioch University (Guskin & Marcy, 2003). Theirs is a bad news/good news argument. The bad news is their analysis of financial trends, which concludes that we are fooling ourselves if we think higher education will ever return to the glory days of funding enjoyed in the past. In the past, the response to times of limited resources has been that they are a temporary phenomenon that can be dealt with by temporary measures—what Guskin and Marcy refer to as "muddling through." Guskin and Marcy argue that we are not facing short-term challenges and that the usual "muddling through" will result in universities becoming places in which none of us will want to work. And, of course, if we do continue to just "muddle through," we can expect that such "extras" as undergraduate research programs will not survive.

The good news from Guskin and Marcy is that these troubled times present us with the opportunity to transform the university, enhancing student learning, improving the quality of faculty work life, and lowering the costs per student. Space does not allow a review of their three organizing principle and seven transformative actions, but their description of the sustainable university of the future and key elements of what they describe are aspects of undergraduate research programs.

The currency of higher education is student credit hours, which distorts the entire system because the underlying assumption is that all learning occurs in "occupied seats." Guskin and Marcy propose that transformative change requires us to shift from a system where seats count to a system where learning counts. If we can establish and certify the learning outcomes that we expect for our students, then what matters is their attainment of those learning outcomes, not how they attained them. At the moment, students earn undergraduate research credits that often only fulfill an elective requirement or, at most, a senior honors thesis requirement. What if an undergraduate research experience led to fulfillment of a significant number of the stated learning outcomes for a given discipline? What if essential baseline information were delivered by technology and/or by a limited number of traditional courses, and faculty time were focused on courses and experiences along the research spectrum described by Trosset et al. in Chapter 3?

And these would not have to be taught only by faculty—graduate students, postdoctoral research associates, and campus professionals could all join the enterprise. Perhaps the junior and senior years would be close to being courseless in the traditional sense, and would instead be long-term research projects with all of the attendant background reading, discussions, and presentations.

A tentative title for this chapter was "Taking Undergraduate Research Seriously," which is a good summary of the proposals above. Taking undergraduate research seriously means that we think of it more as something at the core of a curriculum, not as a supplementary activity. There are significant problems with this idea: maintaining the authenticity of the research, developing mechanisms for certifying that learning outcomes have been achieved, appeasing concerns of graduate schools and medical schools, training mentors for what will now be a more high-stakes enterprise, engaging larger numbers of students in research endeavors, and finding the funds to do so. Challenging indeed, but the alternative will be institutions that are increasingly obsessed with creating and filling seats, and forced to trim anything that detracts from that goal.

CONCLUSION

This chapter began by reminding us that undergraduate research has existed for years and has contributed to the development of scientists, in the absence of any formal undergraduate research programs. Unfortunately, we do not have baseline studies of the impact of undergraduate research prior to the rise of the undergraduate research movement. However, it would be reasonable to propose that the movement served to raise the profile of undergraduate research, involved greater numbers of students in the research enterprise, and diversified the students who engage in research. Future evaluation efforts should help us to identify critical components of undergraduate research programs, including those that could be incorporated into the curriculum so that all students may benefit to some extent from research experiences. The greatest challenge of all to undergraduate research is its sustainability in the face of the fiscal pressures facing colleges and universities. Given the power of these programs to transform the lives of our students, it is critical that we determine how to ensure their sustainability.

REFERENCES

Ali, F., Jadavji, N. M., Ong, W. C. H., Pandey, K. R., Patananan, N., Prabhala, H. K., et al. (2007). Supporting undergraduate research. *Science, 317*, 42.

Allen, G. E. (1978). *Thomas Hunt Morgan, the man and his science.* Princeton, NJ: Princeton University Press.

Bonner, J. T. (2002). *Lives of a Biologist: Adventures in a century of extraordinary science*. Cambridge, Mass.: Harvard University Press.

Boyer Commission on Educating Undergraduates in the Research University. (1998). *Reinventing undergraduate education: A blueprint for America's research universities*. Washington, D.C.: Carnegie Foundation for the Advancement of Teaching.

Browne, J. (1995). *Charles Darwin voyaging: A biography*. Princeton, NJ: Princeton University Press.

Carlson, E. (2006). Scientific publishing 101. *HHMI Bulletin, 19*(3), 44–45.

Cech, T. R. (1999). Science at liberal arts colleges: A better education? *Daedalus, 128*, 195–216.

Ferry, G. (1998). *Dorothy Hodgkin: A life*. Cold Spring Harbor, NY: Cold Spring Harbor Laboratory Press.

Frängsmyr, T. (Ed.). (1990). *Les Prix Nobel, The Nobel Prizes 1989*. Stockholm: Nobel Foundation.

Frängsmyr, T. (Ed.). (1997). *Les Prix Nobel, The Nobel Prizes 1996*. Stockholm: Nobel Foundation.

Gribbin, J., & Gribbin, M. (1997). *Richard Feynmann, a life in science*. New York: Viking.

Guskin, A. E., & Marcy, M. B. (2003). Dealing with the future now: Principles for creating a vital campus in a climate of restricted resources. *Change, 35*, 10–21.

Guterman, L. (2007). What good is undergraduate research, anyway? *Chronicle of Higher Education, 53*, A12–A16.

Hunter, A.-B., Laursen, S. L., & Seymour, E. (2006). Becoming a scientist: The role of undergraduate research in students' cognitive, personal, and professional development. *Science Education, 91*, 36–74.

Levi-Montalcini, R. (1988). *In praise of imperfection: My life and work*. New York: Basic Books, Inc.

Lopatto, D. (2004). Survey of undergraduate research experiences (SURE): First findings. *Cell Biology Education, 3*, 270–277.

Malachowski, M. (2006). Undergraduate research as the next great faculty divide. *Peer Review, 8*, 26–27.

McGrayne, S. B. (1998). *Nobel Prize women in science: Their lives, struggles, and momentous discoveries* (2nd. ed.). Seacaucus, NJ: Birch Lane Press.

Merkel, C. A. (2001). *Undergraduate research at six research universities: A pilot study for the Association of American Universities*. Retrieved November 8, 2007, from http://www.au.edu/education/Merkel.pdf

Mervis, J. (2007). Straight talk about STEM education. *Science, 317*, 78–81.

Nobel Foundation. (1972). *Nobel Lectures, Chemistry 1963–1970*. Amsterdam: Elsevier.

Nobel Foundation. (2007). [Laureate autobiographies located on the Nobel prizes Web site]. Retrieved 8/10/2007, http://nobelprize.org/nobel_prizes/

Reynolds, M. D. (1999). *American women scientists: 23 inspiring biographies, 1900–2000*. Jefferson, NC: McFarland.

Russell, S. H., Hancock, M. P., & McCullough, J. (2007). Benefits of undergraduate research experiences. *Science, 316*, 548–549.

Seymour, E., Hunter, A.-B., Laursen, S. L., & Deantoni, T. (2004). Establishing the benefits of research experiences for undergraduates in the sciences: First findings from a three-year study. *Science Education, 88*, 493–534.

Summers, M. F., & Hrabowski, F. A. (2006). Preparing minority scientists and engineers. *Science, 311*, 1870–1871.

Wasserman, E. (2000). *The door in the dream: Conversations with eminent women in science.* Washington, DC: Joseph Henry Press.

Westfall, R. S. (1980). *Never at rest: A biography of Isaac Newton.* Cambridge: Cambridge University Press.

Wilson, E. O. (1994). *Naturalist.* Washington, DC: Island Press.

Yount, L. (1994). *Contemporary women scientists.* New York: Facts on File.

About the Editors and the Contributors

KAREN WEBBER BAUER is an associate professor in the University of Georgia Institute of Higher Education. Prior to joining the IHE faculty on a full-time basis, she served as director of Institutional Research and interim associate provost for Institutional Effectiveness at the University of Georgia. Bauer came to UGA in 2003, following a 15-year tenure in the Office of Institutional Research and Planning at the University of Delaware. In her role at UD, she served on the 2001 Middle States Accreditation committee and worked successfully on several externally funded grants, including the NSF Recognition Award for the Integration of Research and Education (RAIRE), a second NSF grant on A Model of Evaluation for Undergraduate Research, and a Pew Charitable Trusts grant on Problem-Based Learning. Her primary research interests are the assessment of academic, cognitive, and psychosocial growth of college students, with additional interests in gender studies and higher education data management.

JOAN S. BENNETT is a professor of English at the University of Delaware, where until 2007 she directed UD's Undergraduate Research Program, which she founded in 1980. She earned her PhD from Stanford University. Bennett is coauthor of several studies sponsored by the National Science Foundation that assess the educational benefits of the undergraduate research experience. She is also the author of a book and many articles in her own scholarly field, seventeenth-century British literature.

RICHARD L. BLANTON (Editor) is a professor of plant biology and the director of the University Honors Program at North Carolina State University. He received his BS in botany with highest honors in 1977, and his PhD in botany in 1981, both from the University of North Carolina at Chapel Hill. He was an NSF Graduate Research Fellow, NSF Postdoctoral Fellow, and NATO Postdoctoral Fellow. Following postdoctoral research at the University of Georgia, the Culture Centre of Algae and Protozoa (Cambridge, England), and the University of Texas at Austin, he joined the faculty in the Department of Biological Sciences at Texas Tech University in 1988, where he remained until his departure for North Carolina State in 2003. He served as co–program director on Texas Tech's first grant (awarded in 1992) from the Undergraduate Biological Sciences Education Program of the Howard Hughes Medical Institute and as program director for HHMI grants awarded in 1994, 1998, and 2002. He was also the program director of an NSF Research Experiences for Undergraduates site at Texas Tech. With the HHMI grants and substantial university support funds, he led the development of a multifaceted science education program that featured a large undergraduate research program (notable for multiyear, year-round research experiences), a precollege outreach program (focused on building a seamless community of K–16 science educators), and various curriculum development initiatives. He led the creation of a university center to serve as an administrative home for these endeavors, the Center for the Integration of Science Education and Research. As director of the University Honors Program at North Carolina State, he has guided the transformation of the program to a research- and scholarship-based model, whereby students are encouraged and enabled to integrate experiential learning opportunities into their undergraduate education across all disciplines, not just in the sciences and engineering. He is the program director of North Carolina State's Beckman Scholars program.

LINDA BLOCKUS earned her PhD in higher education from the University of Missouri–Columbia (MU) and is the director of the Office of Undergraduate Research there. Her responsibilities include working with MU students during the academic year and summer and directing science research programs in the summer funded by NSF, NIH, USDA, and a variety of campus sources for approximately 100 MU and visiting undergraduates. She was elected as a councilor in 2002 to the Council on Undergraduate Research (At-Large Division), was a founding councilor of the Undergraduate Research Program Directors Division in 2005, and continues to serve in that division.

CRAIG W. BOWEN is director of Medical Education Services and assistant professor of Anesthesiology and Critical Care Medicine in the School of Medicine at Johns Hopkins University. His PhD work was in science education, and he focused his early research efforts on the assessment of student learning in college-level chemistry. He has served as an external program evaluator for a number of education projects funded by the National Science Foundation and Howard Hughes Medical Institute. He now provides support in the School of Medicine through faculty instructional development, assessment of learning, program assessment, and curriculum development.

TREVOR BRASEL received his PhD in medical microbiology from Texas Tech University Health Sciences Center. He is currently at the Lovelace Respiratory Research Institute. Honorary positions or honors include expert reviewer for several peer-reviewed journals concerning fungal bioaerosols, continued authorship on numerous scientific publications and national presentations, and laboratory supervisor for a newly built ABSL-3 facility. Current research interests include immunotoxicology and microbiology of Risk Group 2/3 microorganisms. Specifics include model and vaccine development and testing for the causative agents of anthrax, plague, tularemia, bird flu, SARS, and others.

ASHLEY CAMPBELL holds bachelor's and master's degrees in biology, and a Doctor of Education degree in curriculum and instruction with a specialization in science education from Texas Tech University. Campbell is certified in composite science, and prior to her graduate work, she taught Biology I, Physics I, and Physical Science in public high school. Currently, she serves as an assistant professor in the Department of Education at West Texas A & M University (WTAMU), where she teaches Educational Psychology and Science Methods. Her current research interests include gender equity in science education.

SARAH R. ELGIN is Viktor Hamburger Professor of Arts and Sciences and professor of Biology at Washington University in St. Louis. She received her PhD from the California Institute of Technology. She is a member of the society of HHMI professors and currently leads a consortium on genomics education.

SANDRA GREGERMAN is the director of the Undergraduate Research Opportunity Program at the University of Michigan. She has directed this program since 1992, overseeing its expansion from 150 students and faculty to over 1,000 students and 600 faculty participants. Prior to 1992, she was the director of Academic Programs for the University of Michigan's School of Natural Resources. She received her bachelor's degree in political science from the University of California–Davis and her master's degree from the University of Michigan School of Natural Resources and Environment. Her academic background is in environmental policy and communication. In her work in higher education, she has focused on issues related to women in science and retention of students of color. She is an expert on the development, implementation, and evaluation of undergraduate research programs and has served as a consultant to other campuses interested in establishing such programs. Gregerman is the recipient of an Outstanding Freshman Advocate Award from the National Resource Center for the Freshman Year Experience. The Undergraduate Research Opportunity Program has won several awards under her leadership: the NSF Recognition Award for the Integration of Research and Teaching; the White House Presidential Award for Excellence in Science, Engineering, and Mathematics Mentoring; and a Hesburgh Award.

ROBIN HENNE received her bachelor of science degree in biological sciences from Texas Tech University. She is currently at the Alzheimer's Research Trust. Her honors include the Earl Camp Award 2005 for Outstanding Senior in the Department of Biological Sciences, Texas Tech University; First Place in the Undergraduate Division at TTU/HSC Student Research Days 2002 and 2003. Current career interests are in the medical research charity sector, facilitating the formation of scientific research collaborations and funding those ventures.

WILLIAM HENNE received his bachelors of science degree in cellular and molecular biology from Texas Tech University. He is currently at the University of Cambridge, MRC Laboratory of Molecular Biology. His honorary positions or honors include Cambridge Overseas Trust Scholar and Trinity College External Research Student. Current research interests include membrane curvature sensing protein domains; lipid-protein biochemistry and biophysics.

ANNE-BARRIE HUNTER is codirector of and a senior professional researcher at Ethnography and Evaluation Research at the Center to Advance Research and Teaching in the Social Sciences, University of Colorado–Boulder. Since 1991 she has worked in collaboration with other group members to conduct research and evaluations on STEM education initiatives seeking to improve quality and access in these fields. Since working with Elaine Seymour and Nancy Hewitt on *Talking about Leaving* (1997), she has also played a major role in evaluations for ChemConnections, Los Alamos National Laboratory student internship program, the College Board, and Project Kaleidoscope, among others. She is coauthor (with Seymour) of *Talking about Disability: The Education and Work Experiences of Graduates and Undergraduates with Disabilities in Science, Mathematics, and Engineering* (1998), the first study of STEM students with disabilities. Hunter has an MA in journalism and mass communication research from the University of Colorado at Boulder.

CAROLANNE M. KARDASH holds a PhD in educational psychology from Arizona State University. She joined the faculty of the University of Nevada–Las Vegas in 2001, where she is professor of Educational Psychology. From 2003 until 2006, she served as associate editor of the *Journal of Educational Psychology*. Her current research interests involve examining how individual differences influence the processing of text, with a particular emphasis on how beliefs and attitudes affect people's memory for controversial information.

SANDRA L. LAURSEN received her PhD in chemistry from the University of California at Berkeley. As codirector and research associate of Ethnography and Evaluation Research at the University of Colorado at Boulder, she collaborates with social scientists on research and evaluation projects on innovative science teaching and on issues of career growth, diversity and leadership in the scientific community. As an outreach scientist for the Cooperative Institute for Research in Environmental Sciences (CIRES), also at CU–Boulder, she teaches courses and conducts professional development workshops on earth science topics, active learning strategies, and inquiry-based science teaching for science educators, college faculty, K–12 teachers, scientists, and the public. She has coauthored several ChemConnections modules and instructor resources for teaching fundamental chemistry concepts through real-world questions and active learning strategies, published by W. W. Norton.

ANGELA M. LOCKS is a doctoral candidate at the University of Michigan's (UM) Center for the Study of Higher and Postsecondary Education. Before beginning her doctoral studies, she served as an assistant director for the Undergraduate Research Opportunity Program (UROP) at UM–Ann Arbor and completed her BA in psychology at UM. As Assistant Director, Locks coordinated all admission, recruitment, and retention activities, cosupervised a 30-member peer advising staff, and served as a member of the program's evaluation team. Her current higher education research interests include the recruitment, retention, and experiences of students of color at predominantly White institutions.

DAVID LOPATTO is professor of psychology at Grinnell College. He received his PhD in experimental psychology from Ohio University. His research includes analysis of the Summer Undergraduate Research Experiences survey (SURE) and the Classroom Undergraduate Research Experiences survey (CURE), as well as other assessment of student learning.

WYATT MCMAHON received his PhD in cell biology and biochemistry from Texas Tech University Health Sciences Center. He is currently at Texas Tech University in Plant and Soil Science. His current research interest is studying the functional genomics of cotton.

NATASHA J. MEHDIABADI received her PhD in ecology, evolution, and behavior from the University of Texas at Austin. She is currently at The Smithsonian Institution's National Museum of Natural History. Honorary positions or honors include W. M. Keck Postdoctoral Fellow, Computational Biology 2003–04; National Science Foundation Postdoctoral Fellow, Microbial Biology 2004–06; Smithsonian Institution Postdoctoral Fellow 2007–08; and Best Poster, Postdoctoral Fellow, Gordon Research Conference, Microbial Population Biology 2005. Current research interests include the evolution and ecology of social interactions, with particular focus on the evolution of cooperation and conflict in group-living organisms and also symbiosis.

ERIC PRENSKY is a clinical psychologist and assistant professor of Clinical Psychology in the Department of Psychiatry at the University of Illinois Medical Center at Chicago. His research includes sensory and behavioral aspects of smokeless tobacco, and he has presented nationally in a variety of areas within health psychology. Dr. Prensky is involved in clinical work, supervising, and teaching.

SUSAN H. RUSSELL, now retired, was director of SRI International's Survey Research Program. She has 30 years of experience designing and conducting a wide variety of survey- and interview-based projects. Federal agencies and organizations for which she has conducted research studies include the National Science Foundation, the National Center for Education Statistics, the State Department, the U.S. Department of Education, the National Institute on Drug Abuse, and the Bureau of the Census. Her research clients also have included many commercial organizations, universities, and nonprofit organizations. For NSF, Dr. Russell has led the most comprehensive assessment yet undertaken of undergraduate research opportunities in the United States, involving more than 18,000 survey respondents.

ELAINE SEYMOUR was for 17 years director of Ethnography and Evaluation Research (E&ER), at the University of Colorado–Boulder. Issues of women in science, technology, engineering, and mathematics (STEM) disciplines have been a special focus of her research; in recognition of this work, WEPAN awarded Elaine its 2002 Betty Vetter Award for Research. Her best-known published work is *Talking About Leaving: Why Undergraduates Leave the Sciences* (1997), coauthored with Nancy M. Hewitt. Recently, she and E&ER members published *Partners in Innovation: Teaching Assistants in College Science Courses* (2005) drawing on studies of three science education innovations. She and her group have been evaluators for several national and institution-based innovations. In response to the learning assessment needs of faculty classroom innovators, Seymour designed two online resources: the Student Assessment of their Learning Gains (SALG) online instrument and the Field-tested Learning Assessment Guide (FLAG). She continues to work with E&ER members on their study of undergraduate research and on a study of the nature and sources of resistance to innovation. Elaine has served as an external evaluator and as a member of national visiting committees and advisory boards for many STEM education change projects. She is a PhD sociologist and a British-American whose education and career have been conducted on both sides of the Atlantic.

GERALD D. SKOOG, Paul Whitfield Horn Professor Emeritus, was a faculty member at Texas Tech University from 1969 to 2004. He is a science educator with experience as a high school science teacher, an author of secondary science textbooks, and a director of several federally funded curriculum and training projects. Skoog served as President of the National Science Teachers Association in 1985–86 and received the organization's Citation for Distinguished Service to Science Education in 1994 and the Robert H. Carleton Award in 2004 in recognition for his leadership in science education nationally. Skoog was named a fellow in the

American Association for the Advancement of Science (AAAS) in 1996 in recognition of his leadership in science education and his research concerned with evolution education. He received the University of Nebraska–Lincoln Teacher's College Alumni Association's Award of Excellence in May 2003.

ROMAN TARABAN (Editor) is a professor and Associate Chair in the Department of Psychology at Texas Tech University, assessment coordinator for the Texas Tech University Howard Hughes Medical Institute (TTU/HHMI) Biological Sciences Education Program, member of the Texas Tech Teaching Academy Executive Council, past president of the Society for Computers in Psychology (SCiP), and associate editor for the *Journal of Educational Psychology*. He received his PhD in cognitive psychology from Carnegie Mellon University. His interests are in how undergraduate students learn, and especially, how they draw meaningful connections in traditional college content materials.

CAROL TROSSET holds a PhD in cultural anthropology from the University of Texas at Austin. She is director of Institutional Research at Hampshire College. Her current research areas include learning outcomes assessment methods and the effectiveness of the liberal arts as preparation for careers.

MICHAEL WALLACE is an assistant professor of Science Education at Morehead State University where he teaches Inquiry-Based Physical Science for Elementary Teachers and Science Methods for Elementary Teachers. He graduated from the University of Missouri in 2002 with a PhD in science education and worked with the Life Sciences Undergraduate Research Opportunities team evaluating the impact that undergraduate research experiences have both on students' self-efficacy doing research-related tasks and their desire to pursue advanced degrees with an emphasis toward research. He is currently focused on developing a strengths-based science teaching approach for preservice elementary teachers.

SUSAN HARRELL YEE received her PhD in ecology and evolution from the University of Chicago. She is currently at the U.S. Environmental Protection Agency, Gulf Ecology Division, National Health and Environmental Effects Research Laboratory (NHEERL). Her current career interest is to continue as a research scientist for the federal government.

Index